Human-Computer Interaction Series

T0134658

Human-Computer Interaction is a multidisciplinary field focused on human aspects of the development of computer technology. As computer-based technology becomes increasingly pervasive – not just in developed countries, but worldwide – the need to take a human-centered approach in the design and development of this technology becomes ever more important. For roughly 30 years now, researchers and practitioners in computational and behavioral sciences have worked to identify theory and practice that influences the direction of these technologies, and this diverse work makes up the field of human-computer interaction. Broadly speaking, it includes the study of what technology might be able to do for people and how people might interact with the technology.

In this series, we present work which advances the science and technology of developing systems which are both effective and satisfying for people in a wide variety of contexts. The human-computer interaction series will focus on theoretical perspectives (such as formal approaches drawn from a variety of behavioral sciences), practical approaches (such as the techniques for effectively integrating user needs in system development), and social issues (such as the determinants of utility, usability and acceptability).

For further volumes:
http://www.springer.com/series/6033

Regina Bernhaupt
Editor

Evaluating User Experience in Games

Concepts and Methods

 Springer

Editor
Asst. Prof. Regina Bernhaupt
Université Paul Sabatier, Toulouse III
Institut de Recherche en
Informatique de Toulouse (IRIT)
118 Route de Narbonne
31062 Toulouse Cedex 9
France
Regina.Bernhaupt@irit.fr

ISSN 1571-5035
ISBN 978-1-4471-2557-0   ISBN 978-1-84882-963-3(eBook)
DOI 10.1007/978-1-84882-963-3
Springer London Dordrecht Heidelberg New York

British Library Cataloguing in Publication Data
A catalogue record for this book is available from the British Library

Printed on acid-free paper

Springer is part of Springer Science+Business Media (www.springer.com)

For Philippe

Foreword

It was a pleasure to provide an introduction to a new volume on user experience evaluation in games. The scope, depth, and diversity of the work here is amazing. It attests to the growing popularity of games and the increasing importance developing a range of theories, methods, and scales to evaluate them. This evolution is driven by the cost and complexity of games being developed today. It is also driven by the need to broaden the appeal of games. Many of the approaches described here are enabled by new tools and techniques. This book (along with a few others) represents a watershed in game evaluation and understanding.

The field of game evaluation has truly "come of age". The broader field of HCI can begin to look toward game evaluation for fresh, critical, and sophisticated thinking about design evaluation and product development. They can also look to games for groundbreaking case studies of evaluation of products.

I'll briefly summarize each chapter below and provide some commentary. In conclusion, I will mention a few common themes and offer some challenges.

Discussion

In Chapter 1, User Experience Evaluation in Entertainment, Bernhaupt gives an overview and presents a general framework on methods currently used for user experience evaluation. The methods presented in the following chapters are summarized and thus allow the reader to quickly assess the right set of methods that will help to evaluate the game under development.

In Chapter 2, Enabling Social Play: A Framework for Design and Evaluation, Isbister examines the neglected area of social games. She reviews the literature and considers sample games and some of the primary factors affecting the experience of social gaming. These include contextual factors, motivational factors, and the conceptual and theoretical ground which shape such evaluations. Isbister points to ecological validity being a primary focus when considering any testing method. She stresses the importance of looking at the entire set of measures including attitudinal and behavioral data. Her chapter creates a context for planning and conducting evaluations of social games.

Chapter 3, Presence Involvement and Flow in Digital Games (Takatalo, Hakkinen, Kaistinen, and Nyman) is a report on a massive study using multivariate analysis to reveal the subcomponents of user experience in games. It reviews the history of classifications of user experience going back to the classic psychological categories of thinking, feeling, and will. The authors compare and analyze current concepts: immersion, fun, presence, involvement, and flow. They also review previous multivariate analysis of game questionnaires. From this analysis, they develop the Presence-Involvement-Flow framework (PIFF) which encompasses both technical game components and psychological determinant of UX. Using a factor analytic study, they evaluate this model. The final questionnaire was assessed by comparing two different groups of gamers in two different games. In addition, the profile for games was compared to Metacritic scores and user ratings. The results were promising, with results of PIFF accounting for the important differences between games and illuminating the learning curves of different users during the first hour of play. PIFF is very broad in scope and shows potential to evaluate user experience at different stages of development.

In Chapter 4, Assessing the Core Elements of the Gaming Experience, Calvillo-Gamez, Cairns, and Cox assume an ambitious goal – creating a new theory of user experience for games. They adopt a novel process to achieve this end. They have chosen to use a bottom-up approach. They build the theory by analyzing video game reviews using the methodology derived from grounded theory. Their analysis is complex containing two core elements: puppetry and video game, each with three elements. They term this theory the Core Elements of Game Experience (CEGE) theory. This theory is integrated into a model and translated into a questionnaire. The questionnaire is then applied to user experience in two versions of a popular game (Tetris). The results are as predicted, i.e., scales show no difference for elements of the game that were not different (visuals and sound) but are different for those that relate to control – puppetry. The ambitious goal that was proposed at the beginning of the chapter is matched by an impressive result – validation of a theory for gaming. Since the theory includes measurement instruments, it represents an advance over previous theories, in which the measurement is unspecified.

Emily Brown reports on the current practice in the gaming industry about the Life and Tools of a Game Designer (Chapter 5).

In Chapter 6, Investigating Experiences and Attitudes Toward Videogames Using a Semantic Differential Methodology, Lemay and Lessard explore the use of the semantic differential to evaluate video games as leisure activities. They offer a new tool for research on perception of games. As they point out, having a standard set of questions and metrics for attitudes about games would provide a foundation for more research. This also could provide a foundation for analyzing the attitudes toward potential market segments for a game. Their results are promising and could help game designers understand their intended audiences.

In Chapter 7, Video Game Development and User Experience, McAllister and White provide a detailed overview of the testing done for three products. The chapter gives a snapshot of how evaluation is currently being done in industry. The methods and procedures are quite broad. The first case study recounts the development of Pure by Black Rock Studio. In that case study, three useful distinctions in test methodology are introduced. These are as free flow (play the game as you normally would) vs. narrow specific (play only a part of the game and play it repeatedly) vs. broad specific (user plays more of the game but plays repeatedly). While these three types of tests are used widely, naming them is a step forward. In the second case study, the development of Zoë Mode illustrates some basic truisms of testing, such as the need for multiple iterative tests not only to refine but also to develop a completely alternative and more effective approach – in this case, changing from text descriptions to visual images to illustrate successful calibration. The third and final case study examines Relentless Software's approach to evaluating Buzz! Quiz TV. Focus group testing was used to collect user ratings of the game. In addition, telemetry from the game was captured remotely postlaunch (a technique also used by Black Rock Studio). The authors see future developments as capturing more data such as facial expressions and physiological data.

In Chapter 8, User Experience Design for Inexperienced Gamers: GAP – Game Approachability Principles, Desurvire and Wiberg provide an insightful analysis and useful guidance to design studios that are developing games for broad audiences. A classic challenge that these studios face is creating a game that is "approachable". That is, the game must be accessible to novices and hold their interest so that they will purchase it and continue to play it. Traditionally, game studios emphasize the "playability" of their games. Playability is usually taken to mean the game is good for experienced players. While traditional methods like the members of the studio playing the game or testing for balance by a quality assurance team might produce a "playable" game (good game balance, few bugs, elimination of "golden" paths, etc.), "approachability" is often a bigger challenge since it addresses the needs of new or novice players. Desurvire et al. address this problem using two "traditional" usability methods: usability testing (UT) and heuristic evaluation (HE). They enrich the HE with Game Approachability Principles (GAP). Heuristic evaluation is only as good as the principles that drive it and the experience of the evaluators. In their chapter, Desurvire et al. describe a study that tested several games using both HE and UT. They found that using the methods together produced actionable insights either method alone would not have uncovered. Their approach is unique, since most of the research literature has attempted to evaluate which method is best. This chapter shows that the combination of UT and HE produces more "value" for the design studio. Value is defined as the most actionable data for the investment made. Any studio hoping to produce an approachable game would be wise to incorporate both HE and UT into their toolkit.

In Chapter 9, Digital Games, the Aftermath, Poels, IJsselsteijn, de Kort, and Van Iersel explore a relatively uncharted area of gaming – the short- and long-term effects of the game on the player. While most past studies have focused on single possible effects of gaming, e.g., gaming leads to isolation or gaming desensitizes one from violence, Poels looks at more global effects. The results show both temporary and long-lasting effects that are not different from exposure to other media such as movies or books. These results are not unexpected, but their implications are consistent with a significant shift in the conceptualization of personality. That is, the rejection of a fixed, trait-like conception of personality in favor of a more malleable personality which evolves and changes over time based on experience. This view can be seen as hopeful. It says we become what we do.

In Chapter 10, Evaluating User Experience Factors Using Experiments: Expressive Artificial Faces Embedded in Contexts, Lankes, Bernhaupt, and Tscheligi present an experimental study investigating the effects of embodied conversational agents in games on the overall user experience. This chapter shows that it is necessary to conduct rigorous experiments to understand influencing factors on the overall user experience.

In their chapter, Evaluating Exertion Games (Chapter 11), on the effect of exertion in producing emotional engagement, Mueller and Bianchi-Berthouze explore four methods for studying the relationship between exertion and user experience. This is an important question from a research perspective, but the question gains additional importance given the rise in popularity of activity-based games (e.g., Wii sports and fit games) and the common criticism that most games are sedentary and contribute to declining fitness in children. Like many of the other chapters, Mueller et al. uses a case study approach testing four games and using different methods for each one. Overall, the results are interesting and promising, albeit for some tests opposite of what was expected. It would be early to standardize on any particular approach. The chapter also points to the promise of automatic encoding of user movements and physiological measures. Fortunately, Mueller et al. raises the often underrated concern that any such measures fall short in capturing the contextual factors which could be major determinants of emotional states and game experience.

In Chapter 12, Beyond the Gamepad: HCI and Game Controller Design and Evaluation, Brown, Kehoe, Kirakowski, and Pitt focus on controllers as a determinant of user experience in a game. They propose a McNamara and Kirakowski framework that categorizes technology into experience, usability, and functionality. They apply this model to the evaluation of three controllers: a steering wheel, the game pad, and the keyboard. Three measures, completion time, subjective mental effort questionnaire, and consumer product are used. They also do a content analysis of user comments about each device classifying in terms of their valence (positive, negative) and category (sensitivity, feedback, learning potential . . .). Brown et al. also captured behavioral data during the test, comparing the steering angle access for the game pad and the steering for both experienced and inexperienced users. This allows them to draw relatively sophisticated conclusions such as that for sophisticated users the more sensitive the controller, the more useful the controller. This is a good example of one of their main conclusions – that a complete collection of measures combined with user comments enabled an analysis of causes and therefore fixes.

In Chapter 13, Using Heuristics to Evaluate the Overall User Experience of Video Games and Advanced Interaction, Koeffel, Hochleitner, Leitner, Haller, Geven, and Tscheligi provide a comprehensive review of the recent literature on game evaluation as an introduction to their approach of using heuristics to evaluate games. In most cases, the heuristics refer to user experiences throughout the course of playing the game. As such, they are user evaluation heuristics, e.g., the game outcome should be perceived as fair. The heuristics do not specify ideal or minimal design parameters, e.g., no more than five enemies should attack a player simultaneously.

Thus, they require a degree of expertise on the part of evaluators. In essence, this expertise is the ability to anticipate the user behavior and reaction to a game. The researchers conducted heuristic reviews of games representing different genres and compared their results to the games' Metacritic scores (a consolidation of published reviewer ratings). The results show that the more user experience issues were uncovered in the heuristic reviews, the lower the Metacritic score. This is an important result for both, user research in games and user experience research in general. It may be the first comparison of results of heuristic reviews to broad industry metrics. The positive relationship can be seen as validation of heuristic reviews in general and the specific heuristics and processes suggested here.

Taken as a whole, the chapters represent an impressive collection of innovative methods and reviews. They illustrate some common themes and some challenges. Several of the chapters point to the need to understand the causes of user reaction. They approach challenge in different ways. Some use qualitative methods such as free-form comments or video, others use a variety of scales.

A number of the chapters include speculation that physiological measures are a next step. This optimism needs to be tempered. These measures often need to be supplemented by understanding of the context and situation in which they are taken. Simply stated, there is no simple relation to physiological measures and emotional or evaluative states. Emotions are an interpretation of physiology and behavior and the context in which it occurs.

Many frameworks to evaluate games are proposed in this volume. They often claim to offer similar advantages, deeper insights into user experience in games, and more actionable data. Their comparative usefulness is not clear at this time. Some factors that determine broad adoption of any of these frameworks are clearly accidental. For example, which organization hires which graduates of which university or broad awareness of a given framework by industry decision makers. Other factors are more closely related to the inherent characteristics of the measure. A number of these have been discussed by the authors, i.e., the ability to provide precise feedback, the ability to provide a complete analysis, and the ability to analyze causes of problems and suggest fixes. Additional factors affecting adoption will depend on the question at hand. For example, LeMay et al. offer a way to analyze attitudes toward gaming experiences, which is clearly relevant to marketing a game to new users. In contrast, Brown et al. offer detailed and multilevel analysis of player experience which can provide for a causal analysis and suggest fixes. One important factor not emphasized by the authors is the face validity or plausibility of the question set. That is, will the question set seem sensible and relevant to a development team? Without buy-in from the design and development team, the insights from testing will go tragically unused.

Given the promise shown in the work represented here, I would call on the authors to take the next step and venture in the world of commercial development of games. The chapter by McAllister et al. provides some good perspective on the current state of the art. The opportunity is there.

User Research Manager – Microsoft Surface Computing   Dennis Wixon

Contents

Contributors

Regina Bernhaupt IRIT, IHCS, Toulouse, France, Regina.Bernhaupt@irit.fr; ICT&S Center, Universität Salzburg, Salzburg, Austria, Regina.Bernhaupt@sbg.ac.at

Nadia Bianchi-Berthouze UCLIC, University College London, London, United Kingdom, n.berthouze@ucl.ac.uk

Emily Brown Sony Computer Entertainment, London, United Kingdom, ems_brown@gmail.com

Michael Brown People and Technology Research Group, Department of Applied Psychology, University College Cork, Cork, Ireland, mab@campus.ie

Paul Cairns Department of Computer Science, The University of York, York, United Kingdom, pcairns@cs.york.ac.uk

Eduardo H. Calvillo-Gámez División de Nuevas Tecnologías de la Información, Universidad Politécnica de San Luis Potosí, San Luis Potosí, México, e.calvillo@upslp.edu.mx

Anna L. Cox UCL Interaction Centre, University College London, London, United Kingdom, anna.cox@ucl.ac.uk

Yvonne de Kort Human Technology Interaction Group, Game Experience Lab, Eindhoven University of Technology, Eindhoven, The Netherlands, y.a.w.d.kort@tue.nl

Heather Desurvire Behavioristics Inc., Marina del Rey, CA, United States, heather3@gte.net

Arjan Geven Center for Usability Research and Engineering, Vienna, Austria, Geven@cure.at

Jukka Häkkinen The Aalto University School of Science and Technology, Espoo, Finland, jukka.hakkinen@tkk.fi

Michael Haller Media Interaction Lab, Upper Austria University of Applied Sciences, Hagenberg, Austria, Michael.Haller@fh-hagenberg.at

Wolfgang Hochleitner Upper Austria University of Applied Sciences, Hagenberg, Austria, Wolfgang.Hochleitner@fh-hagenberg.at

Wijnand IJsselsteijn Human Technology Interaction Group, Game Experience Lab, Eindhoven University of Technology, Eindhoven, The Netherlands, w.a.ijsselsteijn@tue.nl

Katherine Isbister Polytechnic Institute of New York University, Brooklyn, NY, United States; Center for Computer Games Research, IT University of Copenhagen, Copenhagen, Denmark, isbister@poly.edu

Jyrki Kaistinen Psychology of Evolving Media and Technology (POEM), University of Helsinki, Helsinki, Finland, Jyrki.Kaistinen@helsinki.fi

Aidan Kehoe IDEAS Research Group, Department of Computer Science, University College Cork, Cork, Ireland, ak2@cs.ucc.ie

Jurek Kirakowski People and Technology Research Group, Department of Applied Psychology, University College Cork, Cork, Ireland, jkz@ucc.ie

Christina Koeffel Center for Usability Research and Engineering, Vienna, Austria, Christina@c-na.net

Michael Lankes Upper Austria University of Applied Sciences, Hagenberg, Austria, michael.lankes@fh-hagenberg.at

Jakob Leitner Media Interaction Lab, Upper Austria University of Applied Sciences, Hagenberg, Austria, Jakob.Leitner@fh-hagenberg.at

Philippe Lemay Ludosys, 486 chemin de l'Église, Fatima, QC, Canada G4T 2N8, philippe.lemay@ludosys.com

Martin Maheux-Lessard Ubisoft Montréal, 5505 St-Laurent Blvd, Montréal, QC, Canada H2T 1S6, martin.maheux-lessard@ubisoft.com

Graham McAllister University of Sussex, Brighton, United Kingdom, g.mcallister@sussex.ac.uk

Florian 'Floyd' Mueller Interaction Design Group, Department of Information Systems, The University of Melbourne, Melbourne, Australia, floyd@floydmueller.com

Göte Nyman Psychology of Evolving Media and Technology (POEM), University of Helsinki, Helsinki, Finland, Göte.Nyman@helsinki.fi

Ian Pitt IDEAS Research Group, Department of Computer Science, University College Cork, Cork, Ireland, i.pitt@cs.ucc.ie

Karolien Poels MIOS Research Group, Department of Communication Studies, University of Antwerp, Belgium, karolien.poels@ua.ac.be

Jari Takatalo Psychology of Evolving Media and Technology (POEM), University of Helsinki, Helsinki, Finland, Jari.Takatalo@helsinki.fi

Manfred Tscheligi Center for Usability Research and Engineering, Vienna, Austria; ICT&S Center, Universität of Salzburg, Salzburg, Austria, Tscheligi@cure.at

Bart Van Iersel Human Technology Interaction Group, Game Experience Lab, Eindhoven University of Technology, Eindhoven, The Netherlands, b.m.v.iersel@tue.nl

Gareth R. White University of Sussex, Brighton, United Kingdom, g.white@sussex.ac.uk

Charlotte Wiberg Umeå University, Umeå, Sweden, cwiberg@informatik.umu.se

About the Authors

Regina Bernhaupt is invited professor at IRIT, Toulouse, where she defended her habilitation in computer science on usability and user experience evaluation in non-traditional environments in 2009. She received a Ph.D. in computer science in 2002 and a Master in Psychology 1998, both from the University of Salzburg. She is an active member of the HCI community, involved in the organization of several conferences and active in various program committees. Her main interest is to understand how contextual factors influence the evaluation of interactive systems and how new forms of games and entertainment applications (including the interaction technique) should be designed and evaluated to support the overall user experience. For more information on her current work, please visit: http://ihcs.irit.fr/bernhaupt/index.html

Since 2006, **Nadia Berthouze** (http://www.uclic.ucl.ac.uk/people/n.berthouze/) is a lecturer in the UCL Interaction Centre (UCLIC) at the University of London, a leading Centre of Excellence in Human–Computer Interaction (HCI). After her Ph.D. (1995) in Computer Science and Bio-medicine at the University of Milan (Italy), she spent 5 years first as a postdoctoral fellow and then as a COE fellow at the Electrotechnical Laboratory (Tsukuba in Japan), where she investigated HCI aspects in the area of multimedia information interpretation with a focus on the interpretation of affective content. In 2000, she was appointed as lecturer at the Computer Software Department of the University of Aizu in Japan, where she extended her interest in emotion expression to the study of nonverbal affective communication. The premise of her research is that affect, emotion, and subjective experience should be factored into the design of interactive technology. At the center of her research is the creation of interactive systems that exploit body movement as a medium to induce, recognize, and measure the quality of experience of humans. She is investigating the various factors involved in the way body movement is used to express and experience emotions, including cross-cultural differences and task context. She was awarded a 2-year International Marie Curie Reintegration Grant (AffectME) to investigate these issues in the clinical domain and gaming industry. In the area of computer games, she is investigating how an increase in task-related body movement imposed, or allowed, by the game controller affects the player's game experience.

Emily Brown is a designer at Sony Computer Entertainment, where she has worked for nearly 5 years. Projects she has worked on include PlayStationHome and PlayTV and several EyeToy products. During this time, her responsibilities included planning and conducting user evaluations, designing systems, controls, and user interfaces as well as game flow and mechanics.

Emily has a master's degree in Human–Computer Interaction from UCL Interaction Centre. There she began to explore her interest in games usability. With this interest, she conducted her thesis exploring the definition and experience of immersion. Emily has published on games and game usability methods at CHI and British HCI. She continues to give seminars on games usability, interaction design, and immersion at UCL Interaction Centre and the University of York's Master's in HCI programs.

Michael Brown currently works with the University of Nottingham and Ordnance Survey, UK. He has previously worked as a researcher and lecturer, specializing in experimental psychology and human–computer interaction. His main research interest includes exploring the application of user-centered design to non-traditional contexts.

Paul Cairns is a senior lecturer in Human–Computer Interaction in the Department of Computer Science at the University of York. He did his DPhil in Mathematics at Oxford University. From there, he became an analyst programer at The Technology Partnership, an SME in real-time automation. Missing the academic life, he moved to Middlesex University as a lecturer in computing, and in 2001 he moved to the newly formed UCL Interaction Centre. He has research interests in the experience of videogames and modeling user interactions.

Eduardo H. Calvillo Gámez is a member of the New Information Technology Faculty at Universidad Politécnica de San Luis Potosí. He holds a Ph.D. in Human Computer Interaction from University College London, a degree of Masters of Science in Electrical Engineering from Tufts University and a degree of Bachelors of Science in Electronic Engineering from Universidad Autónoma de San Luis Potosi. Eduardo's research interests are user experience, video games, input devices and epistemology of HCI.

Anna L. Cox is a senior lecturer in HCI at the UCL Interaction Centre, Division of Psychology and Language Sciences, University College London. Her research interests are driven by working to understand human–computer interaction through the theories and methods of cognitive science. She has co-edited a book with Paul Cairns on Research Methods for HCI.

Heather Desurvire of Behavioristics is an experienced specialist of usability and playability whose published work on research methodologies has added to knowlededge base of usability testing and game testing research. She is also a faculty at USC game studies program, teaching game usability.

As a practitioner, her clients benefit from Ms. Desurvire's wealth of knowledge and experience with many top publishers and studios, such as Disney Online, THQ publishers, Electronic Arts, Heavy Iron, Relic, Disney Interactive, LucasArts, Sega, Creative Assembly, and many more. She has worked both on consumer and serious games.

Ms. Desurvire has pioneered research on alternative methodologies for evaluating the usability of user interfaces. A summary of her research work is published in "Usability Inspection Methods" (John Wiley & Sons, edited by J. Nielsen and R. Mack) and in an upcoming book "Evaluating User Experience in Games: Concepts and Methods". Her research has appeared in journals and conferences, such as the HCI, INTERACT, and CHI.

Her current research involves developing principles for helping game developers design better access in their game designs for newer gamers.

Arjan Geven studied Technology and Society at the Eindhoven University of Technology (The Netherlands), with specialization in Human–Technology Interaction. He gained international experience in usability and research methods at the University of Linköping (LIU, Sweden). He participated in various national and European research projects and is author of various publications on usability and user experience. At CURE, he deals with issues on user experience research methodology in the context of entertainment and innovation.

Michael Haller is a professor at the Department of Digital Media of the Upper Austria University of Applied Sciences (Hagenberg, Austria), head of the Media Interaction Lab (www.mi-lab.org), head of the Austrian Research Center NiCE, and is responsible for computer graphics, human–computer interaction, and augmented reality. His core areas of expertise are visualization and interaction. He received Dipl.-Ing. (1997), Dr. techn. (2001), and Habilitation (2007) degrees from Johannes Kepler University of Linz, Austria. He is active in several research areas, including interactive computer graphics, augmented and virtual reality, and human–computer interfaces. His current focus is on innovative interaction techniques and interfaces for next generation working environments. Currently, he leads a team of over 10 researchers and students. In 2004, he received the Erwin Schrödinger fellowship award presented by the Austrian Science Fund for his visit at the Human Interaction Technology Laboratory (HITLabNZ), University of Canterbury (New Zealand), and the Integrated Media Systems Center (IMSC), University of Southern California (USA). The research output includes 13 journal papers and book chapters and has been presented already in high-quality academic conferences and several demonstrations, including ACM SIGGRAPH, Eurographics, Disney's New Technology Forum, and Ars Electronica Festival. In 2006, he was also invited to exhibit his work for 5 years at the Singapore Science Center. In 2007, Haller taught the ACM SIGGRAPH course "Interaction Tomorrow." Since 2008, Haller is head of the Austrian Research Studio NiCE, designing natural user interfaces for collaborative environments.

Jukka Häkkinen received his Ph.D. degree in experimental psychology from the Department of Psychology, University of Helsinki, Finland. Later he worked as a principal researcher in Nokia Research Center, Helsinki. Currently, he is working as a post-doctoral researcher at a Department of Media Technology, Aalto University in Espoo, Finland. His research has focused on the ergonomics and experiential aspects of emerging display technologies, like head-mounted, stereoscopic, and paper-like displays. He has also investigated image quality with mobile video and mobile camera technologies. Currently, he is investigating the subjective image quality in stereoscopic movies.

Wolfgang Hochleitner received his master's degree from the Upper Austria University of Applied Sciences, Hagenberg. His major in the program Digital Media were computer games; his thesis dealt with the performance of computer games in the programing language Java. Wolfgang also has practical experience in the field of mobile game development, acquired during an internship at an Infineon subsidiary. Wolfgang is currently working as an assistant lecturer at the Media Technology and Design program at the Upper Austria University of Applied Sciences, with a focus on technical subjects. He is also actively involved in the computer games education.

Bart Van Iersel is a bachelor student in Innovation Sciences at Eindhoven University of Technology. His bachelor thesis focuses on long-term postgame experiences in heavy MMORPG players.

Wijnand IJsselsteijn is an associate professor at the Human–Technology Interaction group of Eindhoven University of Technology. He has a background in psychology and artificial intelligence, with an MSc in Cognitive Neuropsychology from Utrecht University, and a Ph.D. in Media Psychology/HCI from Eindhoven University of Technology on the topic of telepresence. His current research interests include social digital media, immersive media technology, and digital gaming. His focus is on conceptualizing and measuring human experiences in relation to these advanced media. Wijnand is significantly involved in various commercial, nationally funded, and EU-funded projects. He is associate director of the Media, Interface, and Network Design labs (http://www.mindlab.org/cgi-bin/default.pl), and co-director of the Game Experience Lab (http://www.gamexplab.nl). He has published over 100 journal and conference papers and co-edited four books.

Katherine Isbister is an associate professor of both Digital Media and Computer Science at the Polytechnic Institute of New York University. She is director of the Social Game Lab at NYU-Poly, an investigator in the NYU Games for Learning Institute, and an advisory committee member of the NYU Game Center. She also maintains an affiliation with the IT University of Copenhagen's Center for Computer Games Research.

Isbister received her Ph.D. from Stanford University, with a focus on applying human social behavior to the design of digital characters. Since then she has worked in both industry and research venues to create and evaluate interfaces that enhance the player (or user) experience using social and emotional qualities. Current research interests include emotion and gesture in games, supple interactions, design of game characters, and game usability.

Isbister has written two books: Better Game Characters by Design and Game Usability. Better Game Characters was nominated for a Game Developer Magazine Frontline Award. Isbister serves on the advisory board of the IGDA Games Education Special Interest Group, and on the editorial board of the International Journal of Human Computer Studies. In 1999, she was selected as one of MIT Technology Review's TR100 Young Innovators, most likely to shape the future of technology.

Jyrki Kaistinen, M.A. (Psych.), has been studying several human factors and ergonomics areas for last 20 years. He has done numerous projects for public sector and private companies concerning traffic safety, computer-supported collaborative work, user interfaces, organizational development, workplace design, and software development for laboratory work. Currently, he is working as a researcher and teacher in the Psychology of Evolving Media and Technology group, in the Department of Psychology, University of Helsinki, Finland.

Aidan Kehoe works at Logitech Inc. He has worked on product and middleware development for peripherals on a variety of systems, including PC, Sony, and Nintendo platforms. He is co-inventor of a number of patents relating to game controllers. He received his Ph.D. from University College Cork for work in the area of speech interfaces.

Jurek Kirakowski's specialty is quantitative measurement in Human–Computer Interaction and he has contributed numerous books, articles, and workshops to this theme. His major research goal has been to show and indeed prove how the quality of use of information technology products can, and should be, quantitatively measured in an objective manner. Dr. Kirakowski and his group have contributed the Software Usability Measurement Inventory (SUMI) and the Website Analysis and Measurement Inventory (WAMMI) questionnaires, which are by now "de facto" standards in their respective areas. His personal home page is found at http://www.ucc.ie/hfrg/jk.

Yvonne de Kort is assistant professor in environmental psychology and co-director of the Game Experience Lab at Eindhoven University of Technology. She received her Ph.D. in 1999 and since then she has been working in the Human–Technology Interaction Group. She specializes in the interaction between humans and their socio-physical environment. Yvonne's current research focuses on two domains. The first comprises spaces, technology, and social interaction (e.g., situated social interaction in and around digital games, locatedness in mediated social interaction). The second lies at the intersection of spaces, technology, and health (restorative effects of mediated environments, effects of lighting on people's health, mood, and mental restoration). Her research has also covered topics in persuasive technology and norm activation. Yvonne is involved in several European projects under the sixth and seventh framework. She supervises Ph.D. students and postdocs, has published over 70 papers, has co-organized scientific workshops and conferences, and reviews for various journals and conferences. Website: http://www.yvonnedekort.nl.

Christina Koeffel studied Digital Media at the Upper Austria University of Applied Sciences Hagenberg with focus on interactive media. She completed a second master degree in Medialogy at Aalborg University Copenhagen, where she concentrated her studies on international usability and usability issues in virtual reality. Christina has authored several publications in connection to general usability, games and social networks. At CURE, Christina deals with usability issues in advanced user interfaces and usability tools. Her personal emphasis is on usability in connection with new interaction paradigms such as computer games.

Michael Lankes is working at the Department of Digital Media of the Upper Austria, University of Applied Sciences (Hagenberg, Austria), focusing on the topics game art and game design. He earned a Ph.D. in communication studies (focus: Human–Computer Interaction) from the University of Salzburg. Within his doctoral thesis "Artificial Faces in Context – Introducing the Interaction Paradigm to Investigate Facial Expressions Performed by Embodied Conversational Agents," an experimental setting to observe and measure the perception of facial expression performed by embodied conversational agents (ECAs) is proposed.

Michael Lankes also holds a master's degree in Multimedia Art from the University of Applied Sciences, Salzburg. Apart from various research activities, he earned experience as a freelance 3D artist and as an illustrator. Furthermore, Michael Lankes was involved in various projects at the ICT&S Center Salzburg (research fellow), the Ars Electronica Futurelab in Linz (researcher in virtual environments), and the Sony DVDCE (interface designer).

Jakob Franz Leitner is a Ph.D. candidate at the Media Interaction Lab of the Upper Austria University of Applied Sciences, Austria. His research interests include tabletop interfaces, real-time computer graphics, and nontraditional interfaces with a special focus on next-generation gaming. Leitner received an MSc. in engineering from the Upper Austria University of Applied Sciences, Austria.

Philippe Lemay, Ph.D., received his Master Diploma in Cognitive Science from the prestigious École Polytechnique of Paris and his Ph.D. in Psychology from the University of Lausanne. During his 10-year stay in Europe, he also worked at TEChnologies de Formation et d'Apprentissage (TECFA) at the University of Geneva, a reference center for distance teaching and learning environments.

He was a university professor for more than 6 years at University of Montreal and is recognized as the main responsible for the creation and the management of the first university graduate studies program specialized in game design in Canada. Throughout his courses, workshops, and seminars, students have benefited from his expertise in contemporary topics such as experiences, interactions, emotions, learning, and other relevant psychological aspects exhibited in various interactive systems.

His research activities focus on key themes such as: experience and experience design paradigm, and more specifically optimal experiences, the cornerstone of the conceptual and pragmatic approach he puts forward; the bidirectional relationships existing between games and learning, or how to make learning environments more fun and efficient by integrating ludic aspects, and, conversely, how to make games more instructive, even enlightening, by integrating learning principles; the impacts of videogames on quality of life; and finally the development of user-centered methodologies, in particular language patterns, scenarios, experience sampling methods, and semantic differentials.

He now leads design, research, and consulting activities in the game design community with his company Ludosys.

Martin Maheux-Lessard, MSc., works as a user-research specialist at Ubisoft Montreal. Within the GamesLab, his job is to coordinate user-research activities such as focus groups, benchmarks, and playtests. He also offers coaching and support to development teams for early prototype testing, with people from the target audience. Before joining Ubisoft, Martin was a student at the University of Montreal, where he received the Faculty's first master's degree related to the design of videogames. The case study presented within this chapter showcases many facets of the work he submitted for his master's thesis, which was led under the direction of Professor Philippe Lemay.

Martin also holds a bachelor's degree in Industrial Design, where he developed an interest for ergonomics and user-centered design methodologies. As a student, Martin worked as a research assistant on various virtual reality projects and as a teaching assistant for two design-related courses. He also worked as a tester for the mobile division of Electronics Arts in Montreal.

Graham McAllister is a senior lecturer in Human–Computer Interaction at the University of Sussex, United Kingdom. His research is in the area of designing new methods to evaluate the usability and user experience of video games.

Graham is also the director of Vertical Slice, the United Kingdom's first company to focus entirely on the area of video games usability and user experience. Their studios are based in Brighton and feature facilities in which the interaction between players and video games can be observed, captured, and analyzed. Previous to joining the University of Sussex, Graham was a lecturer in Music Technology at the Sonic Arts Research Centre (SARC) at Queen's University Belfast, Northern Ireland. At SARC, his research focused on multimodal technology, in particular how the senses of sound and touch can be used to enhance, or replace, visuals for games and other digital environments.

In 2006, he completed a 3-month industrial secondment at Unity Technologies, makers of the game creation tool Unity based in Copenhagen, Denmark. During his placement, he was able to explore usability and user experience of video games from a different perspective that of the technology which creates games themselves. Graham has a Ph.D. in Computer Science (Computer Graphics) and a B.Eng. in Software Engineering.

Florian 'Floyd' Mueller is researching Exertion Interfaces – computer interfaces that require physical effort – in the Department of Information Systems at the University of Melbourne, Australia. Floyd has degrees in Digital Media from Germany, in Multimedia from Australia, and in Media Arts and Sciences from the

MIT Media Lab, USA. He has extensive work experience from the USA, Australia, Ireland, and Germany, where he worked for industry and research companies such as Virtual Artists, Xerox PARC, FX Palo Alto Laboratory, MIT, and Media Lab Europe. Prior to joining the University of Melbourne, he was a principal scientist at CSIRO, where he led the "Connecting People" group with 12 staff, researching the future of human connectedness.

Floyd received several awards for the games he designed, including being short listed for the European Innovative Games Award. He published for the major human–computer interaction conferences (CHI, Siggraph) and exhibited his work at Wired's NextFest. He is also interested in the business side of bringing research advances into the real world and was semi-finalist of MIT's 50K entrepreneurship competition.

Floyd received several prestigious scholarships to conduct research in the USA and Australia. He is also a fellow with Distance Lab, UK, and London Knowledge Lab, UK, and a Microsoft Research Asia Fellow in China as well as a Fulbright scholar with Stanford University, USA (http://exertioninterfaces.com).

Professor Göte Nyman is the leader of the Psychology of Evolving Media and Technology research group (POEM). He has a specific interest within the scope of research group, which is to understand complex human experiences related to the use of future digital technologies and media environments in various areas of life, e.g., communication, entertainment, and collaborative work. In studying human experiential phenomena, POEM focuses on media and material with real or real-like contents, such as magazines, games, photographs, videos, and movies. Focused psychological methodology is applied for these new technologies and media environments. This includes both qualitative and quantitative data collection as well as psychometric methods to analyze both linear and nonlinear multivariate data.

Ian Pitt lectures in Usability Engineering and Multimedia at UCC. He took his DPhil at the University of York, United Kingdom, then spent a year as a post-doctoral research fellow at Otto-von-Guericke University, Magdeburg, Germany, before moving to Cork in 1997. His research interests include the use of speech and nonspeech sound in human–machine interfaces.

Karolien Poels is an assistant professor of Strategic Communication at the University of Antwerp (Belgium), specializing in consumer psychology and digital gaming research. She has an M.A. in Communication Studies and a Ph.D. in Social Sciences (both from Ghent University). She previously worked as a post doc researcher at the Human Technology Interaction Group of Eindhoven University of Technology (March 2007–September 2009) where she was involved in the FUGA-project (EU-FP6, NEST). Karolien has a proven record of interdisciplinary and multi-method research. Her doctoral dissertation focused on the role of emotions in advertising and mainly discussed how understanding emotions can contribute to better insights into how advertising works. This work was very interdisciplinary in nature, combining insights from communication sciences, marketing, social psychology, and neuroscience. Parts of her dissertation are published in international journals such as *Journal of Advertising and Journal of Business Research*. After her Ph.D., Karolien joined the Game Experience Lab of Eindhoven University of Technology and started integrating her experience and knowledge on emotions into the field of digital gaming. Her current research at the MIOS (Media & ICT in Organisations & Society) Research Group at the University of Antwerp focuses on the experience and consumption of digital media (e.g., digital games, virtual worlds) and strategic communication in digital worlds (e.g., in-game advertising, health communication through digital media).

Jari Takatalo, Lic.A. (Psych.), is working as a researcher in Psychology of Evolving Media and Technology (POEM) research group located at the Department of Psychology, University of Helsinki. Takatalo has several years of experience in developing a psychological theory and measurement method to understand experiences in various computer-generated environments. His research interests concern both work and entertainment applications with various display technologies (for example, head-mounted and stereo displays and CAVE's). Currently, he is finishing his Ph.D. in user experience measurement model for digital games.

Manfred Tscheligi is professor for Human–Computer Interaction & Usability at the University of Salzburg, ICT&S Center (Center for Advanced Studies and Research in Information and Communication Technologies & Society). He is founder and director of CURE, the Vienna (Austria) based Center for Usability Research & Engineering, which is an independent research organization. He is also founder, owner, and managing director of USECON-The Usability Consultants GmbH, an international usability and user experience engineering consultancy company.

Manfred has been active in the areas of Interactive Systems, Human–Computer Interaction, Usability Engineering, User Interface Design, and User Experience Research for more than 20 years. Manfred Tscheligi has done pioneer work to establish the field in Austria (both in university education, as research field and industrially applied field). He is also recognized as an active actor in the international scene. He has been successfully managing numerous research and industrial projects (among these more than 20 EC projects) and established national and international initiatives in this field.

Gareth R. White is a Ph.D. student at the University of Sussex, United Kingdom. His research explores the design and evaluation of usability and user experience for video games, with a particular interest in practical solutions for titles under development by professional studios. Gareth has been playing video games since the Atari VCS 2600 arrived in his living room in the late 1970s, subsequently going on to teach himself how to program computer games on the BBC Micro as a child in the 1980s, and earning a BSc. (Hons) in Computer Science from the University of Brighton in 1998.

Since graduating, Gareth has published several games as a professional programer working for studios in London, England; Adelaide, South Australia; and with Rockstar Games in Vienna, Austria, where he worked on titles in the Grand

Theft Auto and Manhunt series. More recently, Gareth has consolidated his professional and personal interests with academic research, earning an M.A. in New Media from the University of the West of England in 2007, where he wrote about the nature of embodiment in Resident Evil 4: Wii Edition.

He has presented talks at the Australian Game Developers Conference about programing techniques for console development and has helped to launch and run Vertical Slice, a professional video game research company focusing on usability and user experience.

Charlotte Wiberg assistant professor in Informatics, Umeå University, Sweden. Dr. Wiberg received her Ph.D. (2003) and bachelor's degree (1997) from Umeå University in Sweden. Dr. Wiberg is specialized in evaluation methods for evaluating fun and entertainment in digital media and information technology. Her work focuses on games, websites, and other experience-related applications. In her earlier work, she conducted evaluations using traditional usability methods on entertainment IT and she proposed revision of the methods according to results in order to evaluate fun. Wiberg has conducted usability design – as a researcher and practitioner – for Vodafone, Swedish National TV (SVT), TeliaSonera, Coke Zero, and Le Meridien to mention some.

Dennis Wixon currently serves as a user research manager for Microsoft Surface. Over the past 12 years Dennis has managed research for MSN, Microsoft Home Products, and Microsoft Game Studios. Dennis previously worked as a usability manager at Digital Equipment Corporation, where a number of important usability methods such as Usability Engineering and Contextual Inquiry were developed. His primary interest is innovative research methods for more usable, useful, and exciting designs that lead to commercial success. In addition, Dennis has been an active member of the human factors community for many years. Notably, in 1982 he was one of the five founding members of the Greater Boston Chapter of the ACM SIGCHI and was general co-chair of the SIGCHI 2002 conference. He has served as vice chair for Conferences for ACM SIGCHI and has been a member of the SIGCHI Executive Committee. Dennis has authored over 50 articles, book chapters, and talks on HCI and co-edited the book *Field Methods Case Book for Software Design* with Prof. Judy Ramey of the University of Washington.

Wixon holds a Ph.D. in Social Psychology from Clark University and has published in numerous psychological journals, including *The Journal of Personality and Social Psychology* and *The Journal of Experimental Psychology*.

Part I
Introduction to Evaluation of UX

Chapter 1
User Experience Evaluation in Entertainment

Regina Bernhaupt

Abstract Based on an overview on currently used definitions of user experience in human–computer interaction and major concepts from game development like immersion, flow, and playability, this overview describes a set of evaluation methods and their applicability in the various game development phases. Summarizing the contributions in this book, a user experience-centered development process is presented, allowing readers to understand when to use what kind of user experience evaluation methods to achieve a positive user experience.

1.1 Introduction

User experience evaluations in games and more general in interactive entertainment systems have been performed from early on in games development. Programers of the first computing systems started to develop the first versions of digital games and already established a very basic form of user experience evaluation by simply trying to play the game – and trying to understand why it was not fun in the end. The introduction of video games like Tetris showed that small changes in game play or story heavily influence the overall user experience of the game (Novak 2008).

In industry today a variety of methods are deployed to understand the various contributing aspects of the overall gaming experience. The term user experience was only rarely used in the games industry (Federoff 2002), but became extremely prominent in the field of HCI during the last 10 years. Since then the scientific communities of human–computer interaction and game research are starting to learn from each other. On the one hand, user experience evaluation methods from HCI are used during the game development to improve user experience, on the other side HCI was borrowing and investigating aspects of the gaming

R. Bernhaupt (✉)
IRIT, IHCS, Toulouse, France
e-mail: Regina.Bernhaupt@irit.fr

R. Bernhaupt (ed.), *Evaluating User Experience in Games*, Human-Computer Interaction Series, DOI 10.1007/978-1-84882-963-3_1,
© Springer-Verlag London Limited 2010

experience like immersion, fun, or flow to better understand the concept of user experience.

This chapter gives an overview on both aspects. First, an overview on definitions of user experience in the area of HCI is given, followed by some basic terms that are currently used in the games industry like immersion, flow, or playability. Then an overview on currently applied methods for the evaluation of user experience in games is given. This overview also includes all of the methods that are proposed, described, discussed, and presented in the following chapters of the book. To allow an easy overview on the currently applied methods for user experience evaluation, the most commonly used methods are presented. To help identify the applicability of the various user experience evaluation methods, the methods are presented following four major development phases: initial stages of game development, early development stages, prototypical stage and later (implementation) stages, and finally alpha and beta phases.

1.2 Defining User Experience

How user experience should be defined is currently discussed in the HCI community. User eXperience (UX) still misses a clear definition. As of today, the term user experience can be seen as an umbrella term used to stimulate research in HCI to focus on aspects which are beyond usability and its task-oriented instrumental values (Hassenzahl 2003). User experience does include a look on all the (qualitative) experience a user is making while interacting with a product (McCarthy and Wright 2004), or on experiences made during interacting with a special type of product, e.g., a mobile phone (Roto 2006). The current ISO definition on user experience focuses on a person's perception and the responses resulting from the use or anticipated use of a product, system, or service. From a psychological perspective, these responses are actively generated in a psychological evaluation process, and it has to be decided which concepts can best represent the psychological compartments in games to allow to measure the characteristics of user experience (see Takatalo et al., Chapter 3).

User experience in games has been evaluated using a variety of concepts including immersion, fun, presence, involvement, engagement, flow (see Takatalo et al., Chapter 3), play, and playability – and what makes play fun, including social play (see Isbister, Chapter 2). Given that user experience is understood as the subjective relationship between user and application (McCarthy and Wright 2004), Calvillo-Gámez (Chapter 4) proposes the CEGE approach to allow to differentiate between different subjective experiences. Other evaluation approaches focusing on experiences and attitudes toward video games are the use of semantic differentials (Lemay et al., Chapter 6). From an industry perspective, the tools currently in use to enable the evaluation of user experience are closely connected to the game development phases. E. Brown (Chapter 5) describes tools used in games industry according to the various development phases. During the concept phase, classical user-centered development methods like (paper) prototyping are used to allow to understand if the game is fun to play or a tech demo is used to allow not only to understand the robustness of the technology but to enable a first evaluation of the fun potential. In the preproduction phase, evaluation methods like heuristics are used; during production, user testing is one of the most successful methodologies to evaluate user experiences. Post-launch user experience evaluations are based on reviews and online forums. McAllister et al. (Chapter 7) provide more insight into current industrial practices to evaluate user experience based on a set of case studies.

Decomposing various aspects of user experience in games, we have to understand that the user experience depends on the individual player experiences (see Desurvire et al. in Chapter 8 for game approachable principles for inexperienced users), that various phases during the game play will provoke different forms of experiences (see Poels et al. in Chapter 9), and that user experience will be influenced by various aspects of the game including the behavior of nonplayer characters (see Lankes et al. in Chapter 10 on investigating aspects of user experience with experiments).

Evaluation of user experience not only depends on the various constructs and factors that contribute to the general experience, but can be heavily influenced by the interaction technique and format of the game. Mueller et al. present evaluation possibilities for exertion games (see Chapter 11), Brown et al. look into the evaluation of game controllers (see Chapter 12), and Köffel et al. present ways on how to evaluate tabletop games (see Chapter 13).

1.3 Methods to Evaluate UX in Games

Based on the various definitions and concepts used to evaluate user experience, the following section will present an overview on methods that are currently used to evaluate user experience during the various game development phases. Game development can be structured in a set of development phases. Most of these phases are used in standard software development processes; other phases are special for game development. Following Novak (2008), the following phases are used to structure the overview on methods for evaluating user experience in games:

- Concept: This phase is dedicated to the initial game idea and is devoted to producing a first concept document describing the game. The development team in this phase is typically small (e.g., consisting of designer, programer, artist, and producer).
- Preproduction phase: This phase includes the development of art style guides, production plans, and first description of the game design and the technical design document.
- Prototype: Goal of this phase is a first working piece of software allowing to demonstrate key characteristics of the game and enabling to understand basic concepts related to the general user experience of the game ("Is the game fun to play?").

- Production: The production phase can range from few weeks development to years of programing. This phase can be structured additionally, following approaches like an increment to completion approach, a cascade approach, or an "iterative – until you drop" approach (Irish 2005).
- Localization: An important phase for games that will be delivered to different markets (countries) is the localization phase. In this phase, game play can be adjusted to suit the tastes of the market, to allow language translation and modifications due to local regulatory authorities.
- Alpha-phase: This is the phase when a game is playable from start to finish, allowing different evaluation methods to be applied to better understand aspects like fun, playability, and user experience.
- Beta-phase: Main goal during this phase is normally to fix bugs. In terms of user experience in this phase, lots of fine-tuning is necessary to improve the overall user experience. The beta-phase includes steps like certification or submission (the hardware manufacturer of the proprietary platform will test the game).
- Gold: In this phase, the game is sent to be manufactured.
- Postproduction: In this phase, subsequent versions of the game may be released (including patches and updated) and allow to improve the user experience of the game.

Goal of evaluating user experience during the *concept phase* is to understand if the game will be fun to play and what kind of experience the player will have during game play. During the concept phase and other early development phases like the *preproduction and prototype phase*, methods and approaches used are

- Focus groups
- Interviews
- Informal play testing
- Questionnaires

In this book, E. Brown presents methods like (paper) prototyping and tech demos (see Chapter 5), Isbister shows that early (internal) play testing and analysis of existing play patterns can help to understand user experiences in general and especially for social play (see Chapter 2). Methods like semantic differentials (see Chapter 6) and the PIFF questionnaire (Chapter 3) allow to gain a general understanding of the game user experience. Methods like the GAP approach (Chapter 8) investigate user experience for a special user group – the inexperienced gamer.

During the *implementation and testing phases*, the following methods have been successfully used:

- Play testing (including biometrical measurements)
- (Semi-structured) interviews
- Observation
- Video coding
- Quantitative comparisons of gamers' behaviors

- Questionnaires focusing on users' attitudes, experiences,. . .
- Heuristic evaluation (including heuristics for playability, tabletop)

For new forms of game play including new forms of interaction, Mueller et al. (Chapter 11) describe how to evaluate exertion games in the implementation and testing phase and Köffel et al. (Chapter 13) present how to investigate user experience for tabletop games. Other influencing factors on the overall user experience are described by Poels et al. (Chapter 9) for post-game experiences, Lankes et al. (Chapter 10) for the influence of nonplayer characters on the overall user experience, and Brown et al. (Chapter 12) for evaluation of game controller design.

Acknowledgments This book is based on two workshops on methods for user experience evaluation in games which were held during ACE 2007 (Conference on Advances in Computer Entertainment Technology) and at CHI 2008. I would like to thank all participants in these workshops for the fruitful discussions and their engagement to contribute to the book, the workshop co-organizers for their support, and all reviewers of these workshops for their help in improving the first versions of the workshop papers and the book chapters.

This book would not exist without the financial, organizational, or personal support of the following people: Ferdinand Maier, Jean Vanderdonkt, Manfred Tscheligi, Manfred Eckschlager, Astrid Weiss, Michael Pirker, Sandra Steere, and Marco Winckler. And last – but not least, Merci Philippe, for everything.

References

Federoff MA (2002) Heuristics and usability guidelines for the creation and evaluation of fun in videogames. Master's thesis, Department of Telecommunications, Indiana University.

Hassenzahl M (2003) The thing and I: Understanding the relationship between user and product. In: Blythe MA, Monk AF, Overbeeke K, Wright PC (eds) Funology: From Usability to Enjoyment. Kluwer Academic Publishers, Netherlands.

Irish D (2005) The Game Producer's Handbook. Thomson Course Technology PRT, Boston, MA.

McCarthy J, Wright P (2004) Technology as Experience. MIT Press, Cambridge, MA.

Novak J (2008) Game Development Essentials. Delmar Cengage Learning, Clifton Park, NY.

Roto V (2006) Web browsing on mobile phones – Characteristics of user experience. PhD Thesis, University of Helsinki.

Part II
Frameworks and Methods

Chapter 2
Enabling Social Play: A Framework for Design and Evaluation

Katherine Isbister

Abstract This chapter focuses on evaluation and design for successful social play in digital games. It includes an overview of published work in this area and best practices gleaned from professional discussions and descriptions and presents a framework for thinking about an effective evaluation and iteration process. The framework includes issues such as identifying play subgroups and how they differ, interpersonal dynamics that can and should be leveraged and looked for in multiplayer play, hardware factors in supporting social play, and issues of external validity in evaluation of social play. It includes key challenges and work that remains to be done in this area.

2.1 Introduction

There is very little written about testing multiplayer social engagement and enjoyment of games per se, and how this can feed back into the design process, even though 59% of gamers surveyed report playing games with others (Entertainment Software Association 2008). Much of existing practice is based on intuition and on word-of-mouth best practices that spread among industry practitioners. This chapter brings together what has been published about existing practices, and theory and useful practice from related fields, to provide a framework for both practitioners and researchers that can help to further define this important evaluation area.

2.1.1 Brief Overview of Related Work

While there is published material on play testing in general (Fullerton et al. 2004, Collins 1997), there has been until very recently little written discussion of play

K. Isbister (✉)
Polytechnic Institute of New York University, Brooklyn, NY, USA
e-mail: isbister@poly.edu

R. Bernhaupt (ed.), *Evaluating User Experience in Games*, Human-Computer
Interaction Series, DOI 10.1007/978-1-84882-963-3_2,
© Springer-Verlag London Limited 2010

testing of groups to evaluate the success or failure of social play. There is a discussion of methods used by the Microsoft Games User Research group for studying group games in a recent edited book (Amaya et al. 2008). There is also a brief discussion of group dynamics in a piece concerning role-playing games (Tychsen et al. 2008).

There have been arguments made about the importance of social play to games (Lazzaro 2008, Isbister 2008, Colwell et al. 1995, Neimeyer et al. 2005), and research has been conducted showing that there are differences between solo and social play, such as "more positive effect, less tension, and more competence" self-reported in social play (Gajadhar et al. 2008, p. 3103), as well as less frustration in social play versus solo play as measured by physiological indices (Mandryk et al. 2006).

Designers in the pervasive and mobile gaming spaces have, by necessity, innovated effective ways to test their games with groups of players (Koivisto and Suomela 2007, McGonigal 2005, Sanneblad and Holmquist 2004, Szentgyorgyi et al. 2008). Most of the time, though, these designers and evaluators focus on balancing game play in general, rather than investigating the social components of play in particular.

One way we might approach the study of social play is through better understanding of player characteristics and motivations (e.g., Yee's work in massively multiplayer worlds (Yee 2006), Lazzaro's analysis of different types of fun inherent in play (Lazzaro 2008), also Batemen and Boon's taxonomies (2005)). It could also be interesting to examine relationships among members of a heterogeneous play group – for example, between parents and children (Bryant et al. 2008) or between grandchildren and grandparents (Khoo et al. 2007). The uses and gratifications model from traditional media research could also be valuable in this context (Vorderer and Bryant 2006).

The aim of this chapter is to bring together these interesting strands of prior work into a synthesis focused upon social game play as a value in and of itself, alongside other game design concerns.

2.1.2 Defining Social Play

What is meant here by social play is active engagement with a game (through use of its controls or through observation and attention to ongoing game play) by more than one person at once. There is a range of formats that this can take. It may be two or more people playing in the same room, as with a fighter game such as Guilty Gear or party game such as Mario Kart, or across a network in different locations, as with a massively multiplayer game such as World of Warcraft. The game itself may be designed to support multiplayer simultaneous play, as in the previous examples, or the game may be a single-player game that players have decided to engage with using a technique like controller passing that allows for cooperative play (see Narcisse 2008 for a detailed description of an experience with controller passing while playing Portal and Assasin's Creed).

It is also the case that there is important social interaction taking place among colocated players, even when they are not all taking an active role in game play in a given play round. Observers in a colocated social group may provide coaching and critical commentary that substantially adds to the gaming experience for those who are playing, and over the course of a play session, may in turn become active players. This is a subarea of social play that also deserves consideration in design and evaluation and is included in this chapter.

Finally, there are some who believe that interacting with nonplayer characters in games is a form of social play (Isbister 2006, Lazzaro 2008). While this may indeed be a legitimate form of social play, it is not included in the analysis in this chapter.

2.1.3 Why Focus on Social Play

There are several reasons social play is an important place to focus our efforts in understanding the game play experience.

A primary reason is that games, even single-player games, are often played in social contexts. As mentioned above, the ESA reports that 59% of their survey respondents played games with others. If we want to understand the user experience of games thoroughly, we must include consideration of the social nature of the experience.

Another reason to turn our attention toward social play is that adding people to the play session creates a fundamentally different end experience. It isn't as if two players are having the same experience as a single person would on his/her own. There are many social phenomena that contribute to this. For example, the presence of others in a play session has an impact on each player's learning curve and mastery of a game. People model game play behavior that others learn from, and those who have already figured out new mechanics or challenges may offer coaching to those who have not yet arrived at these insights. Spectators and coplayers can create priming and framing effects for players with the comments they make about what is happening – drawing attention to some things and not others, creating extra-game competitions or other narratives that players take part in, reminiscing about past play sessions and framing the goals for the present session in ways that may transcend or run counter to explicit game goals, and the like. And it seems to be the case (as mentioned in Section 2.1.2) that playing with others can affect each player's moment-to-moment experience of game play (e.g., raising positive affect, lowering frustration).

Social play sessions also end up serving as a forum for ongoing evolution of relationships among players, and play activities are thus contextualized within the larger framework of strengthening ties, building trust, forging alliances, flirting, and the like, among a community of players.

From a designer's point of view, there are compelling reasons to focus on social play explicitly. In terms of designing multiplayer games, it is essential to approach evaluation and iteration from the perspective of supporting social play.

Even with single-player games, the "over-the-shoulder" appeal of a game becomes an important factor in adoption and sales of the game.

For all these reasons, social play is an important aspect of the player's experience for the user experience (UX) research and practice community to address.

2.1.4 A Framework for Understanding Social Play

In order to grasp how social play will affect the UX of gaming, and to come up with appropriate design and evaluation tactics, it's important to have a nuanced understanding of the many factors that shape the nature of social play. This section covers some key factors presenting a preliminary framework for understanding and analyzing social play.

It may be helpful to hold in mind several very different examples of social play, as a backdrop against which to apply these factors:

- A Nintendo DS play session among colleagues taking a break from work, which takes place in a stairwell of their office complex (a play pattern reported in Szentgyorgyi et al. 2008).
- Members of a World of Warcraft guild, having met in person for the very first time at a convention, playing together online once they all travel back home (taken from experiences described by Taylor 2006).
- Contestants going head-to-head in an all-day competition in Dance Dance Revolution, sponsored by a campus DDR club (personally observed by author).
- A child, grandparent, and mother trying out an RFID-enabled physical game developed by researchers interested in supporting cross-generational play (experience created by Age Invaders research team, reported in Khoo et al. 2007).

There are many differences among these situations that help to illustrate some of the key dimensions of social play.

2.1.4.1 Contextual Factors

It is helpful when analyzing social play to take a look at contextual factors that frame the play: e.g., the form factors of the gaming platform upon which the game is played and the physical context of play. Often these are intertwined – that is to say certain platform characteristics lend themselves to certain settings.

Consider the platforms mentioned in the examples above. The Nintendo DS, with its wireless access and portable format, allows players to cluster almost anywhere and play a game together. There is no need to travel to a place that houses the game equipment. The small personal screens take away one component of most colocated social play sessions – viewing of a large shared screen with shared audio as well. Each person has his/her own inputs, and this also affects how many people can play (depending upon choices the designers have made). It also profoundly affects some of the possibilities for social play. For example, it's very difficult to engage in observational learning or do active mentoring when using the Nintendo DS because there isn't a readily available shared visual reference. It can become unclear who is who onscreen, in a multiplayer game, a confusion that players can learn to exploit in ways that enhance everyone's experience. Gaming sessions can start and stop very quickly and informally, allowing players to form fluid play sessions that come together in spare moments in a day.

The DDR competition example involves shared access to arcade quality game machines for a contest among players who typically play together using home equipment in a campus recreation room. The arcade machine gives the contest a "professional" feel for the players and seems to "up the ante" for them in their interactions. It marks a formal competition from the usual weekly matchups.

Using custom equipment, like Age Invaders' RFID tags in player shoes, which are tracked as players move around on a custom LED-block play grid, while aiming Bluetooth-enabled toy guns, brings its own challenges to social play. Players must get familiar with how the equipment works and how to manage it to engage in game play. Glitches in performance of custom and still research-grade hardware, such as failure to connect properly, can profoundly impact the play experience and muddy any results in examining social interactions around the play. Being in a lab setting may make participants self-conscious or uncomfortable in ways that affect their social interactions, as well.

Finally, even the typical person-sitting-at-PC platform social play scenario can be shaped by context . . . in the case of the MMO player returning home, memories of interacting in person are still fresh and make her notice the ways in which she interacts with the others. She can hold in her mind images of how these people look in person, and how they interact "live," and this impacts how she perceives the interface she has to them through the game avatars and controls. The platform constraints and typical physical context of MMO play (each person sitting at his/her own PC alone at home) become newly relevant and visible.

To summarize, in order to fully understand the user experience of social play, we need to make visible to ourselves as designers and researchers, the contextual factors that will influence the shape that social play takes. Screen size and control schemes, portability, network access, novelty of equipment, and typical versus atypical or special contexts all have an impact on how social play will unfold.

2.1.4.2 Motivational Factors

Social play experiences are also highly determined by the composition of the group that is playing. Who are the players? Why did they choose to play with one another? What are their prior relationships and how does play serve to enhance these?

A group of officemates playing DS games as a break from work may be solidifying their ties as co-workers as well as building extra-office friendships. They may be making a statement to one another about how they feel about work, by choosing to play during work hours.

A formal competition among clubmates is part of the official "work" of the club and also sets the pecking order among club members in terms of skill and performance under pressure. Players may behave differently in head-to-head matches if they are trying to support and sustain ongoing relationships (e.g., a couple playing against one another).

MMO players who've newly strengthened ties with an in-person convention meeting may end up playing differently as they work to accomplish goals together, forming new alliances within their party and chatting about extra-game interactions they've had.

A family playing a research game like Age Invaders that is supposed to support intergenerational ties brings dynamics from other family interactions to the play space. Choosing to volunteer for research probably adds a layer of complexity of motivation to the social interactions going on during play – some of the family members may want to show off their relations in the best possible light, and so forth.

All of these examples point to the complexity of understanding what is going on in a social play session, in terms of how it supports larger social goals and relationships among the players.[1]

Researchers have developed some strategies for weaving complex individual motivations into patterns that can be understood and designed for – creating taxonomies of player motivations (Yee 2006, Batemen and Boon 2005, Lazzaro 2008) that revolve around in-game aims such as Yee's achievement, social and immersion factors, or Lazarro's serious fun, easy fun, people fun, and hard fun categories. These kinds of taxonomies share similarities in approach to the uses and gratification strategies for understanding media that come from the Communication literature (e.g., Vorderer and Bryant 2006). Such taxonomies may be valuable in future, but as of yet, there is not yet much specific information in current taxonomies that focuses on social play in enough detail to truly guide design and evaluation.

2.1.4.3 Conceptual and Theoretical Grounding

Game designers (e.g., Schell 2008, Koster 2004) have done considerable thinking and writing about what makes play fun, including social play. In such cases, the designer shares intuitions based upon practice and observation with his/her target users, working in particular genres that she/he is familiar with. This is very helpful information, but doesn't always lead to reliable and replicable approaches to a broader array of social play situations.

Some have begun to bring a broader conceptual framework about human interaction to their work in analyzing social play – for example, Lazzaro (Lazzaro 2008) grounds her analysis of social play (which she calls "people fun") in an examination of the particular emotions that arise when engaging with others in play, such as love, gratitude, generosity, and embarrassment. She links these emotions to particular choices in game play mechanics. Some of these include offering chances

---

[1] Another factor that has not been addressed in this chapter is the large and complex literature on intrinsic motivational factors (such as personality and baseline arousal preferences) that would of course also come into play in social gaming situations. Readers are encouraged to explore this literature as well.

for players to mentor others, allowing players to personalize their avatars and create profiles that enhance their self-expression, and providing time and mental space during game play for relationship formation to take place.

User experience researchers and designers can benefit from this kind of more broadly based approach, because it can transcend specific design cases and be applicable to emerging platforms and genres as well. Ideally, when possible, this would also draw upon the rich body of knowledge that social scientists such as Social Psychologists, Anthropologists, Communication scholars, and Sociologists have collected through their empirical work on human interaction and media use.

For example, here are three useful concepts drawn from Social Psychological literature, which can be valuable in understanding and evaluating what is happening during social play (there is more detail about these findings and how they can inform design in Isbister 2006 and Isbister 2008).

Social Learning

Social Psychologists have demonstrated that we gain much of our knowledge of how the world works through observation of others moving through the world and acting (e.g., Bandura 1977). One way designers of social games can make social play work well is to think ahead about how their game will support social learning. Is it possible to follow along over-the-shoulder and understand what someone is doing, or is it difficult? Keeping the connection between a player's actions and game progress trackable by observers will make learning happen much faster and may help hesitant players get drawn into play more quickly. Evaluators can confirm whether the design is truly supporting over-the-shoulder learning in play sessions and make suggestions for improvements.

Emotional Contagion

Both social scientists (Hatfield et al. 1994) and neuroscientists (Iacoboni et al. 1999) have gathered evidence that people are very susceptible to one another's moods – emotions are very "contagious." Simply by observing another feeling a certain way, we start to take on that emotion. In social play situations, this means that if the designer can get some players feeling happy, that others are more likely to follow along and feel that same way, creating a sort of snowball effect among the group. It helps to explain why party games can be so fun. Having to take actions very quickly, and do goofy things that may make you laugh, can put the player into a high energy, positive mood, which gets "caught" by those watching, creating a positive feedback loop among the group, leading to mood elevation for everyone. Conversely, something annoying to one player can have a ripple effect among the others and "break the mood."

Physical Feedback Loop

Social Psychologists have conducted experiments (e.g. Strack et al. 1988) that show that part of how people figure out how they are feeling is by tuning into bodily signals of emotion, and then self-labeling about feeling. So if the player feels her body acting as if it were happy and high energy (jumping around excitedly), she will conclude that she must be in a positive mood and will end up feeling more upbeat. With the emergence of physical controller-based games like those for the Nintendo Wii, it's possible to use this physical feedback loop to help induce player emotions that can then spread through the group through emotional contagion.

2.1.5 Evaluation Tactics

Given the many factors and nuances involved in the social play experience, evaluation of effectiveness of design choices toward a strong end user experience must vary accordingly, and a full discussion of the permutations involved is beyond the scope of this chapter. However, there are some general recommendations that can be made about evaluating the success of a given social play experience, which build upon the various aspects discussed in the prior sections.

The first recommendation is a strong focus on ecological validity in testing. The design team must be clear about the expected parameters of use – setting, relational groups and their qualities, known social phenomena (such as emotional contagion or social learning) that should be supported – and should craft a test plan that allows a fair examination of these groups engaging in these activities in these settings. For example, it is helpful to test out mobile or handheld platforms in a setting in which players might engage in game play embedded in their daily lives, rather than in a laboratory setting. It is crucial to test a game directed at preschoolers and their parents with members of the appropriate demographic groups (e.g., Druin et al. 2008). When one is testing a social/party game, it is best to bring in a cohort of players who already are familiar with one another, perhaps recruited through one core player who meets all the target requirements (e.g., Amaya et al. 2008). This can sometimes make testing more costly and complex but may save a development team from essential errors in design that do not take these important environmental and contextual variables into account. Of course these recommendations are easier to follow when a prototype is fairly mature, but even early stage prototyping may benefit from in situ testing, to capture requirements that are otherwise invisible to developers in supporting engaging social play.

In some cases, a company may be able to generate early insights into social play without relying on external testers, by conducting internal tests that mimic the end social experience. For example, Harmonix, when developing Rock Band, had every employee join a "band," play weekly builds of the game, and provide feedback to the design team (Kohler 2007).

Designers may also want to do some exploratory studies of play patterns with other similar games for the target platform, like those conducted in the Nintendo DS project (Szentgyorgyi et al. 2008), to help generate design specifications for social play before a project even begins.

Another general recommendation is to craft questions that are asked to players with the target social experience in mind. That is to say, if the design team hopes to provide a great over-the-shoulder viewing experience, opportunities for creating emotional contagion, encouragement of performance, and the like, it is important to actually ask testers whether these effects were achieved. There are not yet standard questionnaires about these issues available to user experience evaluators, and this is an important area for further research and refinement and for the pooling of resources among both commercial developers and user experience researchers.

In addition to attitudinal measures such as questionnaires, it's ideal to look for behavioral evidence of effects as well, and recording tactics should support this process. For example, if a user researcher is conducting test sessions that include a larger play group, and is video recording game play, it is vital to include those who are watching as well as those who are playing in the recording. It's not too difficult to rig multiple camera composited video records of play (see for example Fig. 2.1), and these will vastly improve analysis of the social effects of the game after the sessions are over.

In terms of general procedure for studies with groups of gamers, the Microsoft group reports that groups of people who already know each other tend to talk about the experience much more readily as they play than solo players, giving high-quality comments about the design, thus making think-aloud much more viable and straightforward (Amaya et al. 2008). They also report that one should rethink task lists for a group study – instead of highly specific task lists, a general list that emphasizes certain game elements that the experimenters want the group to cover seems much more effective. The group also mentions that they hold off on asking specific questions of play groups until the end, in order to allow playful banter and discussion to develop that they feel gives them valuable information about the game design issues

Fig. 2.1 Video recording with multiple cameras and screen capture allows for rich analysis of play

they are testing. Instead, they make note of any issues that seem to arise and include them in a post-play discussion with the play group.

These are some preliminary recommendations for how to conduct evaluation of social play. This is still an emerging practice, and it will be important for developers and researchers to work together to evolve best practices for social play user experience evaluation.

2.1.6 Challenges and Future Directions

User experience researchers and industry practitioners can certainly do a better job of sharing experiences and converging upon common practices and measures for evaluating and understanding social play. Amaya et al.'s chapter (2008) is an excellent beginning (as described in Section 2.1.5). We may all benefit from grounding our intuitions and observations in an understanding of the social phenomena that underpin social interaction in the context of play, such as those mentioned in Section 2.1.4.3. A recent paper in Computers in Entertainment (de Kort and IJsselsteijn 2008) provides a "framework describing social processes underlying situated social play" that may be of practical value for creating a more systematic and nuanced understanding of the mechanics at work in social play. Work in supporting social play among diverse groups (such as multi-generational games) is only just beginning and will require sophisticated design and evaluation strategies.

Developing for novel interaction styles, such as the accelerometer-based physical play possible with the Nintendo Wii system, iPhone, and other mobile platforms, or the camera-enabled play made possible by the Sony eyeToy, should also lead us to new insights into what elicits fun and engagement in social play and how to measure it.

Some believe that games are innovating modes of social interaction and enabling social engagement in new ways (Dyck et al. 2003, Jørgensen 2004), and so work in design and evaluation for social play may turn out to be an important driver in the field of social user experience with technology more broadly.

I hope that this chapter will initiate further discussion of tactics for social play design and evaluation, helping us all to solidify our practice and innovate.

References

Amaya G, Davis JP, Gunn DV, Harrison C, Pagulayan R, Phillips B, Wixon D(2008) Games user research (GUR) – Our experience with and evolution of four methods. In: Isbister K, Schaffer N (eds) Game Usability: Advice from the Experts. Morgan Kaufmann, San Francisco, CA.
Bandura A (1977) Social Learning Theory. Prentice Hall, Englewood Cliffs, NJ.
Batemen C, Boon R (2005) 21st Century Game Design. Charles River Media, Boston, MA.
Bryant JA, Akerman A, Drell J (2008) Wee Wii: Preschoolers and motion-based game play. Presented at the International Communication Association Annual Conference, May 2008, Montreal, Canada.
Collins J (1997) Conducting in-house play testing. Game Developer Magazine, February 1997 (retrieved from www.gamasutra.com).

Colwell J, Grady C, Rhaiti S (1995) Computer games, self-esteem and gratification of needs in adolescents. Journal of Community and Applied Social Psychology 5(3): 195–206.

De Kort YAW, IJsselsteijn WA (2008) People, places and play: Player experience in a socio-spatial context. ACM Computers in Entertainment 6(2): Article 18.

Druin JA, Akerman A, Drell J (2008) Wee Wii: Preschoolers and motion-based game play. In: Proceedings of the International Communication Association Annual Conference, Montreal, Quebec, Canada.

Dyck J, Pinelle D, Brown B, Gutwin C (2003) Learning from games: HCI design innovations in entertainment software. In: Proceedings of the 2003 Conference on Graphics Interface, Halifax.

Entertainment Software Association (2008) Essential facts about the computer and video game industry. Downloaded from http://www.theesa.com/facts/pdfs/ESA_EF_2008.pdf on July 17.

Fullerton T, Swain C, Hoffman S (2004) Game Design Workshop: Designing, Prototyping and Playtesting Games. CMP Books, Gilroy, CA.

Gajadhar BJ, de Kort YAW, IJsselsteijn WA (2008) Influence of social setting on player experience of digital games. In: Proceedings of CHI 2008, April 5–10, Florence, Italy, pp. 3099–3104.

Hatfield E, Cacioppo JT, Rapson RL (1994) Emotional Contagion. Cambridge University Press, Paris.

Iacoboni M, Woods RP, Brass M, Bekkering H, Mazziotta JC, Rizzolatti G (1999) Cortical mechanisms of human imitation. Science 286(5449): 2526–2528.

Isbister K (2005) Extroverted play. Presentation at the Game Developers Conference.

Isbister K (2006) Better Game Characters by Design: A Psychological Approach. Morgan Kaufmann, San Francisco, CA.

Isbister K(2008) Social psychology and user research. In: Isbister K, Schaffer N (eds) Game Usability: Advice from the Experts for Advancing the Player Experience. Morgan Kaufmann, San Francisco, CA.

Jørgensen AH (2004) Marrying HCI/usability and computer games: A preliminary look. In: Proceedings of NordiCHI 2004, Tampere, Finland, pp. 393–396.

Khoo ET, Merritt T, Cheok A, Lian M, Yeo K(2007) Age invaders: User studies of intergenerational computer entertainment. In: Ma L, Nakatsu R, Rauterberg M (eds) ICEC 2007, LNCS 4740, pp. 231–242.

Kohler C (2007) A glimpse into Harmonix punk rock design process. Wired 15(10): Dated September 14, 2007, accessed October 4, 2008, http://www.wired.com/gaming/gamingreviews/magazine/15-10/mf_harmonix_sb

Koivisto EMI, Suomela R (2007) Using prototypes in early pervasive game development. In: Proceedings of Sandbox Symposium 2007, San Diego, CA, August 4–5, pp. 149–156.

Koster R (2004) Theory of Fun for Game Design. Paraglyph, Scottsdale, AZ.

Lazzaro N (2008) 4 Fun Keys: Testing Emotions and Player Experiences. In Game Usability: Advice from the Experts for Advancing the Player Experience. Morgan Kaufmann, San Francisco, CA.

Mandryk R, Atkins MS, Inkpen KM (2006) A continuous and objective evaluation of emotional experience with interactive play environments. In: Proceedings of CHI 2006, April 22–27, Montréal, QC, Canada, pp. 1027–1036.

Mcgonigal J (2005) Supergaming! Ubiquitous play and performance for massively scaled community. Worthen WB (ed) Modern Drama. Special Issue on Technology 48(3) (Fall): 471–491.

Narcisse E (2008) Don't Bogart that controller: Freelance journalist Evan Narcisse gives us the SCOOP on shared single-player gaming. Posted March 5, 2008, downloaded December 2, 2008 from Level Up blog: http://www.blog.newsweek.com/blogs/levelup/archive/2008/03/05/evan-narcisse-on-shared-single-player-gaming.aspx .

Niemeyer G, Perkel D, Shaw R, McGonigal J (2005) Organum: Individual presence through collaborative play. In: Proceedings of Multimedia 2005, November 6–11, Singapore, pp. 594–597.

Sanneblad J, Holmquist LE (2004) "Why is everyone inside me?!" Using shared displays in mobile computer games. In: Proceedings of the International Conference on Entertainment Computing, ICEC 2004, pp. 487–498.

Schell J (2008) The Art of Game Design: A Book of Lenses. Morgan Kaufmann, San Francisco, CA.

Strack F, Martin LL, Stepper S (1988) Inhibiting and facilitating conditions of the human smile: A nonobtrusive test of the facial feedback hypothesis. Journal of Personality and Social Psychology 54: 768–776.

Szentgyorgyi C, Terry M, Lank E (2008) Renegade gaming: Practices surrounding social use of the Nintendo DS handheld gaming system. In: Proceedings of CHI 2008, pp. 1463–1472.

Taylor TL (2006) Play Between Worlds: Exploring Online Game Culture. MIT Press, Cambridge, MA.

Tychsen A, Hitchens M, Brolund T, McIlwain D, Kavakli M (2008) Group play – Determining factors on the gaming experience in multiplayer role-playing games. ACM Computers in Entertainment 5(4): Article 10.

Vorderer P, Bryant J (2006) Playing video games: Motives, responses and consequences. Lea's Communication Series.

Yee N (2006) Motivations of play in online games. CyberPsychology and Behavior 9: 772–775.

Chapter 3
Presence, Involvement, and Flow in Digital Games

Jari Takatalo, Jukka Häkkinen, Jyrki Kaistinen, and Göte Nyman

Abstract Digital games elicit rich and meaningful experiences for the gamers. This makes games hard to study solely with usability methods that are used in the field of human–computer interaction. Here is presented a candidate framework to analyze multidimensional user experience (UX) in games. Theoretically, the framework is grounded both on previous game studies and on relevant psychological theories. Methodologically, it relies on multivariate data analysis of approximately 320 games ($n = 2182$), with the aim of revealing the subcomponents of UX in games. The framework captures the essential psychological determinants of UX, namely, its quality, intensity, meaning, value, and extensity. Mapping these determinants to the game mechanics, the narrative and the interface offers a rich view to UX in games and provides added value to those who want to understand why games are experienced in certain ways.

3.1 Introduction

Entertainment computer and video games, that is, digital games, elicit rich and personally meaningful experiences for the gamers. This makes games hard to study solely with methods that are used to analyze the functionality or productivity of software in the field of human–computer interaction (HCI). The emergence of research into user experience (UX) in HCI has opened new ways of evaluating digital games. The critical criteria in making these evaluations are psychological in nature. Thus, there is a need for a relevant research framework that concerns both technical game components and user psychology in UX that evolves from game playing. Here, we present a theoretical and methodological background of a candidate empirical framework for analyzing UX in games. Theoretically, it is grounded both on previous game studies and on relevant psychological theories. Methodologically, it

J. Takatalo (✉)
Psychology of Evolving Media and Technology (POEM), University of Helsinki,
Helsinki, Finland
e-mail: Jari.Takatalo@helsinki.fi

R. Bernhaupt (ed.), *Evaluating User Experience in Games*, Human-Computer
Interaction Series, DOI 10.1007/978-1-84882-963-3_3,
© Springer-Verlag London Limited 2010

relies on multivariate data analysis of approximately 320 games ($n = 2182$), with the aim of revealing the subcomponents of UX in games. We emphasize the multidimensional approach in both the analysis of the game and the gamer. This enables capturing the essential psychological determinants of UX, namely, its quality, intensity, meaning, value, and extensity. These basic determinants have already been outlined in the early days of psychology (James 1890, Wundt 1897) and they still provide relevant metrics to evaluate such rich psychological experiences.

The proposed framework is applied and demonstrated here with two different cases to disclose the holistic UX. First, it is used to analyze the differences between two different games. The results are then related to expert reviewer's critics (METASCORE®) and user ratings provided by the Metacritic.com (Metacritic.com 2009). Second, we show how the framework can be utilized in an individual-level analysis of evaluated difficulty of playing and skill development during the first hour of play. Performance analysis and qualitative interview of the gamers are integrated into this case. The examples demonstrate the multifaceted nature of UX and show how it is related to technical game components. In both cases, the utilization of the framework in different phases of the game development life cycle is discussed.

3.1.1 Games and Playing

Any digital game can be considered a system that can be controlled and tuned by its designers. The available technology, their designing skills, and desired end-user UX are typical constraints on designers. The components of the game system can be broadly described as the mechanics, the narrative, and the interface (Hunicke et al. 2004, Winn 2006). Game mechanics include the goals of the game, the rules and rewards of action, and the choices provided the gamers. The narrative creates the game world, setting the stage for the storyline. Closest to the gamers is the interface, that is, what the gamers actually see, hear, perhaps even feel, and how they interact with the game (e.g., control system). Although the designer may have a clear idea of the UX that the game system should provide, this experience will not necessarily be the gamers' experience. The UX is founded on the above components of the game system, but it evolves from the game play.

When games are played, the game dynamics emerge from the mechanics (Hunicke et al. 2004). Meaningful game goals direct gamers' actions. Within the game rules and choices, gamers pursue these goals, earn rewards, make decisions, and face challenging situations. Gamers consistently evaluate, consciously or unconsciously, their performance in the game; are they reaching the desired goals and do they have the abilities to meet the challenges? When they reach the goals after overcoming obstacles, positive feelings and a sense of competence emerge. Game narrative turns into storytelling, in which the gamer has an active role. Curious places in spaces draw the gamers' focus to the game world and provide escape from the real world. The gamers become engaged in their role with the events in the game. The creation of the game world is also supported by the interface, which sets limits on both physical and social interactions in the game. The interface provides an environment to explore, discover, and collect new things. There gamers interact with other agents and adapt and become drawn deeper into the game world. All this is inseparably accompanied by rich emotions, which are an essential part of playing games. But how can we measure the UX in such a rich interaction?

Many authors have presented different motivating aspects of game play, such as challenges, sensations and feelings, other gamers, and narrative that encourage gamers to play and elicit fun experiences (Hunicke et al. 2004, Lazzaro 2004, Sherry et al. 2006). Motivation to play is also explained by rewards and achievements. Seeking game rewards is believed to reinforce playing chiefly in order to obtain more rewards (Ducheneaut et al. 2006). The above studies show clearly what playing affords the gamers, and they provide a useful list of game-relevant issues. But to help designers in their efforts to offer gamers the chance to "think clever thoughts and feel profound emotions" (Pagulayan et al. 2003, p. 891), an analysis of the UX that goes beyond fun, gratification, and the behavioristic reward cycle is needed. Understanding games is approaching a phase where it is close to understanding the psychology of individual life experiences in general.

3.1.2 Psychology of User Experience

There is no one unified and general definition of the UX, but there have been serious attempts to achieve such a definition. Current research on the UX concentrates on a person's perceptions and responses resulting from the use or anticipated use of a product, system, or service (ISO 9241-210:2008 2008). Here, both "perceptions and responses" are considered psychological in nature. According to this view, for example, the perception of a reward by the gamer will not simply lead to an impulsive response to play more. Even if both "perception and response" are considered psychologically, the perceived reward will not lead to fun either. Responses are actively generated in a psychological evaluation process that includes basic psychological compartments. For example, we perceive and focus our attention on stimuli that motivate and interest us (James 1890). Only those perceptions that are interesting and meaningful enough to us will be evaluated in our consciousness and will form a part of our inner world. Some perceptions are evaluated subconsciously, whereas others are evaluated in awareness. Awareness can best be understood through the concept of trilogy of mind, namely, the psychological set consisting of thinking, feeling, and will (Hilgard 1980). Over decades, this trilogy has concerned human cognition, emotion, and motivation (Mayer 2001). As the research paradigms in psychology have changed from the stimulus-response paradigms to information-processing paradigms, this traditional trilogy has been cut to pieces and studied separately (Lubart and Getz 1998). However, for example, cognitions and emotions are so intimately connected that studying emotions without cognitions makes a little sense (Lazarus 1991a). When we look at the UX by integrating cognition, emotion, and motivation with perception and attention, we obtain a realistic set of psychological compartments that make an analysis of "person's perceptions and responses" relevant and valid in any given context. Naturally, our past experiences (memories) and attitudes have an impact on this experiential process (Särkelä et al. 2004).

Although the foundations of these psychological compartments can be traced back to the history of psychology, they have not changed significantly. An excellent example of this is that such compartments are present when today's gamers spontaneously describe their experiences: They report emotional feelings (e.g., enjoyment), cognitive evaluations (e.g., game challenge), and motivations (e.g., curiosity) while playing games (Komulainen et al. 2008). Thus, the content we are dealing with orients the psychological compartments. If we are able to recognize how these psychological compartments are shaped by the game and represented in the game play, we can achieve many advantages for evaluating the UX. Measuring gamers' cognition, emotion, motivation, perception, and attention will reveal relevant determinants of the UX, such as its quality, intensity, meaning, value, and extensity (i.e., voluminous or vastness, a spatial attribute). Taken together, these determinants allow the profiling of experiences and give them their special and distinctive characteristics. Although the determinants have also been outlined already in the beginning of the psychology (James 1890, Wundt 1897), their importance in understanding any mental phenomena and human behavior should not be overlooked.

Together with the external game components, these internal psychological compartments help us to understand different aspects of the multidimensional UX in games (Fig. 3.1). By using these psychological compartments as lenses through

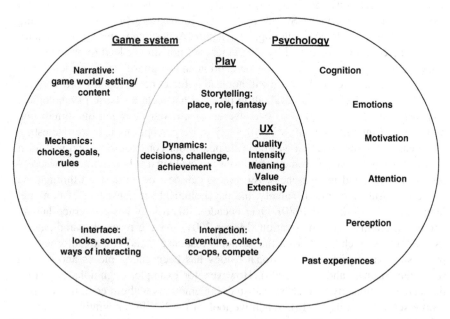

Fig. 3.1 The game system can be affected by the game designer. Play is when the user interacts with a game. Within this interaction UX characteristics evolve. Besides the game system, the UX is strongly affected by the ever-present basic psychology and the user background. The way psychology is represented in UX depends on the content, that is, the game

which we observe the gamers' inner world, we can consider the game achievements and rewards discussed earlier in a new light. Because not all rewards motivate gamers equally to continue playing, it is likely that there is a deeper psychological evaluation process underlying human motivation. A reward will be evaluated based on how relevant it is, how challenging it was to achieve, whether it required the use of special skills and abilities, and how enjoyable and satisfying it was to achieve. Such an evaluation assigns a particular reward to its intrinsic value. If some specific behavior pattern in a game has no intrinsic value but is done because of an external reward (e.g., one gets paid), then it is said to be extrinsically motivating (Atkinson 1964). In general, intrinsically rewarding behaviors are experienced as more enjoyable and are more likely to be repeated (Csikszentmihalyi 1975). Whether some rewards are intrinsically or extrinsically rewarding is difficult or even impossible to know by looking at the outer behavior only. Evaluating UX from the outer behavior possesses its own challenges as well. But what are the relevant game-related concepts that best represent the psychological compartments in games and could enable us to measure the true characteristics of the UX?

3.1.3 User Experience in Games

Numerous candidate concepts, such as, immersion, fun, presence, involvement, engagement, and flow have been used to describe the UX in games (Brown and Cairns 2004, IJsselsteijn et al. 2007, McMahan 2003, Nakatsu et al. 2005, Sweetser and Wyeth 2005). Often these concepts are defined quite broadly, for instance, presence is "the sense of being there," while flow describes "an optimal experience." Various psychological compartments are attached to these concepts, for example concentration, emotions, and cognitive evaluations of the game's challenges are each referred to as immersion (McMahan 2003). Thus, there is a great overlap among the concepts and as a consequence, numerous challenges to understanding and actually measuring them. For instance, considering flow as an "optimal experience" by definition (Csikszentmihalyi 1975) and restricting it to extreme situations only (Jennett et al. 2008) would diminish its applicability to the analysis of the UX in typical games. The subcomponents of flow, such as, skills and challenges (Csikszentmihalyi 1975) provide psychologically valid metrics to evaluate games, even if the gamers would never reach the actual "optimal experience." Concentrating on the subcomponents instead of the concept that has a complex underlying structure itself has other advantages as well. We have shown, for example, how equally high "meta-presence" scores in four different games actually hide clear experiential differences between the games found in five measured presence subcomponents (e.g., physical presence, attention, and co-presence) (Takatalo et al. 2006a).

There are empirical user-centered data that provide evidence for potential subcomponents of the UX in games across the concepts. Jennett and her colleagues (2008) studied immersion in games. They extracted five experiential subcomponents in a principal component analysis ($n = 260$) and named them as *cognitive involvement* (curiosity and interest), *real-world dissociation* (attention, temporal dissociation), *challenge, emotional involvement* (empathy, enjoyment), and *control* (ease of controls, interacting with a game). Similarly, Ermi and Mäyrä (2005) studied immersion. Although their model is based on the interviews of children who played the games with their parents, the model was further supported by a factor analysis of a sample ($n = 234$) collected from grown-up gamers. Their three extracted subcomponents were: *sensory immersion* (e.g., "The sounds of game overran the other sounds from the environment"), *challenge-based immersion* (challenges and abilities), and *imaginative immersion* (use of imagination, empathy, and fantasy).

Sherry et al. (2006) used factor analysis ($n = 550$) to extract uses and gratification dimensions. They named the six extracted motivations to play as *competition, challenges, social interaction, diversion* ("I play instead of other thing I should do"), *fantasy* (to be someone else), and *arousal* (excited, adrenaline). Lazzaro (2004) found four main motivations to play from the qualitative and quantitative analysis of 15 gamers and 15 nongamers. Included were *hard fun* (meaningful challenges), *easy fun* (excitement and curiosity of exploring new adventures), *altered states* (emotions inside), and *people factor* (compete and co-ops with others). Likewise, Ryan et al.'s (2006) Player Experience in Need Satisfaction (PENS) framework deals with the reasons that keep gamers playing the games. Measures in this framework are composed of summed scales that have been used in previous studies: *in game competence* (capable and effective), *in game autonomy* (free to do things that interest), *presence* (physical, emotional, and narrative), and *intuitive controls* (easy to remember). In addition to PENS measures, *subjective vitality* (energy and aliveness), *self-esteem, mood, game enjoyment, preference for future play*, and *continued play behavior* were measured. Sweetser and Johnson (2004) investigated, which issues in games impact player enjoyment. Their principal components analysis ($n = 455$) resulted five subcomponents, *physics* (gravity, life-like graphics), *sound* (effects and soundtrack), *narrative, intuitiveness* (interaction with objects), and *the freedom of expression* (many different as well as unique ways of using objects).

Pagulayan et al.'s (2003) four important factors in game evaluation were *overall quality* (e.g., fun), *ease of use* (controls, interface), *challenge*, and *pace* (the rate of new challenges) are based on strong empirical data gathered in various studies conducted in Microsoft Game Studios. Poels and her colleagues' (2007) study revealed nine relevant subcomponents that were based on both qualitative gamer interviews and expert evaluations. Included were *enjoyment* (fun, pleasure, and relaxation), *flow* (concentration, absorption), *imaginative immersion* (story, empathy), *sensory immersion* (presence), *suspense* (challenge, tension, and pressure), *negative affect* (disappointment, frustration), *control* (autonomy, power), *social presence* (being connected with others, empathy), and *competence* (pride, euphoria). An overview of the 10 general UX subcomponents found in the above empirical studies is presented in Table 3.1. There is conceptual overlapping between the subcomponents depending on both the scope and the methodology of the approach. However, common to majority of the studies is some kind of a reference to both emotions and challenges. We have developed the Presence-Involvement-Flow Framework (PIFF) (Takatalo et al. 2004) in order to integrate the vast amount of relevant UX subcomponents

Table 3.1 A summary of game-related studies introducing potential empirically derived UX subcomponents. Marked x indicates that the authors have considered that subcomponent. The main scopes (e.g., motivation to play, immersion) and the methodologies used (e.g., qualitative, quantitative) vary across the studies

	Skill, competence	Challenge	Emotions	Control, autonomy, freedom	Focus, concentration	Physical presence	Involvement, meaning, curiosity	Story, drama, fantasy	Social interaction	Interactivity, controls, usability
Jennett et al. (2008)	–	x	x	–	x	–	x	–	–	x
Poels et al. (2007)	x	x	x	x	x	x	–	x	x	–
Ryan et al. (2006)	x	–	x	x	–	x	–	x	–	x
Sherry et al. (2006)	–	x	x	–	–	–	–	x	x	–
Ermi and Mäyrä (2005)	–	x	–	–	–	x	–	x	–	–
Lazzaro (2004)	–	x	x	–	–	–	x	–	x	–
Sweetser and Johnson (2004)	–	–	–	x	–	x	–	x	–	x
Takatalo et al. (2004)	x	x	x	x	x	x	x	x	x	x
Pagulayan et al. (2003)	–	x	x	–	–	–	–	–	–	x

into one framework and to study the UX in games as multidimensional and psychological in nature.

3.1.4 Presence-Involvement-Flow Framework (PIFF)

PIFF is a psychological research framework to study experiences in digital games. It has been constructed on the basis of the extensive concepts of the sense of presence, involvement, and flow. They represent the psychological compartments in digital games well: Presence (Lombard and Ditton 1997) describes the perception of and attention to the game world and both spatial and social cognitions in game play, involvement (Zaichkowsky 1985) is considered a measure of gamer motivation, and flow (Csikszentmihalyi 1975) refers to the subjective, cognitive-emotional evaluation of the game. Each concept includes subcomponents that are relevant to both technical game components and psychological determinants of the UX.

3.1.4.1 Presence and Involvement

Gamers often mention realistic high-quality graphical interface and an engaging narrative as central game components responsible for various game-related feeling (Sweetser and Johnson 2004, Wood et al. 2004). The feeling of being in a realistic place with others is indeed the core idea of the concept of presence (Lombard and Ditton 1997). Presence has been studied in a variety of different media, for instance, in virtual environments, movies, and television (Schuemie et al. 2001). The research on presence has extensive theoretical and empirical foundations. Hence, it provides valid and tested metrics to study experiences in games (Pinchbeck and Stevens 2005). The subcomponents of presence are proven to be especially useful when the intensity and extensity of the UX is evaluated (Takatalo et al. 2006a).

The following three subcomponents of presence have been used to study the "sense of being there" or spatial presence in mediated environments: attention (psychological immersion), perceptual realness (naturalness), and spatial awareness (engagement) (Lombard and Ditton 1997). This threefold construct has also been reliably extracted in empirical studies (Lessiter et al. 2001, Schubert et al. 2001). Additionally, the level of arousal and the range and consistency of the physical interaction are integral parts of spatial presence (Lombard and Ditton 1997). Social content is a significant factor in many games and it elicits the sense of social presence. In Lombard and Ditton's (1997) explication, social presence was composed of social richness, social realism, and co-presence (shared space). These aspects correspond well to the social features found in digital games, such as, narrative and the engagement with one's own role in a story. Social richness refers to the extent to which a game is perceived as personal and intimate. Social realism refers to the sense of similarity between real-world and game-world objects, people and events. Co-presence is the feeling of being and acting in a game together with other agents.

We have found out a clear distinction between presence and the motivational concept of involvement (Takatalo et al. 2006b). Psychologically, involvement is defined as a motivational continuum toward a particular object or situation (Rothschild 1984). Involvement concerns the level of relevance based on inherent needs, values, and interests attached to that situation or an object (Zaichkowsky 1985). Thus, involvement determines the meaning and value of the UX. The main interest here is not in what motivates gamers to play, but in understanding the meaning and personal relevance of the game. Weather we want to understand UX in a high-end technological setup or mobile device in a rush-hour subway meaning plays always a key role. Involvement is a central and well-established concept in the field of buyer behavior studies (Brennan and Mavondo 2000). It includes two distinct but closely related dimensions: importance and interest (McQuarrie and Munson 1992). Importance is dominantly a cognitive dimension concerning the meaning and relevance of the stimulus, whereas interest is composed of emotional and value-related valences (Schiefele 1991). This makes importance similar to the cognitive involvement subcomponent that was extracted by Jennett et al. (2008). On the other hand, interest is close to Lazzaro's (2004) curiosity and the will to find out something new in a game. Curiously enough, we have found out that first-person shooters are less involving compared to third person role-playing games (Takatalo et al. 2006a), but it is difficult to point out exactly which game components affect involvement the most.

Taken together, presence and involvement indicate the switch between the real world and a game, namely, the way gamers willingly form a relationship with the physical and social features of the game.

3.1.4.2 Flow

The concept of flow in PIFF describes the subjective, qualitative direction of the UX. In psychological terms, it explains the cognitive evaluation and emotional outcomes of the game play. The cognitive evaluation is often related to game mechanics. In PIFF, the cognitive evaluation of the game concerns, for example, game challenges and gamer skills. These evaluations are related to a number of emotional outcomes (e.g., enjoyment, boredom). This way of looking at the subcomponents of flow is based on different flow-channel models, such as the four-channel flow model (Csikszentmihalyi 1975). The flow-channel models share the idea that there are certain cognitions that are followed by emotions. In an ideal situation where skills and challenges are high and in balance, an optimal state of flow occurs. Such a close coupling of cognitions and emotions is widely acknowledged in psychology in cognitive theories of emotion (Lazarus 1991b). Cognitive evaluations by the gamers and the related emotional outcomes provide useful subcomponents for analyzing the UX from the first hour of play to the full completion of the game.

In addition to describing the subjective evaluations of challenge and skill, the flow theory (Csikszentmihalyi 1975) also considers clear goals and instant feedback as important features that are evaluated cognitively in a given situation. The theory also includes the sense of control, the level of arousal, concentration, time distortion, the loss of self-consciousness, and the merging of action and awareness as prerequisites or correlates of the flow experience. In PIFF, the level of arousal, concentration, and time distortion are included as subcomponents of presence. This theoretical overlap between flow and presence supports the findings of presence being a pre-requisite of flow (Novak et al. 2000). Losing self-consciousness and merging action and awareness have been difficult for respondents to recognize in previous studies (Rettie 2001). The actual state of flow is often characterized as ease of doing, enjoyment and positive valence (pleasure), and the absence of boredom and anxiety (Csikszentmihalyi 1975). Previously, flow has been related to playfulness (e.g., cognitive spontaneity) (Webster and Martocchio 1992) and the sense of control (Ghani and Deshpande 1994, Novak et al. 2000). In addition to these, a wide variety of other emotional feelings has been reported in games, such as, pleasantness, strength, and impressiveness of the experience, amazement, and excitement (Lazzaro 2004, Schubert et al. 2001).

Although all the above PIFF subcomponents have a strong theoretical foundation, we have studied them psychometrically in a large empirical data set.

3.2 PIFF: Methodological Background

PIFF is based on the quantitative data gathered with the Experimental Virtual Environment Experience Questionnaire-Game Pitkä (i.e., long) (EVEQ-GP). EVEQ-GP is composed of approximately 180 items presented in previous studies concerning the sense of presence (Kim and Biocca 1997, Lessiter et al. 2001, Lombard et al. 2000, Schubert et al. 2001, Usoh et al. 2000, Witmer and Singer 1998), involvement (McQuarrie and Munson 1992), and flow prerequisites and correlates (Della Fave and Massimini 1988, Fontaine 1992, Ghani and Deshpande 1994, Mehrabian and Russell 1974, Novak et al. 2000, Webster and Martocchio 1992). All the items were translated into Finnish and transformed either into a seven-point Likert-scale (1 = Strongly Disagree to 7 = Strongly Agree) or into seven-point semantic differentials. The items were modified so that they were assessing experiences received from one game playing session. EVEQ-GP is administered to an individual gamer after a playing session. The gamers who fill in the questionnaire are encouraged to reflect on their subjective experiences of the game they just played. The method enables the participants to report, within the boundaries of the 180 items, how they experienced that particular game. In the field of behavioral sciences, the use of questionnaires has proved to be a valid way of assessing various mental phenomena (Rust and Golombok 1999).

The first version of the PIFF was based on two smaller data sets ($n = 68$ and $n = 164$). Of the 180 EVEQ-GP items, 146 were used to form 23 subcomponents measuring the UX in games (Takatalo et al. 2004). Thereafter, a heterogeneous data from 2182 Finnish gamers who filled in the questionnaire were collected. Data from laboratory experiments and an Internet survey are included in the data set. The data include approximately 320 different games, various displays (HMD, TV, and CRT), and contexts of play (online, offline, home, and laboratory), giving a broad scope to the UX in games. This data enabled more advanced statistical analyses of the PIFF subcomponents. As a result of these analyses, a refined version of the framework, i.e., PIFF^2 was developed.

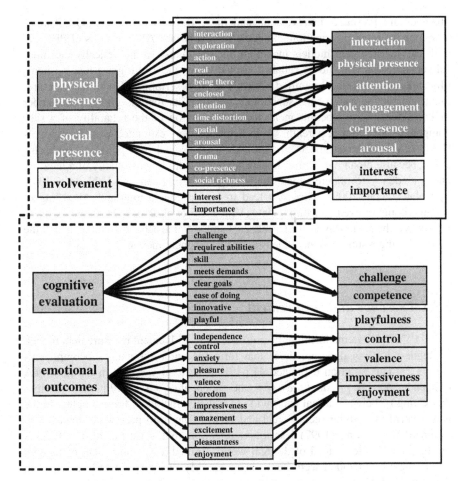

Fig. 3.2 The two measurement models that form the PIFF^2. On the *left*, measured latent variables in five boxes, in the *middle*, 139 measured questionnaire items (observed variables) represented in 34 boxes. On the *right*, 15 factor-analytically (PFA) extracted subcomponents of UX in games

Methodologically, PIFF^2 is grounded on two separate multivariate measurement models (Tarkkonen and Vehkalahti 2005), which assessed presence and involvement as well as flow (Fig. 3.2). In psychometrics, measurement models include latent variables (i.e., those difficult to measure straightforwardly), which are measured with observed variables such as questionnaire items. These observed variables are analyzed with multivariate methods to form subcomponents (i.e., measurement scales). These subcomponents thus formed can then be used to assess latent variables.

We used principal axis factor analysis (PFA) with an oblique direct Oblimin rotation (delta $= 0$) independently in both measurement models to compress a large number of questionnaire items into the subcomponents. Of the 180 EVEQ-GP items,

163 measure presence, involvement, and flow. The rest of the EVEQ-GP items assess background information and game-related issues. After a series of PFA's in both the measurement models including the 163 items, 15 theoretically meaningful subcomponents could be reliably formed out of the 139 highest loading items (Takatalo et al. 2006b, Submitted). Next, a short description of both the measurement models and each of the subcomponents forming them is given. The number of items forming a subcomponent and an estimation of the reliability of a subcomponent are given in parenthesis. Reliabilities were estimated with Tarkkonen's rho (ρ) (Vehkalahti et al. 2006). Rho was used instead of a popular Cronbach's alpha, because alpha has a build-in assumption of one-dimensionality of a measure and a tendency to underestimate the measures (Tarkkonen and Vehkalahti 2005, Vehkalahti et al. 2009). This may lead to biased conclusions and discarding of suitable items or even subcomponents (Vehkalahti et al. 2006). Tarkkonen's rho is interpreted the same way as the Cronbach's alpha: Values above 70 indicate that the items forming a subcomponent measure the same phenomenon.

3.2.1 Presence and Involvement

Of 93 EVEQ-GP items forming the presence and involvement measurement model, 83 highest loading ones are those that form the eight extracted subcomponents (Fig. 3.2). This solution explained 41.67% of the total variance in the final PFA (Appendix A). The *physical presence* subcomponent ($\rho = 0.82/17$ items) describes the feeling of being in a real and vivid place. Items included, for example, "In the game world everything seemed real and vivid." The third presence dimension in Lombard and Ditton's (1997) description, *attention*, that is, time distortion, focuses on the game world instead of the real world, formed a subcomponent of its own ($\rho = 0.88/12$). Included were items, such as, "My vision was totally engaged in the game world" and "I was not aware of my 'real' environment." Two subcomponents for different aspects of social presence were also extracted. *Co-presence* ($\rho = 0.89/14$) includes the feeling of sharing a place with others and being active there (e.g., "I felt that I was in the game world with other persons"). *Role engagement* ($\rho = 0.80/12$) describes being transported into the story: how captivated gamers were by the role provided in the narrative (e.g., "I felt that I was one of the characters in the story of the game"). Two more subcomponents measuring emotional *arousal* ($\rho = 0.70/5$ items, e.g., active, stimulated vs. passive, unaroused) and game world's interactivity were extracted. *Interaction* subcomponent ($\rho = 0.72/9$) was composed of items assessing, for example, speed, range, mapping, exploration, and predictability of one's own actions in the game world (e.g., "The game responded quickly to my actions"). In our further analysis (Takatalo et al. 2006b), the *interaction* subcomponent did not fit with the rest of the subcomponents extracted in the presence and involvement measurement model. One explanation could be the nature of the interaction subcomponent: It is more of a cognitive evaluation of the game interactivity than a subjective perceptual experience as pointed out by Schubert and his colleagues (2001). Similarly, Jennett and her colleagues (2008) considered their control subcomponent (i.e., "using the controls as travelling somewhere and interacting with the world") as a game factor instead of a person factor. Thus, we have analyzed interaction among the other cognitive game evaluations extracted in our flow measurement model.

In the same PFA, the two theoretical subcomponents of involvement, namely, importance and interest, were extracted. *Interest* ($\rho = 0.72/6$) is composed of emotional and value-related valences, such as, "the game was exciting." *Importance* ($\rho = 0.89/8$) is dominantly a cognitive dimension showing how meaningful, relevant, and personal the game was (e.g., "the game mattered to me"). More details of the extraction and utilization of the eight presence and involvement subcomponents can be found in our previous studies (Takatalo et al. 2006a, b).

3.2.2 Flow

Of the 70 EVEQ-GP items forming the flow measurement model, 56 highest loading ones are those that form the seven extracted subcomponents (Fig. 3.2). This solution explained 41.30% of the total variance in the final PFA (Appendix B). The *challenge* subcomponent ($\rho = 0.76/5$ items) assesses the degree to which abilities were required to play the game as well as how challenging the gamer felt it was to play (e.g., "playing the game felt challenging"). *Competence* ($\rho = 0.86/11$) combined measures of user skills and positive feelings of effectiveness. It also included items, which assessed clear goals and items that evaluated both demand and competence (e.g., "I felt I could meet the demands of the playing situation"). Furthermore, five subcomponents with emotional content were extracted. Hedonic *valence* ($\rho = 0.77/10$) is the bipolar subcomponent having pleasure on one end and displeasure on the other. It was composed of semantic differentials, such as, "I felt happy/I felt sad." The *enjoyment* subcomponent ($\rho = 0.74/7$) included aspects such as pleasantness and enjoyment. Playing was also somehow special (e.g., "I will recommend it to my friends" and "I had peak experiences while playing"). Items forming the original *playfulness* scale (Webster and Martocchio 1992) (e.g., "I felt innovative" and "I felt original") formed a subcomponent of their own ($\rho = 0.78/9$). Items measuring actual feelings of flow, such as ease of doing, loaded on the playfulness subcomponent as well. *Control*, that is, being dominant and independent, formed one subcomponent ($\rho = 0.74/5$) composed of semantic differentials, such as, "I was dominant/I was submissive." Feelings of being amazed and astonished formed the *impressiveness* subcomponent ($\rho = 0.79/9$), which included items, such as, "I was astonished and surprised at the game world" and "I felt something dramatic in the game world." For more details of the extraction and utilization of the seven flow subcomponents, see our previous studies (Takatalo et al. 2008, Submitted).

Factor scores with Bartlett's method (Tabachnick and Fidell 2001) were computed from the 15 PIFF^2 subcomponents. Next, these subcomponents are used to analyze different aspects of the UX in games.

3.3 PIFF^2 in Practice

We have demonstrated here the multidimensional and psychological nature of the UX in games. The rest of the chapter presents two distinct practical examples of how to utilize the mapping of PIFF^2 subcomponents in different phases of the game development life cycle. First, all the subcomponents are used to compare groups of expert gamers in two different games. Psychological profile provided by the PIFF^2 is compared against METASCORE® and user ratings provided by the Metacritic.com (Metacritic.com 2009). However, sometimes more detailed information about a specific game feature is needed as quickly and efficiently as possible. Using only selected PIFF^2 subcomponents in a more qualitative manner would then be a better choice. Our second case deals with an individual-level analysis of experienced game difficulty and learning of skills during the first hour of play. Analysis of game mechanics and qualitative interview are integrated into this case. However, the use of complete subscales with several participants guarantees more extensive and reliable results.

3.3.1 Between Groups: PIFF^2 in Two Different Games

A standard way of using PIFF^2 is to gather post-game experiences with an EVEQ-GP questionnaire. This would be most beneficial, for example, in the production phase when all content can be represented, but there is still time and possibility to introduce changes before releasing the game. If used as a post-launch study, a PIFF^2 analysis can provide useful information and facilitate evaluation of the released product. Here, we conduct such a post-launch analysis to two first-person shooters (FPS) and compare PIFF^2 profiles with the METASCORE® and the user ratings of these games. Both these numeric values are provided by the Metacritic.com (Metacritic.com 2009). METASCORE® is based on a weighted average of various scores assigned by expert critics to that game. The user ratings are means of all the ratings given to a game by the users. Metacritic.com provides the amount of users that have rated a particular game. This comparison will demonstrate the added value of the psychological and multidimensional analysis of the UX based on gamers' own reflections from the game.

The data included 109 expert male gamers, who played either Valve's *Half-Life 2* (*HL2*; $n = 62$) or *Counter Strike: Source* (*CS*; $n = 47$), both run by the same Source® game engine. This makes the interface in studied games exactly the same. After they finish playing either *HL2* or *CS*, each gamer filled in the EVEQ-GP in our Internet survey. *HL2* is described as "it opens the door to a world where the player's presence affects everything around him, from the physical environment to the behaviors even the emotions of both friends and enemies. The player again picks up the crowbar of research scientist Gordon Freeman, who finds himself on an alien-infested Earth being picked to the bone, its resources depleted, its populace dwindling" (Half-Life 2 2004). In *CS*, gamers can "engage in an incredibly realistic brand of terrorist warfare in this wildly popular team-based game" (Counter-Strike: Source 2004). In addition, "*CS* modifies the multiplayer aspects of 'Half-Life' to bring it a more team-oriented game play. *CS* provides the player with an experience that a trained counter-terrorist unit or terrorist unit experiences" (Metacritic.com 2009). Thus, there were differences in game mechanics and narrative between *HL2* and *CS*.

HL2 has received a METASCORE® of 96/100 based on 81 reviews and *CS* 88/100 based on nine reviews. A METASCORE® between 90 and 100 is considered as a "Universal Acclaim" and between 75 and 89 a "Generally favorable reviews" (Metacritic.com 2009). The users rated *HL2* 9,3/10 (3487 votes) and *CS* 9,2/10 (7532 votes) (situation in March 22, 2009). Although the background of the players rating the games was not standardized in any ways (e.g., skill, gender), this variation between scores and ratings gives an interesting starting point for the inspection of the $PIFF^2$ profiles. Two distinct between-subjects multivariate analyses of variance (MANOVA) were conducted for both presence and involvement as well as flow subcomponents. Significant differences in MANOVA's were further studied in univariate analyses. The UX determinants are included in bold face.

Figure 3.3 shows that the levels of both *presence* and *involvement* differed between the games (Wilk's Lambda = 0.70, $F(8,100) = 5.46$, $p <0.001$, $\eta^2 = 0.30$). *HL2* was considered more *interesting* (**value**) than *CS* (one-way ANOVA, $F(1, 4,05) = 4.10$, $p <.05$, $\eta^2 = 0.04$). The presence profiles of the games were also quite different. *CS* was high in *co-presence* ($F(1, 5,46) = 5,93$, $p <0.05$, $\eta^2 = 0.05$), *attention* (NS), and *arousal* ($F(1, 5,90) = 4.23$, $p <0.05$, $\eta^2 = 0.04$), whereas characteristic for *HL2* was quite steady scores in each of the subcomponents. Especially high it was in *role engagement* ($F(1, 16,38) = 14.89$, $p <0.001$, $\eta^2 = 0.12$) and *physical presence* ($F(1, 8,08) = 5.41$, $p <0.05$, $\eta^2 = 0.05$) compared to *CS*. Both the games were considered equally *important* and *attentive*. These differences show, quite simply, how

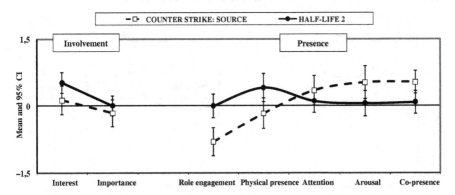

Fig. 3.3 Group means in involvement and presence subcomponents in *Half-Life 2* and *Counter Strike: Source*. The *error bars* represent a 95% confidence interval. An overlap by half the average arm length of the *error bar* indicates a statistical difference between the groups ($p \approx 0.05$). If the tips of the *error bars* just touch, then the difference is $p \approx 0.01$. A *gap* between the *error bars* indicates $p < 0.001$

the narrative affects the UX: *HL2* builds on the realistic game world, the city seven (**extensity**), and provides the role of the Gordon Freeman to an individual gamer (**meaning**). With a similar interface, *CS* provides teamwork and **intensive** performance. Naturally, the difference in game narrative is linked to the game mechanics, which was studied with the flow subcomponents.

Figure 3.4 shows that the cognitive-emotional flow subcomponents in both games were significantly different (Wilk's Lambda = 0.59, $F(7,101) = 10.10$, $p < 0.001$, $\eta^2 = 0.41$). Especially, in cognitive evaluations the games were quite different. Gamers evaluated *CS* more *challenging* ($F(1, 12,13) = 4.04$, $p < 0.01$, $\eta^2 = 0.07$), *interactive* ($F(1, 14,35) = 11.64$, $p < 0.01$, $\eta^2 = 0.10$), and themselves more *competent* to play ($F(1, 5,50) = 10.58$, $p < 0.01$, $\eta^2 = 0.09$). However, the emotional **quality** of their UX was somewhat "thinner" compared to *HL2*. *HL2* was more positive in *valence* (pleasure) ($F(1, 4,80) = 5.68$, $p < 0.05$, $\eta^2 = 0.05$), *enjoyable* ($F(1, 5,38) = 4.64$, $p < 0.05$, $\eta^2 = 0.04$), *playful* ($F(1, 3,40) = 4.40$, $p < 0.05$, $\eta^2 = 0.04$), and *impressive* ($F(1, 14,44) = 13.60$, $p < 0.001$, $\eta^2 = 0.11$). There was no difference between the games in the sense of *control*. Game mechanics providing competition and co-operative performance are the most likely cause for the flattened emotional profile in *CS*. However, it should be emphasized that the UX in *CS* is still far from being negative or boring. Heightened attention and arousal and highly evaluated cognitive and social features in the game are enough to keep gamers in *CS* for hours.

Both the PIFF^2 analysis and a METASCORE$^®$ found the differences between *HL2* and *CS*. A well-prepared narrative combined with good AI-based action seems to be engaging and heart-touching compared to extreme challenge and action with live comrades. The advantage of the PIFF^2 is its potential use in any phase of the game development cycle: stimulating, supporting thinking, and giving ideas for the UX goals in concept phase and providing a facilitative tool to evaluate these goals

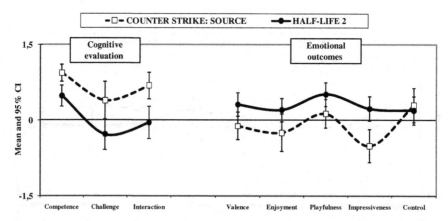

Fig. 3.4 Group means in flow subcomponents in *Half-Life 2* and *Counter Strike: Source*. The *error bars* represent a 95% confidence interval. An overlap by half the average arm length of the *error bar* indicates a statistical difference between the groups ($p \approx 0.05$). If the tips of the *error bars* just touch, then the difference is $p \approx 0.01$. A *gap* between the *error bars* indicates $p < 0.001$

in beta versions in a production phase, as it was show here. Relating PIFF^2 to user ratings provides a good demonstration of our content-oriented approach in media psychology in general. In order to understand the user rating, one needs to understand both the content and the psychology involved. Gamers rated both *HL2* and *CS* as about equally high, but clearly for different reasons, which were out of the reach of the single rating grade given. However, these nuances could be disclosed by a multidimensional psychological profile of PIFF^2. The analysis of the profile indicated that the two games were equally interesting and attentive, which could explain the similar ratings given by the gamers. It is an old psychological fact that we perceive and focus our attention on stimuli that motivate and interest us (James 1890). This part of the UX cannot be reached by an outside observer, thus a measure which considers meaning and personal relevance in that particular game is needed. As presented in this example, the involvement concept fits well into this purpose.

3.3.2 Between Users: Competence and Challenge in the First Hour

In the previous example, games were evaluated by groups of gamers at a general level. User ratings and PIFF^2 profiles were based on hours of playing. However, sometimes a finer detail, such as, a particular game feature or user group needs to be investigated. Critical issues in production phase are often related to game mechanics and could include, for example, evaluating the learning curve or adjustment of the difficulty level. Usually, such issues take place in the first hour of play, which should convince the gamer to keep on playing instead of suffocating an evolving enthusiasm (Davis et al. 2005). To study these, a large data and a heavy questionnaire are not the best option. It is enough to (1) define the investigated problem well, (2) know what to measure, and (3) how to measure. Here, we give an example where the focus is on understanding how competence develops and game challenges are evaluated during the first hour of play. The cognitive-emotional flow subcomponents provided by PIFF^2 serve this purpose well, disclosing both the cognitive game evaluations and the quality of UX. In addition, a lighter way of utilizing PIFF^2 dimensionality is introduced and PIFF^2 findings are integrated into gamer interviews and the observed performance in the game.

Evaluations of challenge and competence by two male gamers' (Mr. 1 and Mr. 2) were analyzed during their first hour playing Valve's *Portal*. *Portal* is a single-player game, in which "players must solve physical puzzles and challenges by opening portals to maneuvering objects, and themselves, through space." *Portal* has been called "one of the most innovative new games on the horizon and will offer gamers hours of unique game-play" (Portal 2007). *Portal* provides game mechanics with clearly distinguished levels (i.e., chambers) that enable study of the process that gives the UX its quality. This process was captured by suitably interrupting the gamers twice during the 1 h of play. The breaks were timed so that the gamers were in "the elevator" between the chambers. The third evaluation was made after 60 min of playing. The gamers were in the laboratory by themselves, and the interruptions were made as natural as possible. During the breaks, the gamers rated one item in each of the

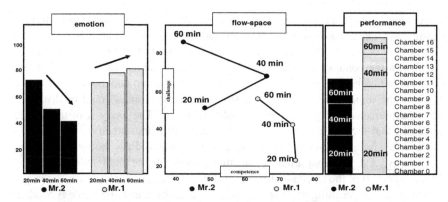

Fig. 3.5 (**a**) Composite measure of emotions of the two gamers during the first hour of play. (**b**) Flow space and evaluations of challenge and competence of the two gamers during the first hour of play. (**c**) The number of chambers finished by the two gamers during the first hour of play. Each measure was taken after 20, 40, and 60 min of playing

selected PIFF^2 subcomponents in the touch-screen next to them. Thus, the method was called PIFF^2-in-breaks analysis. The first page on the touch-screen included a flow space (Fig. 3.5b). The flow space is formed from the *challenge* and *competence* subcomponents. The idea of the flow space was to evaluate both competences and challenges together in each game period. So, during each break the gamers marked the point in the flow space that best corresponded to their evaluations in that particular game period. Flow space is based on the flow-channel models, such as the four-channel model (Csikszentmihalyi 1975) and the flow grid (IJsselsteijn W and Poels K, personal communication, April 24, 2008). The second page of the touch screen presented one question in each of the emotional subcomponents (*pleasure/valence, control, enjoyment, impressiveness,* and *playfulness*). These five individual scores were summed and used as a composite measure of emotional outcomes in this example (Fig. 3.5a). Gamers could not see their previous evaluations when using the touch-screen. While using the touch-screen, the instructor interviewed the gamers in order to deepen their answers. This qualitative–quantitative data collection procedure during each break took approximately 2–3 min. The performance in the game was evaluated based on how many chambers the gamers finished in each of the approximately 20-min game periods (Fig. 3.5c). Although both gamers fulfilled the prerequisite for participating in the experiment, namely, that they had no prior experience on *Portal*, there were other background differences between them.

Mr. 1 is 21 years old and plays games on average for 300 min at a time. He considers that "I have played games for a long time... My little brother has told me that this is an easy one." Mr. 2 is 30 years old and plays games on average 60 min at a time. He thinks that "I have not played this kind of game before. I'm not an expert at these games." Although both play games equally often (50% or more of days), Mr. 1, being younger, invests more time in playing. He seems to be a more experienced gamer and more confident when starting a game. This difference in the gamers' backgrounds is seen both in their cognitive evaluation shown in the flow space (Fig. 3.5b) and in their performance (Fig. 3.5c) after the first 20 min of play. They began their cognitive evaluation at different points, Mr. 2 being more challenged and less competent. Consequently, Mr. 2 completed only four chambers compared to Mr. 1's 10 chambers. However, the composite measure of the two users' emotions was on the same level after 20 min of playing. This shows the complexity of measuring the UX. Gamers have the same level of emotions for different reasons. That is why, for example, measuring only fun in games is not enough; multidimensional measures are needed to uncover the underlying experiential subcomponents.

The shape and magnitude of the two gamers' flow-space profiles disclose the evaluation process that took place during the first hour. After 40 min of play, Mr. 1 had completed only four chambers more, shown in the flow space as increased challenge and stagnation in competence. However, Mr. 1's positive feelings kept increasing. Mr. 2 did essentially the same number of chambers as in his first 20 min. He considered himself competent and the game more challenging. Although his competence increased after 40 min, his feelings dropped dramatically. In the interview he said: "(the level of) arousal decreased and I felt tired"; "The game doesn't feel novel any more; I have become numb"; "It has become more demanding... so many things should be used and considered." This indicates a clear mental collapse, which is seen in his cognitive evaluation of the last period. During the last 20-min period, he reached Chamber 11, never finished it, and experienced a dramatic decrease in competence. At the end he described his UX: "My skills decreased; I lost the logic. It is frustrating because I cannot proceed and do not understand what is going on... I lost concentration and started to try solutions randomly. The Portals were confusing; there were so many things that I could not control." Clearly, after an hour of play, Mr. 2 was giving up. The choices and challenges provided by the game were too overwhelming. He was not ready to commit himself to the game and work to meet its demands. By contrast, Mr. 1 was just getting warmed up. In the last period, he managed to do only two more chambers, but he considered the game to be challenging: "Clearly more challenging. I needed to really think of what to do. The feeling of skill is getting stronger when I learned what I can do... I'm becoming more and more impressed with it." Although his evaluations of competence dropped somewhat in the last period, he was learning to play the game and was confident about continuing.

This simple example shows what kind of information can be obtained with the PIFF^2 subcomponents to support a specific design problem concerning, for example, the game mechanics. Cognitive-emotional flow subcomponents show how the learning curve, difficulty of the game, and the quality of the UX evolve and change during the critical first hour of play. PIFF^2-in-breaks method utilizes reliable measures drawn from a large data more efficiently. This example shows one way of utilizing the PIFF^2-in-breaks method. If the interest is in the analysis of the interface or narrative, then the presence and involvement subcomponents could be included in the PIFF^2-in-breaks analysis. It can also be accompanied by other measures (e.g., usability) in order to analyze design goals at particular game levels, game features, or user groups. The touch-screen can be used at home as well as in the laboratory and the time period evaluated can range from minutes to days, depending on the scope of the study.

3.4 Contributions and Future Challenges

Numerous concepts have been proposed to describe and explain the UX in games. Clearly, there is no one concept alone, but rather a wide and multidimensional array of psychologically relevant subcomponents that can capture the experiential richness provided by digital games. PIFF^2 provides one way of integrating such subcomponents into a single framework. Although it is based on the wider concepts of presence, involvement, and flow, PIFF^2 aims at understanding the subcomponents of "being there" and "optimal experience," for example, when playing games. Theoretically, PIFF^2 is founded on previous studies conducted in the field of game research, while it takes into consideration the basic psychology and the game content, that is, fundamental game components (i.e., the mechanics, the narrative, and the interface). Methodologically, it is based on a large multivariate data set that is psychometrically analyzed in order to establish a reliable and valid set of subcomponents. These analyses have provided 15 subcomponents for analyzing the UX in games. These subcomponents disclose the content, quality, meaning, value, intensity, and extensity of the UX.

It was shown here how PIFF^2 can be utilized to analyze the UX in a group and individual contexts. Because in PIFF^2 gamers are considered to be in a game world instead of merely using a game, this framework enables consideration of a broad range of psychological phenomena occurring in games. This is beneficial for basic research in games. As it was shown in the two cases presented, PIFF^2 metrics can be incorporated into different phases of the game development cycle. In the concept and prototyping phases, a multidimensional framework will be helpful in determining the desired psychological attributes for the UX. Designers can use the psychological information as inspiration and support for their own thoughts when creating new and added value for their games. In the production phase, quality assurance professionals and those evaluating beta versions of the games appreciate validated and reliable tools when evaluating the UX alongside game usability.

Although EVEQ-GP seems to work well in the research settings, future work will involve condensing it into a more convenient tool to be used in various experimental settings. It will then be used to collect multicultural data to support the current framework. The use of the individual PIFF^2 subcomponents for the study of specific game design problems will also be considered in more detail. This will include studying the relationships between different PIFF^2 subcomponents and the game components. In future, we will deepen the social and story-related subcomponents of the PIFF^2 in order to deal with socially rich game contents, such as massively multiplayer online role-playing games. The current multidimensional structure of PIFF^2 provides a firm foundation for these future goals.

Acknowledgments We thank prof. Takashi Kawai, Antti Hulsi, Heikki Särkelä, Jeppe Komulainen, Miikka Lehtonen, Maija Pekkola, Jaakko Sipari, and Jari Lipsanen for help in collecting and analyzing the data and sharing thoughts. This work has been supported by the User Centered Information Technology graduate school, Oskar Öflund's Foundation and the Kone Foundation.

Appendix 1: The Final PFA of the Presence and Involvement Measurement Model

Total variance explained

Factor	Initial Eigen values			Extraction sums of squared loadings			Rotation
	Total	Percentage of variance	Cumulative percentage	Total	Percentage of variance	Cumulative percentage	Total
Role engagement	19,650	23,674	23,674	19,125	23,042	23,042	9,382
Attention	6,189	7,456	31,130	5,657	6,816	29,858	8,310
Interest	3,394	4,089	35,220	2,811	3,387	33,245	4,235
Importance	2,715	3,271	38,491	2,204	2,656	35,900	10,179
Co-presence	2,025	2,439	40,930	1,496	1,803	37,703	11,823
Interaction	1,803	2,172	43,103	1,193	1,438	39,141	5,613
Arousal	1,782	2,148	45,250	1,147	1,382	40,523	4,498
Physical presence	1,485	1,789	47,040	954	1,150	41,673	11,537

Extraction method: Principal axis factoring.

Appendix 2: The Final PFA of the Flow Measurement Model

Total variance explained

Factor	Initial Eigen values			Extraction sums of squared loadings			Rotation
	Total	Percentage of variance	Cumulative percentage	Total	Percentage of variance	Cumulative percentage	Total
Valence	13,279	23,713	23,713	12,762	22,788	22,768	7,543
Impressiveness	4,055	7,241	30,955	3,458	6,175	28,963	4,573
Competence	2,540	4,535	35,490	2,020	3,608	32,571	7,453
Challenge	2,013	3,594	39,084	1,445	2,581	35,152	3,272
Enjoyment	1,898	3,371	42,454	1,261	2,252	37,404	4,848
Playfulness	1,695	3,027	45,481	1,140	2,036	39,440	6,707
Control	1,627	2,906	48,387	1,041	1,860	41,298	4,628

Extraction method: Principal axis factoring.

References

Atkinson JW (1964) An Introduction to Motivation. D. Van Nostrand Company, New York.

Brennan L, Mavondo F (2000) Involvement: An unfinished story? In: Proceedings of ANZMAZ 2000, pp. 132–137.

Brown E, Cairns P (2004) A grounded investigation of game immersion. In: Proceedings of CHI 2004, ACM Press, pp. 1297–1300.

Counter-Strike: Source (2004). http://store.steampowered.com/app/240/. Accessed March 22, 2009.

Csikszentmihalyi M (1975) Beyond Boredom and Anxiety. Jossey-Bass Publishers, San Francisco, CA.

Davis JP, Steury K, Pagulayan R (2005) A survey method for assessing perceptions of a game: The consumer playtest in game design. Game Studies 5: 1.

Della Fave A, Massimini F (1988) Modernization and the changing context of flow in work and leisure. In: Csikszentmihalyi I, Csikszentmihalyi M (ed) Optimal Experience: Psychological Studies of Flow in Consciousness. Cambridge University Press, Cambridge.

Ducheneaut N, Yee N, Nickell E, Moore RJ (2006) "Alone together?": Exploring the social dynamics of massively multiplayer online games. In: Proceedings of CHI 2006, ACM Press, New York, pp. 407–416.

Ermi L, Mäyrä F (2005) Fundamental components of the game play Experience: Analysing immersion. In: Proceedings of DiGRA 2005.

Fontaine G (1992) The experience of a sense of presence in intercultural and international encounters. Presence: Teleoperators and Virtual Enviroments 1: 482–490.

Ghani JA, Deshpande SP (1994) Task characteristics and the experience of optimal flow in human-computer interaction. Journal of Psychology 128: 381–391.

Half-Life 2 (2004). http://www.half-life.com/overview.html. Accessed March 22, 2009.

Hilgard ER (1980) The trilogy of mind: cognition, affection, and conation. Journal of the History of the Behavioral Sciences 16: 107–117.

Hunicke R, LeBlanc M, Zubek R (2004) MDA: A formal approach to game design and game research. In: Proceedings of AAAI Workshop on Challenges in Game AI: 4.

IJsselsteijn W, de Kort Y, Poels K, Jurgelionis A, Bellotti F (2007) Characterising and measuring user experiences in digital games. In: Proceedings of ACE 2007.

ISO 9241-210:2008 (2008) Ergonomics of human system interaction – Part 210: Human-centred design for interactive systems (formerly known as 13407). International Standardization Organization (ISO).

James W (1890) The Principles of Psychology. H. Holt and Company, New York.

Jennett C, Cox AL, Cairns P, Dhoparee S, Epps A, Tijs T, Walton A (2008) Measuring and defining the experience of immersion in games. International Journal of Human Computer Studies 66: 641–661.

Kim T, Biocca F (1997) Telepresence via television: Two dimensions of telepresence may have different connections to memory and persuasion. Journal of Computer-Mediated Communication 3(2).

Komulainen J, Takatalo J, Lehtonen M, Nyman G (2008) Psychologically structured approach to user experience in games. In: Proceedings of NordiCHI 2008, ACM Press, New York, pp. 487–490.

Lazarus RS (1991a) Cognition and motivation in emotion. American Psychologist 46: 352–367.

Lazarus RS (1991b) Progress on a cognitive-motivational-relational theory of emotion. American Psychologist 46: 819–834.

Lazzaro N (2004) Why we play games: Four keys to more emotion without story. http://www.xeodesign.com/whyweplaygames/xeodesign_whyweplaygames.pdf. Accessed November 2007.

Lessiter J, Freeman J, Keogh E, Davidoff J (2001) A cross-media presence questionnaire: The ITC-sense of presence inventory. Presence: Teleoperators and Virtual Enviroments 10: 282–297.

Lombard M, Ditton T (1997) At the heart of it all: The concept of presence. Journal of Computer-Mediated Communication 3: 2.

Lombard M, Ditton TB, Crane D, Davis B (2000) Measuring presence: A literature-based approach to the development of a standardized paper-and-pencil instrument. In: Proceedings of Presence 2000.

Lubart TI, Getz I (1998) The influence of heuristics on psychological science: A case study of research on creativity. Journal for the Theory of Social Behaviour 28: 435–457.

Mayer JD (2001) Primary divisions of personality and their scientific contributions: From the trilogy-of-mind to the systems set. Journal for the Theory of Social Behaviour 31: 449–477.

McMahan A (2003) Immersion, engagement and presence: A method for analyzing 3-D video games. In: Wolf MJP, Perron B (ed) The Video Game Theory Reader. Routledge, New York.

McQuarrie EF, Munson JM (1992) A revised product involvement inventory: Improved usability and validity. Advances in Consumer Research 19: 108–115.

Mehrabian A, Russell JA (1974) An Approach to Environmental Psychology. MIT Press, Cambridge, MA.

Metacritic.com (2009). http://www.metacritic.com/games/. Accessed March 22, 2009.

Nakatsu R, Rauterberg M, Vorderer P (2005) A new framework for entertainment computing: From passive to active experience. In: Proceedings of ICEC 2005, IFIP, pp. 1–12.

Novak TP, Hoffman DL, Yung YF (2000) Measuring the customer experience in online environments: A structural modeling approach. Marketing Science 19: 22–42.

Pagulayan RJ, Keeker K, Wixon D, Romero RL, Fuller T (2003) User-centered design in games. In: JA Jacko and A Sears (eds) The Human–Computer Interaction Handbook: Fundamentals, Evolving Technologies and Emerging Applications. Human Factors and Ergonomics Society, Hillsdale.

Pinchbeck D, Stevens B (2005) Schemata, narrative and presence. In: Proceedings of Presence 2005, pp. 221–226.

Poels K, de Kort YAW, IJsselsteijnWA (2007) "It is always a lot of fun!" Exploring dimensions of digital game experience using focus group methodology. In: Proceedings of Future Play 2007, pp. 83–89.

Portal (2007). http://orange.half-life2.com/portal.html. Accessed March 22, 2009.

Ryan R, Rigby C, Przybylski A (2006) The motivational pull of video games: A self-determination theory approach. Motivation & Emotion 30: 344–360.

Rettie R (2001) An exploration of flow during Internet use. Internet Research: Electronic Networking Applications and Policy 11: 103–113.

Rothschild ML (1984) Perspectives on involvement: Current problems and future directions. Advances in Consumer Research 11: 216–217.

Rust J, Golombok S (1999) Modern Psychometrics: The Science of Psychological Assessment. Routledge, London & New York.

Särkelä H, Takatalo J, Komulainen J, Nyman G, Häkkinen J (2004) Attitudes to new technology and experiential dimensions of two different digital games. In: Proceedings of NordiCHI 2004, ACM Press, New York, pp. 349–352.

Schiefele U (1991) Interest, learning, and motivation. Educational Psychologist 26: 299–323.

Schubert T, Friedmann F, Regenbrecht H (2001) The experience of presence: Factor analytic insights. Presence: Teleoperators and Virtual Enviroments 10: 266–281.

Schuemie MJ, van der Straaten P, Krijn M, van der Mast CAPG (2001) Research on presence in virtual reality: A survey. CyberPsychology & Behavior 4: 183–201.

Sherry JL, Lucas K, Greenberg BS, Lachlan K (2006) Video game uses and gratifications as predictors of use and game preference. In: Vorderer P, Bryant J (ed) Playing Video Games: Motives, Responses, and Consequences. Lawrence Erlbaum Associates, Mahawa, NJ.

Sweetser P, Johnson D (2004) Player-centred game environments: Assessing player opinions, experiences and issues. In: Proceedings of ICEC 2004, Springer, pp. 321–332.

Sweetser P, Wyeth P (2005) GameFlow: A model for evaluating player enjoyment in games. Computers in Entertainment 3(3): Article 3a.

Tabachnick BG, Fidell LS (2001) Using Multivariate Statistics. Allyn & Bacon, Needham Heights, MA.

Takatalo J, Häkkinen J, Kaistinen J, Komulainen J, Särkelä H, Nyman G (2006a) Adaptation into a game: Involvement and presence in four different PC-games. In: Proceedings of FuturePlay 2006.

Takatalo J, Häkkinen J, Lehtonen M, Kaistinen J, Nyman G (Submitted) Experiencing flow in digital games.

Takatalo J, Häkkinen J, Lehtonen M, Komulainen J, Kaistinen J, Nyman G (2008) User Experience in playing a digital game in different situations. In: Proceedings of IADIS Gaming 2008, pp. 3–10.

Takatalo J, Häkkinen J, Särkelä H, Komulainen J, Nyman G (2004) The experiential dimensions of two different digital games. In: Proceedings of Presence 2004, UPV, pp. 274–278.

Takatalo J, Häkkinen J, Särkelä H, Komulainen J, Nyman G (2006b) Involvement and presence in digital gaming. In: Proceedings of NordiCHI 2006, ACM Press, Norway, pp. 393–396.

Tarkkonen L, Vehkalahti K (2005) Measurement errors in multivariate measurement scales. Journal of Multivariate Analysis 96: 172–189.

Usoh M, Catena E, Arman S, Slater M (2000) Using presence questionnaires in reality. Presence: Teleoperators and Virtual Enviroments 9: 497–503.

Vehkalahti K, Puntanen S, Tarkkonen L (2009) Implications of dimensionality on measurement reliability. In: Schipp B, Kräer W (ed) Statistical Inference, Econometric Analysis and Matrix Algebra. Springer, New York.

Vehkalahti K, Puntanen S, Tarkkonen L (2006) Estimation of reliability: A better alternative for Cronbach's alpha. Reports on Mathematics, Preprint 430, Department of Mathematics and Statistics, University of Helsinki, Finland. http://mathstat.helsinki.fi/reports/Preprint430.pdf. Accessed March, 2009.

Webster J, Martocchio JJ (1992) Microcomputer playfulness: Development of a measure with workplace implications. MIS Quarterly 16: 201–226.

Winn B (2006) Serious games construction workshop. Half-day workshop given at FuturePlay 2006. In: Proceedings of FuturePlay 2006.

Witmer B, Singer M (1998) Measuring presence in virtual environments: A presence questionnaire. Presence: Teleoperators and Virtual Environments 7: 225–240.

Wood RTA, Griffiths MD, Chappell D, Davies MNO (2004) The structural characteristics of video games: A psycho-structural analysis. CyberPsychology & Behavior 7: 1–10.

Wundt WM (1897) Outlines of psychology [Judd CH, Trans.] http://psychclassics.yorku.ca/Wundt/Outlines/. Accessed April 2002.

Zaichkowsky JL (1985) Measuring the involvement construct. Journal of Consumer Research 12: 341–352.

Chapter 4
Assessing the Core Elements of the Gaming Experience

Eduardo H. Calvillo-Gámez, Paul Cairns, and Anna L. Cox

Abstract This chapter presents the theory of the Core Elements of the Gaming Experience (CEGE). The CEGE are the necessary but not sufficient conditions to provide a positive experience while playing video-games. This theory, formulated using qualitative methods, is presented with the aim of studying the gaming experience objectively. The theory is abstracted using a model and implemented in questionnaire. This chapter discusses the formulation of the theory, introduces the model, and shows the use of the questionnaire in an experiment to differentiate between two different experiences.

In loving memory of Samson Cairns

4.1 The Experience of Playing Video-games

The experience of playing video-games is usually understood as the subjective relation between the user and the video-game beyond the actual implementation of the game. The implementation is bound by the speed of the microprocessors of the gaming console, the ergonomics of the controllers, and the usability of the interface. Experience is more than that, it is also considered as a personal relationship. Understanding this relationship as personal is problematic under a scientific scope. Personal and subjective knowledge does not allow a theory to be generalised or falsified (Popper 1994). In this chapter, we propose a theory for understanding the experience of playing video-games, or gaming experience, that can be used to assess and compare different experiences.

This section introduces the approach taken towards understanding the gaming experience under the aforementioned perspective. It begins by presenting an

E.H. Calvillo-Gámez (✉)
División de Nuevas Tecnologías de la Información, Universidad Politécnica de San Luis Potosí, San Luis Potosí, México
e-mail: e.calvillo@upslp.edu.mx

R. Bernhaupt (ed.), *Evaluating User Experience in Games*, Human-Computer
Interaction Series, DOI 10.1007/978-1-84882-963-3_4,
© Springer-Verlag London Limited 2010

overview of video-games and user experience in order to familiarise the reader with such concepts. Last, the objective and overview of the whole chapter are presented.

4.1.1 Introduction to Video-games

A video-game is, at its most basic level, the implementation of a game in a computer-based console that uses some type of video output. Providing a formal definition of a video-game was one of the first challenges that game studies faced. Since many things can be considered a game, the following definition is used:

> A game is a rule-based system with a variable and quantifiable outcome, where different outcomes are assigned different values, the player exerts effort in order to influence the outcome, the player feels emotionally attached to the outcome, and the consequences of the activity are negotiable (p. 36) (Juul 2005).

We extend the definition by specifying that the rules are covered by a story, as suggested by Koster (2005). The key part in the above definition is that the player "exerts effort". In other words, the user of the video-game has an active role in the interaction process. Thus, when discussing the experience of playing video-games, we are referring to the process of interaction between player and video-game. Our focus is not on the creation, implementation or design of the video-game. Nor is it the motivation of the user to engage with a particular game or the psychological implications that the user may have after engaging with it. The focus is, as we have called it, the gaming experience, the experience of playing video-games on a one-to-one basis of the interaction between player and game. This concept will be untangled as we move forward within the chapter. First, in order to understand what we mean by experience, we proceed with a discussion of the concept of user experience.

4.1.2 Introduction to User Experience

The concept of user experience is understood as the subjective relationship between user and application (McCarthy and Wright 2004). It goes beyond the usability of the application, focusing on the personal outcome that the user gets from interacting with the application while performing a task. Considering user experience only as a personal or subjective outcome is problematic within the scope of scientific knowledge. Scientific knowledge allows us to generalise about our understanding of the world. If we identify the phenomenon being studied as personal, then it would not be possible to provide a general description of the phenomenon. For this reason, unlike video-games, we do not provide a current definition for user experience. Rather, we will provide a definition which we build and use to understand the experience of playing video-games.

4.1.3 Overview of the Chapter

We divided the chapter into six sections. First, we present a definition for user experience and then we look at how user experience relates to the experience of playing video-games. We proceed by presenting a qualitative study for identifying a theory for the gaming experience. We then present a model and a questionnaire, which is included in the Appendix, based on the theory. Then the theory is used in an example to differentiate among two different gaming experiences. Finally, we present concluding comments.

4.2 The Concept of User Experience

As we have discussed above, defining and understanding the concept of User Experience as only personal or subjective seem to be insufficient for providing a scientific approach. In this section, we present a definition of user experience that helps in bringing the concept of user experience towards an objective understanding. The discussion is grounded in different concepts about user experience, from the colloquial use to the different uses within Human Computer Interaction and philosophy.

4.2.1 Understanding Experience

In our everyday life, we usually do not need further explanation when talking about experiences. In the Merriam-Webster's Collegiate Dictionary (Experience 2009), experience is defined as something intrinsic to human life. Every activity that a human performs constitutes and produces an experience; it is both constituent and product. Experience is the result of the individual interacting with the environment (Dewey 1938). In Human Computer Interaction (HCI), the term designing for experience is about considering the user, the task and the context when designing a computer application (Buxton 2007). But as experience is part of the human everyday life, evaluating experience is not as clear-cut as designing for experience appears to be. Experience is defined as personal and subjective, so evaluating experience is about evaluating a subjective appreciation of the user.

Evaluating experience places the emphasis on going beyond usability by looking at the relation between the user and the task. Usability is how an application is implemented to let the user perform a task effectively and efficiently; the main focus is productivity, to let the user do the tasks with good quality at an optimal time. Secondary goals are user preference and satisfaction (Bevan 1995). It is the evaluation of this relationship between the user with task and context mediated by the application (Beaudouin-Lafon 2004). Preece et al. (2002) define experience as how the interaction *feels* to the users; an application taps into experience, when during the interaction process, factors such as fun, enjoyment, pleasure or aesthetics have an influence on the user. That is, the evaluation of experience is associated with evaluating enjoyment, fun, pleasure, etc. (Kaye 2007). To evaluate experience, HCI usually focuses on the end result of the experience. The user has a relationship with the object within a specific context (Hassenzahl 2003). From this interaction, the user can isolate or share the experience with more individuals (Forlizzi and Battarbee 2004). Or the experience is just personal and transitory, formed by a series of threads that the users mix together in order to make sense of it (McCarthy and Wright 2004). All these approaches require a close understanding of a user to understand how that particular experience was effected. The explanation cannot be generalisable as it was dependent on an individual sense-making process. The current methods that exist look into the evaluating experience (Light 2006, Mahlke and Thüring 2007, Swallow et al. 2005), while they do offer insight to understand the experience, they do not generate objective knowledge out of it.

However, even if experience is personal, it is possible to share it and empathise with it among social groups. In the interaction process, the individual is not focusing on the application at hand, but on the task being done (Heidegger 1927). The actions performed by the individual using the application have resonance in the world (Winograd and Flores 1986), and even if this resonance is particular to the individual, the process of the interaction is common among many individuals.

4.2.2 Definition of User Experience

Experience is both the process and outcome of the interaction. And here we build on the theories discussed by Winograd and Flores (1986), Dourish (2001) and McCarthy and Wright (2004). During the interaction process, the different elements that form the experience are blended to form a personal outcome. To formalise the discussion, we propose the following definition for experience, based on Dewey's definition of experience (Dewey 1938):

> Experience is both the process and outcome of the interaction of a user with the environment at a given time.

In the interaction process, the environment is formed by the goal to be achieved, the tool to be used and the domain in which the interaction is taking place. The domain and tasks are selected by the user, e.g. the user can decide to write a document, this becomes the goal; the domain could be to write the document for college-level class or to be published by a newspaper; the tool could be a personal computer or a PDA, or may even be a typewriter. In order for the user to focus on the task, we identify three properties that have to be present in the application: functional, usable and aesthetically pleasing. The functional quality is the ability of the tool to perform the desired task, e.g. a hammer can be used to nail something to the wall, and so can be a shoe, but not a tomato. Usable relates to how well the properties of the tool match those of the user, using concepts such as effectiveness, efficiency and affordance, e.g. both a hammer and a shoe can be used to nail something to the wall, but a hammer is more usable than a shoe. The final property aesthetics is, in lay terms, how the tool looks, e.g. given enough options of identically usable hammers for the user to nail the object to the wall, the user would select the most appealing based on aesthetic value. These three properties allow evaluating the application. An application letting the user focuses on the task.

It is doing the task which would lead to a positive experience. By looking at the elements that form the process of this interaction between user and task, we are able to understand the common elements of the experiences among many users. Even though the experience at the end is personal, there are common elements in the process of the experience that allow us to compare and share them with other users with similar experiences. User experience is in a feedback loop, as past experiences affect future experiences (Dewey 1938). The resulting experience can create changes in the mood of the person. This could be optimal experiences such as happiness or Flow (Csikszentmihalyi 1990), or at least a sense of satisfaction. Not satisfaction in the classic usability sense of comfort towards using the tool, but as a holistic approach in which the user is able to integrate all the elements of experience while doing a task. The user should feel that all the elements of the experience acted in symphony during the interaction producing a positive experience. So, evaluating the experience can be done by evaluating the elements that are present in the process of the interaction.

4.3 The Experience of Playing Video-games

A video-game is a game played with the aid of the computer. The computer can take the role of a game companion, either foe or ally. Also, it can be used as a rule enforcer and to draw the story that covers them. The design of current video-games requires a big enterprise to pull together graphics experts, game designers and story tellers involved in a process of pre/post-productions (McCarthy et al. 2005). But even with all the complexities that are demanded for commercial video-games, they are still designed following the guidelines of the experts. Video-games, from the designer's point of view, are formed by a three-tier structure: I/O, program and game (Crawford 1984, Rollings and Adams 2003). The I/O structure defines the interaction between the user and the video-game. The program structure details how the game would be implemented at the code level. Game structure defines the objective and rules of the game. The program structure is not discussed in this chapter. The I/O structure is the interface of the program. Looking at the game as a computer interface does not offer any contradictions in terms of what it is expected to provide: an interface that lets the user perform a task efficiently, effectively and with a sense of satisfaction (Federoff 2002). Interfaces are just tools in order to do a task, so there was no reason to expect that this would differ from traditional interfaces.

To understand the relation between game and interface, the Mechanics, Dynamics and Aesthetics (MDA) model (Hunicke et al. 2004) tries to bridge what the designer is creating with what the player is expecting from the game. The mechanics describes the components of the game, such as representation and algorithm. Dynamics describes the behaviour of the mechanics as responses of the player's inputs. And Aesthetics is about the desirable emotional responses evoked in the player. For the designer, the game is built from the mechanics on, whereas for the player, the game builds from the aesthetics on. The model explains this relationship in which dynamics is the bridge between aesthetics and mechanics, between player and designer. Considering only the player's perspective, the experience can be explained in terms of different immersions. Looking further at the relation between dynamics and aesthetics, the Sensory, Challenge-based and Imaginative (SCI) immersions for the game-play experience model (Ermi and Mäyrä 2005) integrates the different aspects of game-play that have an effect on the experience. This model is based on what are considered the three different "immersions", sensory, challenge based and imaginative, which occur, and interact, while playing video-games. The sensory immersion is about the player recognising how the implementation of the game. Challenge-based immersion is "when one is able to achieve a satisfying balance of challenges and abilities" (p. 8). Finally, the imaginative immersion is the area when the player "use[s] her imagination, empathise with the characters, or just enjoy the fantasy of the game" (p.8). The intersection between the three senses of immersion is what provides the player with a fully immersive game-play experience. The sensory immersion is the link of the interface with the game, while challenge-based and imaginative immersions are the link of the player with the game. Both the MDA and SCI models make a clear differentiation between the game and the player. The MDA model proposes that it is the interface where the player establishes contact with the game, while the SCI argues through challenge-based and imagination. Both models are in resonance by providing a separation of the "game" with the "play", the implementation from the interaction. These models, however, include an element in which the interface is not only a series of widgets, but a series of realistic graphics which the player manipulates. The imagery produced in the interface is the story that covers the rules of the game; these were called the "aesthetics" in the MDA model and "imagination" and "sensory in the SCI model. These models provide an understanding of the outcome of the experience. They explain how the different parts of the game are needed so the user can have a playing experience; however, they fail in providing an objective metric to understand the process that forms the overall experience.

4.3.1 Optimal and Sub-optimal Experience in Video-games

Playing games is supposed to produce a positive experience. They are usually associated with the term immersion (Brown and Cairns 2004). Besides immersion, other two terms try to describe these states: Flow (Csikszentmihalyi 1990) and Presence (Slater and Wilber 1997). Flow is a state that an individual achieves after completing a series of steps while engaged in a task. Immersion is the sense of being away from the real world, and Presence is the sense of being inside a virtual world. It has been suggested that Flow, the optimal experience, can be achieved by playing video-games (Sweetser and Wyeth 2005). The GameFlow model translates the stages needed to reach Flow into a series of qualities that video-games offer. Flow was formulated as a model of the stages achieved by the individual, while GameFlow is being proposed as a series of characteristics that video-games posses. That is, this model only suggests that video-games might allow an individual to reach Flow. On the other hand, Immersion and Presence do not automatically mean that the player is having an enjoyable activity, but it is assumed that they are valued but sub-optimal experiences. It is the activity which determines the degree of the experience. Playing video-games can produce an optimal experience, such as Flow, or sub-optimal, such as Immersion; a well-implemented video-game might help the individual to reach a state of Presence.

4.3.2 The Need for a New Approach to Understand Experience in Video-games

The experience is both process and outcome. While playing video-games, the ideal experience is for the player to have fun. In order to build that fun, a series of elements have to be amalgamated together. The MDA and SCI models try to understand the outcome of the experience by looking at the different elements that could form the process, but these elements are not measurable. Outcomes such as Flow, Immersion or Presence, are only concerned with extreme experiences, ignoring the prosaic experience of playing. For example, playing for 5 min while using public transport is overlooked in favour of the extreme experience, such as playing a game for hours and hours until the real world fades away.

   In some sense, these theoretical approaches are top down, applying large frameworks to the study of gaming experience. Our approach is, by contrast, bottom up, approaching empirically the question of how the gaming experience feels in order to operationalise such concept within HCI. In order to measure or design for experience, we should be able to look at those elements of the interaction process that are common among users.

4.4 Defining the Gaming Experience

We believe that by looking at the process of experience, it is possible to study objectively and eventually generalise about experience. We are looking at the elements of the process of the interaction that build the basic experience; those elements that without them the experience would be poor. The hygienic factors of the gaming experience (Herzberg 1968). We are deliberately leaving aside the social aspect of playing video-games. The social aspect of playing video-games has been documented (Lazzaro 2004), but this is a secondary aspect of playing, once the bond between the player and the game has been established. We are interested in looking as closely as possible at the process of playing video-games, not just from our own reckoning of what makes a good experience, but with the idea of grounding our results in qualitative data. We call this one-to-one relationship between player and video-game, the gaming experience.

The section is divided as follows: First, we present an overview of the qualitative method that we used. Second, we present our analysis to formulate the grounded theory. Last, we present an overview of the theory.

4.4.1 A Grounded Theory Approach

The question driving this analysis is what are the necessary conditions to procure a positive gaming experience? The nature of the question suggests that the route to finding the answer should be bounded by qualitative methodologies (Green and Thorogood 2004). In particular, we used Grounded Theory (Strauss and Corbin 1998) to propose a theory for the gaming experience. The interest is to grasp a better understanding of the process of the experience that emerges from the data itself. The method to develop Grounded Theory is composed of a series of coding procedures. First, the data are *openly coded*, in which quotes or words are selected and labelled; this process produces a set of labels, or codes, which can be related to each other producing a set of meta-codes or *axial codes*. These axial codes are the axis on which the forming theory stands. This process is done iteratively until no new codes emerge from the data. The codes are then *selectively coded* where each category is fully developed in order to produce the theory. The data that formulate the theory are different quotations presented throughout the discussion.

The data used for this analysis are game reviews. Game reviews are aimed at telling the general player the reasons that certain games should be played. They do not tell the ending of the game, but just try to describe what it is like to be playing. Game reviews, in some sense, convey the experience of playing video-games. Four over-the-counter magazines from the month of August 2006 and three websites, all of them with a focus on video-games, were used as source data; see Table 4.1 for details of the sources. Besides game reviews, interviews and articles within the magazines were also used on a smaller scale.

The fact that the four magazines are from the same month and year should not hinder the results of the study. One reason is that Grounded Theory is robust enough to overcome the variances that are innate to commercial influences. The second reason is that the interest is in the common parts of the experience. The experience of playing the same video-game described by different magazines should still have the same common elements. Also, the use of websites adds some variance to the types of games reviewed, as well as the fact that two magazines specialised in console games and two in PC games. Since it has been suggested that using only magazines could bias the results of the study, five interviews were conducted once the Grounded Theory study was finished. One game designer, two game reviewers and two players took part in this process. The interviews were semi-structured, transcribed and then analysed. The interviews asked the participants to explain what they focus on while

Table 4.1 Sources of data for the qualitative study. The abbreviation within brackets is how that source is referred within the document. Magazines are quoted, providing the page number from where the quotation was taken; websites are quoted, providing the name of the game from where the quotation was taken, as it is more manageable than providing the complete URL

Source	Material
PC-Gamer. 64, August 2006 – {PCG}	24 Reviews and 2 articles
PlayStation 2 Official magazine, 75, August 2006 – {PSO}	11 Interviews and 1 editorial
Edge. 165 August 2006 – {Edge}	31 Reviews, 3 interviews and 7 articles
PC-Zone. 171, August 2006 – {PCZ}	20 Reviews and 3 articles
GameSpot – {GS} http://www.gamespot.com	3 Reviews and rating system
GameFaqs – {GF} http://www.gamefaqs.com	3 Reviews
ReviewsGameSpy – {GP} http://www.gamespy.com	3 Reviews and rating system
Designer 1 {d1}	Interview
Reviewer 1{r1}	Interview
Reviewer 2 {r2}	Interview
Player 1 {p1}	Interview
Player 2 {p2}	Interview

playing/designing/reviewing a video-game, what makes a game enjoyable and what factors made them stay playing a game. As the interviews were semi-structured, the questions that followed aimed at deepening the answers that the participants gave to the previous questions.

The objective of this study is to find the core elements of the process of the experience. Core elements are those necessary but not sufficient to ensure a positive experience; they can also be understood as *hygienic factors* (Herzberg 1968). Herzberg argues that the opposite of satisfaction is not dissatisfaction, but no satisfaction; satisfaction and dissatisfaction are then two different concepts that are not necessarily related to each other. He argues that motivator factors are those that lead to satisfaction, and the lack of hygienic factors lead to dissatisfaction. With a similar concept in mind, this study looks for those elements that if missing they would mar the experience, but that their presence would not necessarily imply an optimal experience.

4.4.2 Defining the Core Elements

The Core Elements of the Gaming Experience (CEGE) incorporate the video-game itself and the interaction between it and the user, which we labelled "puppetry"; a full discussion of the selection of this label can be found elsewhere (Calvillo-Gámez and Cairns 2008).

4.4.2.1 About the Video-game

The video-game is intrinsic to the experience, without it there would not be a gaming experience. The forming theory does not try to describe what makes a good video-game, rather it focuses on how it is perceived in terms of the forming experience.

> (**PCZ, p.20**): The premise, if you're not familiar with the multiplayer modes of *Pandora Tomorrow* and *Chaos Theory*, is one of spies versus mercenaries. Three spies must hack three security terminals, controlling from a standard *Splinter Cell* third-person viewpoint and using many of the main game's acrobatic tricks. Three mercs [sic] must prevent the spies from doing this, from a first-person viewpoint, using a gun and a flashlight. Sound familiar? Well it should, because it's based on the much-played ancient Egyptian sport of hide-and-seek, albeit on a far more deadly and technological level.

The preceding quote is the typical way in which a review refers to a video-game. The game being discussed, "Splinter Cell: Double Agent", is related to others with similar story lines or rules. The story of the game is about "spies versus mercenaries", the reader of the review could have a better perception of that story in case of familiarity with the two games mentioned. The rules of the game are bounded by the classic play of hide-and-seek, two teams are playing each with three members. Each team has a different goal in the game, and, presumably, the player can select the team of his choice. This excerpt of the review also describes the basic environment of the game, "security terminals", and a third-person view point (the character is fully visible), or first person (the player can only see what the player sees).

The video-game is perceived by two elements: **game-play** and **environment**. The former can be thought of as the soul of the game while the latter as the body. Game-play defines what the game is about, its rules and scenario. Environment is the way the game is presented to player, the physical implementation into graphics and sounds.

The rules are somehow implicit within a game. This can be due to the fact that the number of rules in a video-game is many to be listed:

> (**Interview, p. 2**): I like games that challenge your intellect: strategy, politics, and so on.

Those types of comment refer to the rules, to the "do's and don'ts" that the player can do in the game. The story is the dressing of the rules, taking the abstraction of the rules into characters and scenarios. Sometimes, the story of the game can be inferred with the title of the game:

> (**Edge, p. 46**): Miami Vice opens with an option screen that says as much about gaming's potential as you wish fulfilment in four words as you could in 40,000.

The story is also presented.

> (**Edge, p. 42**): B-Boy. A dance-combat game that's not so much turn-based as headstand, toprock [sic] and spin based.

Those rules and scenarios are considered within the game-play of the video-game. The video-game is also experienced in terms of the environment it creates. This is done by providing the game with graphics and sound. In the printed data, they use pictures as aids to describe the graphics, with usually one or two lines to help in the description:

(**Edge, p. 89**): There is a huge amount of destructible scenery [...] rocks, however, seem to be made of polystyrene.

But not only are the graphics responsible for creating the environment, there are also sounds:

(**PCZ, p. 12**): Sound is hugely important for creating atmosphere and character in games – can you imagine being as tense in *Counter Strike* without hearing 'the bomb has been planted'?

Both sound and graphics make the environment of the game. The environment describes then what the game looks and sounds like:

(**GameSpy, "Flatout2"**): Car impacts are loud and violent, and never fail to be utterly satisfying.

Once the video-game has been defined in terms of the game-play and the environment, it is the turn of the player to take those elements to his disposal.

4.4.2.2 About Puppetry

The interaction of the player with the video-game is the puppetry. Puppetry describes how the player starts approaching the video-game until eventually the game being played is the outcome of the actions of the player. This process of inter-action is affected by three conditions: **control**, **ownership** and **facilitators**. Control is formed by the actions and events that the game has available to the player. Once the player takes control of the game, by using the game's resources the player makes the game respond to his actions, he makes the game his own. Ownership is when the player takes responsibility for the actions of the game, he feels them as his because they are the result of his conscious actions and the game has acknowledged this by rewarding him. Also, there are external factors that have an impact on the interaction process. These external factors relate to the player's subjectivities, such as previous experiences with similar games or aesthetic value. Even if the player fails to rapidly grasp control, these factors can facilitate the ownership of the game by the player.

Control is the player learning to manipulate the game. It is about the player learning how the objects in the game move, understanding the goals of the game and keeping the player occupied. It is also learning about the controllers, getting used to the objects and angles in which the objects are displayed, and the ability of the player to memorise the relationship between controllers and the actions of the game. The first two elements of control, controllers and small actions, relate the basic actions that the characters in the game can do and the manipulation of the controller to make them do something. Without losing generality and to facilitate the discussion, the manipulable objects of the game would be called characters. The process of gaining control is formed by six members: goal, small actions, controllers, memory, something to do (S2D) and point of view (POV). Goal is the objective, the player has to understand what is the overall objective of the game, even if still not clear on the details. Small actions are the basic actions that the player can do on the characters, such as moving to the left or right. Controllers are the way through which the player can exercise the small actions, for example pressing a button makes the object move to the left. Memory is the ability of the player to recall the connection between small actions and controllers. S2D refers to the concept that the player must be kept busy, or doing something. Last, POV is the way that the player sees the environment of the game.

The *controllers* are the basic tools that the player needs to take control of the game. This is how the player starts to manipulate the different characters or objects on the screen.

(**PCZ, p. 53**): Wave your mouse means wave your sword.

Controllers only refer to the player's manipulation of the physical tool, the set of actions that the character can perform is the *Small Actions*. These are the other side of the controllers. Small actions are the basic blocks that allow the player to get the character to do something on the screen. Pressing button "x" is part of the controller, the fact that the character jumps is a small action. Consider the following quote:

(**PSO, p. 32**): By targeting civilian and pressing L2 to shout at them.

From this quote, the player has to relate the act of pressing with the act of shouting that the character can do. In order to make the character shout, then, the player has to press L2.

Memory is the element of control that gives the player the repertoire of actions to get into the game and that can be recalled at a given moment. After learning about the controller and the small actions, the player has to memorise the bindings between controllers and small actions.

(**PCZ, p. 47**): 250 skills for you to master.
(**Interview, r2**): [...] you may find very hard to explain why you need to press that button to reload [...].

Point-of-view is how the information is displayed to the player. The player is able to see what is going on in the game from different angles, depending on the game. The reviews do tell the player what to expect from the point of view, and it is also used as a way to classify games:

(**PCZ, p. 52**): First person makes a combat that actually works.

Point-of-view is not Environment, POV is how the environment affects the control of the game.

The *goal* is the overall objective of the game. That is, the player learning what is to do. It is the player grasping the game-play of the game:

(**PCG, p. 45**): Village pillaging is hard work, get your posse of goblin minions to do it for you.

The goal is the top-level objective of the game, as in the preceding quote, there are no details of what the player is exactly to do, but the player understands that the overall objective is to do village pillaging while directing an army of goblins.

The player must be clear in what is the overall objective of the game in order to get control of the game.

The final element is *something to do*, that is, to keep the player busy doing something:

(**Interview, r2**): Say an interesting example is going to be [...] it is a driving game set in Hawaii, huge free space for you to drive around, but it is just roads like roads on an island, they are not race track roads they are not fake need for space curses they are just roads. And quite a lot of people who kind of sat with thought this just really boring just drive 40 miles and nothing happens and no one chases me and I don't have a gun and you know what is the point and it took all of us I think a while to adjust to this new experience is different kind of driven challenge, it is a different kind of experience the fun is in a different place where you are just used to looking for the game does do at all wrong it is just a genuinely new idea and it takes a while for your brain to adjust.

In the above quote, the player can identify the goal; however, the experience failed to become positive because the player got the sense that there were large spaces without things to do.

Once the player starts to grasp control of the game, the player gears the game with his own intentions in order to make it his. The process of ownership is about using the elements that give the player control in his favour to enjoy the game. The elements that influence ownership are big actions, personal goals, rewards and you-but-not-you. Big actions are those actions that the player implements as strategies, by using a collection of small actions, in order to complete the goal of the game. The player can also draw his personal goals and use big actions to complete them. This process of the player achieving the game and personal goals through his actions is the basis of the process of ownership. The game acknowledges the ownership of the player by providing rewards. Last, you-but-not-you refers to the idea that the player is engaging in activities that are alien to his everyday actions, which allows the player to create his personal goals.

(**Interview, d1**): But also use tend to set their own challenges in their head, not to how much you script the challenge, or, they are actually really playing their own, you can tell them what to do, but they'll play it by themselves, they made their own mini-challenges subconsciously, they don't even know they are doing it half the time, but if you are playing a game [...], you may be on a mission to do something, but in their back of their heads they are oh, last time I did this bit, I did not this street, how did I get to here? Where am I going? some people are mapping the game in their backs of their heads, other people are searching for radio stations, others are concentrating in shooting civilians, everyone plays the game in their own little way, I think is were game-play comes from, as their own challenge. a lot of multiplayer games tend to take on because want that level of challenge that someone else brings, you have 30 people playing the same game at the same time but not one of them is playing quite the same game, they are all playing from their own viewpoint, from their own idea, and that is comes from.

This quote summarises the concept of ownership quite well. The player gets hold of all the elements of the experience and starts doing his own game. To gain ownership, the player starts implementing *big actions*. Big actions are the set of smaller actions that the player uses in order to achieve the goal of the game.

(**PCZ, p. 53**): Knock out a strut from a nearby shelf and barrels can tumble your foes.

Besides the objectives that the game imposes, the player also has *personal goals* while playing.

(**Interview, p1**): On more recent games, sort of on the online games, I actually enjoy helping people, but to be able to help other people you usually have to achieve more than they have. So it is kind of self-fulfilling, the more you achieve the more you can help more people.

The personal goals can also appear while the player is engaging with the game and decides to do something that has no influence on the outcome of the game, but rather just a personal goal:

(**PCZ, p. 53**): Giving you the option to ally yourself with the good or the ill without actually changing the trajectory of the story-arc.

Or it could also be to use the environment, game-play and controls that the game provides to create your own game:

(**Interview, r1**): I'll take this as an example, is a game where you are a boy who lives just to wonder around the world which is instead of cars they have this little bumpy trucks they call walking mock machines and part of the game you can indulge in is to get your own mock, customize it, play around with it but also around town is this beautiful cartoonish kind of town, you can join a band you can start playing the harmonica in a street corner and people wouldn't listen until you get better, you can hang out with other people and you will group people to get a band and it is completely pointless and is just another way for you just to enjoy the game, you can play through the entire story with your big robot or you can become many other things as well but you can stay in the corner playing the harmonica people gather around clapping and you play a bump note and it just doesn't matter that it looks a bit rough and it sounds a bit cheap.

The game acknowledges the ownership of the player by providing *Rewards*.

(**Interview, d1**): [Question: What do you think is the thing that keeps a player for the same game?] It is bit a dough and bullet, it has to be continuously rewarding, but I am not sure, continuously challenging, there is something always that you want to do, even though, there is always rewards given to you, as completing little micro bits, and also larger sections, so there is always a feeling of you moving forward, so you always feels the potential, you can feel this you know, there are more cool things around the corner or something you haven't seen before or just in the next screen, it comes down to I want to find out what is next, I want to find out if I press that button I am so engross that I can't stop now I have to keep going now, until I find a nice place to stop, is not you pushing the user to do more, is the user pushing themselves to do more, to discover what is around the corner, take the next turn, is that little intangibility of the more turn, or next door, or five more minutes.

These rewards can be achieved via sub-goals or by finishing missions:

(**Interview, p1**): You fight a big boss at the end of may be 5 or 6, or several sub bosses and then a final big boss at the end with many characters over the final area, and then you share the loot and you go off and do something else.

Or a continuum of challenges to the player.

(**Edge, p. 83**): We were fed up with games that if someone starts to win, it becomes easier for them to win outright.

Or could also be those actions that have no direct impact on the game development, but amuse the player:

(**PSO, p. 36**): Also funny is princess Leia's mêlée attack – a cheek-stinging slap.
(**PCG, p. 45**): It's clearly wrong to run into an inn and cut [sic] decapitate the cook, but your heart melts when one of them puts the chef's hat on.

While the player is taking big actions and personal goals, the player engages in actions that would not necessarily do in real life, it is a *You-but-not-You* effect:

(**PCZ, p. 51**): Before you offer them a quick painful smiting.

Most games would set the player in activities foreign to his everyday life:

(**Interview, p. 2**): [Question: Why do you play video-games?] To have fun, to be someone else.

Until this, activities can be seen as something that the player has done himself:

(**PSO, p. 3**): Movies and books use real life war as rich source material, so why shouldn't games? (Although you don't get to pull the trigger yourself in a movie).

Not only is the player able to do things otherwise illegal or alien to his own reality, but the player is also making the character grow under his control.

(**PCZ, p. 49**): Who you meet, how you treat them and how you solve their problems determines what recruits you can gather.

This suggests players would take responsibility for their actions as if they themselves are to blame, and not the result of lack of control.

(**Interview, p. 2**): I don't like games where you get stuck because you can't do the button combination in the precise second to jump over the pitfall.

Ownership lets the player see the game as part of his daily life activities:

(**PCZ, p.10**): Well let's see. I can leave my house and wander around the streets of east London to witness filthy roads [. . .] or I can ride around Cyrodiil's beautiful forests on my horse, while slashing any potential thieves.

The last element of the theory to be discussed is the facilitators. Facilitators are the most subjective elements of the CEGE. It has been discussed so far that in order to have a positive experience the player should achieve ownership, and to do so the player must first get control of the game. However, it is possible for the player to achieve a level of ownership, then a positive experience, even if the player fails to get control. Also, the player may fail to achieve ownership even if getting control. This is done by the use of facilitators. These facilitators are time, aesthetic values and previous experiences. The amount of time that the player is willing to play, the previous experiences with similar games or other games, and the aesthetic values of the game.

The *aesthetic values* of the game are important in facilitating ownership. If the game looks attractive to the player, then he may be willing to try longer:

(**PSO, p. 3**): How the increased graphical fidelity changes the way you feel about your action?

These values also influence the player, if the music is attractive:

(**Edge, p. 82**): Locoroco is a nursery rhyme you can play.

Or it may be because they see something about the game that is just amusing to observe.

(PCZ, p. 59): There are also Indian naked female archers that'll have your men furiously polishing their spears.

The *previous experiences* of the player motivate the player to play longer and to assume the consequences, or benefits, of his actions while playing:

(PCZ, p. 2): I don't know about everyone else out there, but I'm really pining for a *Max Payne*. Fans are still churning out mods for the stylish fall of our hero. I'd love nothing more than to see a beautiful new incarnation to empty my clips at. Payne didn't look like he was going anywhere fun after the last game. Well, I say whatever it takes, we want him back. For all I care he can wake up from a cheesy *Dallas*-like dream and start all over again.

Previous experiences may not only be about similar video-games, but just relate to a similar goal:

(PCG, p. 86): I've never lost the heady sense of excitement when I first read about Alexander, and I've been waiting for a game to bring his story to life ever since. Rome: Total war let me live out my fantasies of conquest.

The *time* facilitator is about the time the user is willing to dedicate to play. The time can be intrinsic to the type of game:

(PCG, p. 87): 30 cities in 100 turns is an alarming tight schedule, and it radically changes the way you play. You can't sit back, develop your economy, and gradually build up your mega-army: there isn't time.

Or just to the experience in that moment:

(Interview, d1): [It] is that little intangibility of the more turn, or next door, or five more minutes.

The lack of those extra 5 min could make the player not want to play again, as there is an acknowledgement that without it the game would not be enjoyed fully.

4.4.3 About the Theory

Both elements, video-game and puppetry, are part of the process of the experience. The theory states that if elements are missing, then the experience would be negative. But if they are present, then the experience could be positive. Users first identify the game and then their relationship with it. Ownership is eventually the link that leads to enjoyment. Ownership is achieved when the player has control over the game; if the control is low, then the facilitators have to be high to allow the player to have a sense of ownership. The game is then used by the player to create his own story. The way the player starts making the game his own is by first applying his own actions towards playing the game. Those actions can be used to win the game, or accomplish the player's own goals. As the game progresses, the player starts to receive different types of rewards, which can be helpful towards winning the game, or just something that the player enjoys doing. It is also an opportunity so that the player can do something alien to his reality. The facilitators that influence puppetry

Table 4.2 The core elements of the gaming experience: The two guiding elements are Puppetry and Video-game, followed by Control, Ownership and Facilitators

Puppetry			Video-game	
Control	Ownership	Facilitators	Game-play	Environment
Small actions	Big actions	Time	Rules	Graphics
Controllers	Personal goals	Aesthetic value	Scenario	Sound
Memory	You-but-not-you	Previous experiences	–	–
Point-of-view	Rewards	–	–	–
Goal	–	–	–	–
Something-to-do	–	–	–	–

are part of the subjective relationship of the player with the game: a previous experience with a similar game, the amount of time willing to play or the aesthetic value that the player can perceive from the game. See Table 4.2 for a listing of all the core elements of the gaming experience in their corresponding categories.

4.5 Operationalising the Theory

Once we have formulated the theory, we proceed to operationalise it. We do this in two ways: First, we create a model for the theory and then a questionnaire. The model provides an abstraction of the theory, which shows the relationship among the different elements of the theory. It identifies the elements in two categories, those that can be directly measured versus those that are theoretical constructs. The former are known as observable variables and the latter as latent variables. The questionnaire is created using the observable variables, which allow us to understand the changes for the latent variables.

4.5.1 The CEGE Model

The theory can be summarised in the following three points:

1. A positive experience (enjoyment) while playing games is achieved by the player's perception of the video-game and the interaction with it. These are the Core Elements of the Gaming Experience: Video-game and Puppetry.
2. Puppetry, the player's interaction with the game is formed by the player's sense of control and ownership. Control produces ownership, which in turn produces enjoyment. Ownership is also produced by Facilitators to compensate the sense of control.
3. The player's perception of the video-game is formed by the environment and the game-play, which also produces enjoyment.

All the elements just mentioned are latent variables. In order to observe the change in the Facilitators, for example, we have to be able to observe the forming

elements, namely, Aesthetic Value, Time and Previous Experiences (Table 4.2).
Facilitators are a latent variable, while Aesthetic Value, Time and Previous
Experiences are observable variables. These relationships among variables can be
modelled graphically in the following way: Latent variables are represented as circles and observable as squares. We draw an arrow from a causing variable to a
receiving variable. In Fig. 4.1, we present the relationships among the different
latent variables based on above statements.

All the latent variables depend on the observable variables. However, the observable variable is a consequence of the latent one. That is, the observable variable
exists because it belongs to the construct specified by the latent variable (Nunnally
and Bernstein 1994). See Fig. 4.2 for a graphical representation between latent and
observable variables.

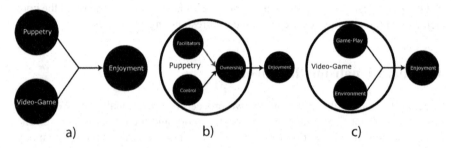

Fig. 4.1 The CEGE model: The figure depicts all the relationships among the latent variables.
(**a**) Inside CEGE, Video-game and Puppetry produce Enjoyment. (**b**) Inside Puppetry, Control and
Facilitators produce Ownership, which produces Enjoyment. (**c**) Inside Video-game, Game-play
and Environment produce Enjoyment

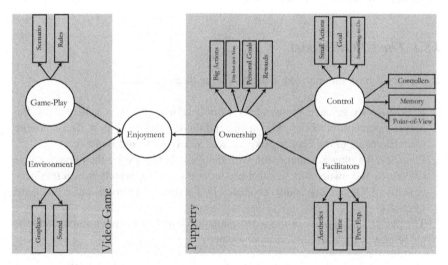

Fig. 4.2 The CEGE model: The figure depicts the relationships among observable (*squares*) and
latent (*circles*) variables

4.5.2 A Questionnaire for the Gaming Experience

The CEGE Questionnaire (CEGEQ) was developed to measure the observable variables in order to understand the behaviour of the latent constructs. The questionnaire was developed using an iterative process following the usual psychometric guidance (Loewenthal 2001, Nunnally and Bernstein 1994). The questionnaire is presented in the Appendix.

Observable variables are considered as items in the questionnaire context and latent variables as scales. The questionnaire is created with 38 items and 10 scales. The scales are Enjoyment, Frustration, CEGE, Puppetry, Video-game, Control, Facilitators, Ownership, Game-play and Environment. The first two scales were included as a reference to see the relationships between CEGE and Enjoyment and Frustration. If the CEGE are present, then Frustration should be low and uncorrelated. The remaining scales are the latent variables produced from the theory. See Table 4.3 for a relationship between items and scales. Due to the hierarchical formulation of the theory, items may belong to more than one category. An item can belong to the Puppetry and Control scales, for example.

Table 4.3 The items in the questionnaire belong to different scales

Items	Scale 1	Scale 2
1, 4, 5	Enjoyment	–
2, 3	Frustration	–
6–38	CEGE	–
6–12, 38	Puppetry	Control
13–18	Puppetry	Facilitators
19–24	Puppetry	Ownership
25	Puppetry	Control/ownership
26–31	Video-game	Environment
32–37	Video-game	Game-play

4.6 An Example of Using the Questionnaire

In this section, we present an example of how to use the CEGE theory to differentiate among different experiences. The experiment explores the differences when two different input devices are used to play Tetris. The results of the experiment are discussed using the CEGE theory to differentiate among the different experiences.

4.6.1 Method

4.6.1.1 Design

The experiment used a within-subjects design. The independent variable was the type of controller used. Two types of controllers were used and the order in which the controllers were used was balanced. The dependent variable was the gaming experience, which was assessed using the CEGEQ.

4.6.1.2 Participants

Fifteen participants took part in the experiment. There were seven women and eight men. The age group of the participants was divided as follows: four were between 18 and 20; two between 21 and 25; two between 26 and 30; two between 31 and 35; two between 36 and 40; one between 41 and 45; and one above 51. Participants were recruited with emails to students within UCL and neighbouring colleges.

4.6.1.3 Apparatus and Materials

Tetris was installed in a PC using a shareware Java-implemented version. This version of Tetris does not have sound. The input devices used were the standard QWERTY keyboard and a knob-like device. Both devices can be used to play Tetris, the mappings of the devices are presented in Table 4.4.

The CEGEQ (see Appendix) has 38 items with a 7-point Likert scale. It was modified by removing the 4 items that query about sound, leaving a total of 34 items. The questionnaire provides seven different scores: Enjoyment, Frustration, CEGE, Puppetry, Video-game, Control, Facilitators, Ownership, Environment and Game-play. A general survey asking about the participants' data, such as age and gender, was also used.

4.6.1.4 Procedure

Participants carried out the experiment individually. They started the experiment with a briefing of the experiment, verbally and written, after which they were asked to sign a consent form and complete the general survey form. Participants were asked to try to forget they were in a lab and think they were in the place where they usually engaged with video-games.

The order in which the participants used the input device was randomised. Each participant was given an explanation of how to play the game with each device. Participants would play for approximately 15 min for each condition and then they would complete the questionnaire and perform the second condition.

Table 4.4 Mappings of both input devices in order to play Tetris

Tetris	Keyboard	Knob
Drop	Down arrow	Push
Move left	Left arrow	Rotate counterclockwise
Move right	Right arrow	Rotate clockwise
Rotate counterclockwise	Up arrow	Push-rotate counterclockwise
Rotate clockwise	Shift-up	Push-rotate clockwise

4.6.2 Results

A related samples *t* test was used to compare the mean of the Enjoyment score for the Keyboard condition (*M* = 0.739, *SD* = 0.176) with the Knob condition (*M* = 0.568, *SD* = 0.169), as the keyboard provided a better experience. The alpha level was 0.01 two tailed. The test was found to be statistically significant, *t(14)* = 3.24, *p* = 0.006. Since there was significance in the results, we proceeded to look further into the CEGE scores. Comparing with a related samples *t* test, the mean score for the Keyboard condition (*M* = 0.644, *SD* = 0.051) with the Knob condition (*M* = 0.610, *SD* = 0.044) using the same alpha level as before. The test was found to be statistically significant, *t(14)* = 3.08, *p* = 0.008.

Hence, we proceeded to look into the two major categories of CEGE: Videogame and Puppetry. The *t* test comparing the means of Video-game (Keyboard condition: *M* = 0.485, *SD* = 0.056; Knob condition: *M* = 0.484, *SD* = 0.052) resulted in a non-significant result, *t(14)* = 0.20, *p* = 0.840. While the *t* test of the means of the Puppetry score (Keyboard condition: *M* = 0.735, *SD* = 0.071; Knob condition: *M* = 0.682, *SD* = 0.063) was found to be statistically significant, *t(14)* = 2.97, *p* = 0.01.

Pursuing further the variables that constitute Puppetry, it was found that comparing the Control scores of the Keyboard condition (*M* = 0.817, *SD* = 0.118) with the Knob condition (*M* = 0.728, *SD* = 0.093) was significant, *t(14)* = 3.28, *p* = 0.005. The other two variables, facilitators (Keyboard: *M* = 0.657, *SD* = 0.118; Knob: *M* = 0.628, *SD* = 0.117) and ownership (Keyboard: *M* = 0.690, *SD* = 0.078; Knob: *M* = 0.666, *SD* = 0.081) were not significant with the following *t* test respectively: *t(14)* = 1.545 and *t(14)* = 1.221.

Finally, the score of Frustration (Keyboard: *M* = 0.476, *SD* = 0.180; Knob: *M* = 0.685, *SD* = 0.196), was also found to be statically significant higher for the knob condition, *t(14)* = –3.55, *p* = 0.003.

4.6.3 Discussion

Using the CEGE questionnaire, it is possible to identify what produces the difference in both experiences. The CEGE theory provides a hierarchical approach to understand the gaming experience. This approach allows identifying that there is a significant difference in the level of enjoyment with each device. Methodically, it is identified that this difference is due to the sense of CEGE, the puppetry, specifically to the level of control that the participants had over the game. Participants experienced the video-game in similar way with both devices. This was to be expected as the graphics, rules and scenario of the game did not change. The low score for video-game could be explained by the fact that it had no sound, and the graphics were quite simple. Regarding puppetry, the main difference is in the sense of control. The sense of ownership and facilitators did not change between both games. That meant that players were still able to overcome the lack of control in order to concentrate on the game.

The difference in control did have a final impact on the level of enjoyment. Answering the original question, the difference between both input devices is that the keyboard gives the player better control of the experience. Even though both devices let users perceive the game equally while making it their own, it was the lack of control with the knob made the difference in the gaming experience. Furthermore, there was such a lack of control with the knob that it actually marred the experience. That is, one of the CEGE was missing thus providing a negative experience.

With this example, we have shown how to use the CEGE theory to objectively study different gaming experiences. The theory provided an explanation of the outcome of the experience.

4.7 Summary

In this chapter, we have presented a novel approach to User Experience. We have argued that by looking at the experience as a twofold phenomenon, process and outcome, and by studying the elements of the process it is possible to formulate an objective theory regarding experience. We acknowledged that experience is indeed a personal endeavour, but there are also common elements in the experience that allow it to be shareable among different users.

We presented the Core Elements of the Gaming Experience (CEGE) theory to understand the experience of playing video-games. The theory describes those elements that are necessary, but not sufficient, to provide a positive experience while playing video-games. The formulation of the theory using a grounded theory approach is presented. The theory can be summarised as follows: If the CEGE are present, then there is no guarantee that the experience would be positive, but it will not be negative; if they are missing, then the experience would be negative. A model that abstracts the relationship between the CEGE and a questionnaire to assess them was also presented.

An example of using the theory to study two different experiences was also presented. Following a hierarchical approach to find the element of the process that affected the outcome of the experience, we showed how to compare two different experiences. The results showed that in one case the lack of control produced a negative experience, while in the other example it produced a positive experience. The theory allowed to formulate and test an objective hypothesis regarding the user experience of playing video-games.

The CEGE theory can be used to evaluate different experience. Future work can look at the theory to evaluate single instances of experience, instead of comparing two similar experiences. The CEGE theory can be used to assess experience in an objective way, it is not about assessing the game or the user, but the interaction of both of them. Further work can look at the elements that might be sufficient to obtain a positive experience, or that complement the CEGE.

Acknowledgements The authors wish to thank Dr. Sarah Faisal, Dr. Lidia Oshlyansky and Charlenne Jennett for valuable comments on this work. Eduardo H. Calvillo-Gámez is sponsored by SEP-PROMEP.

Appendix

Core Elements of the Gaming Experience Questionnaire (CEGEQ)

Overview: This questionnaire is used to assess the core elements of the gaming experience. Each item is rated with a 7-point Likert scale. The questionnaire is to be administered after the participant has finished playing with the game.

Scales: There are eight scales in the questionnaire: CEGE, Video-game, Puppetry, Game-play, Environment, Control, Ownership and Facilitators.

Reliability: The Cronbach alpha for the whole questionnaire is 0.794 and for the CEGE scale is 0.803.

Instructions: Please read the following statements and answer by marking one of the numbers that best describes your experience.

1. I enjoyed playing the game
2. I was frustrated at the end of the game
3. I was frustrated whilst playing the game
4. I liked the game
5. I would play this game again
6. I was in control of the game
7. The controllers responded as I expected
8. I remember the actions the controllers performed
9. I was able to see on the screen everything I needed during the game
10. *The point of view of the game that I had spoiled my gaming
11. I knew what I was supposed to do to win the game
12. *There was time when I was doing nothing in the game
13. I liked the way the game looked
14. The graphics of the game were plain
15. *I do not like this type of game
16. I like to spend a lot of time playing this game
17. I got bored playing this time
18. *I usually do not choose this type of game
19. *I did not have a strategy to win the game
20. The game kept constantly motivating me to keep playing
21. I felt what was happening in the game was my own doing
22. I challenged myself even if the game did not require it
23. I played with my own rules
24. *I felt guilty for the actions in the game
25. I knew how to manipulate the game to move forward
26. The graphics were appropriate for the type of game
27. The sound effects of the game were appropriate
28. *I did not like the music of the game
29. The graphics of the game were related to the scenario
30. The graphics and sound effects of the game were related
31. The sound of the game affected the way I was playing

32. *The game was unfair
33. I understood the rules of the game
34. The game was challenging
35. The game was difficult
36. The scenario of the game was interesting
37. *I did not like the scenario of the game
38. I knew all the actions that could be performed in the game

*Denotes items that are negatively worded.

References

Beaudouin-Lafon M (2004) Designing interaction, not interfaces. In: AVI: Proceedings of the Working Conference on Advanced Visual Interfaces, ACM Press, New York.

Bevan N (1995) Measuring usability as quality of use. Software Quality Journal 4: 115–130.

Brown E, Cairns P (2004) A grounded investigation of game immersion. In: Extended Abstracts of CHI '04, ACM Press, New York.

Buxton B (2007) Sketching User Experiences. Morgan Kaufmann, San Francisco, CA.

Calvillo-Gámez EH, Cairns P (2008) Pulling the strings: A theory of puppetry for the gaming experience. Günzel S, Liebe M, Mersch D (eds) Conference Proceedings of the Philosophy of Computer Games 2008, In, Potsdam University Press, Potsdam.

Crawford C (1984) The Art of Computer Game Design. Osborne/McGraw-Hill, New York.

Csikszentmihalyi M (1990) Flow: The Psychology of Optimal Experience. Harper Perennial, New York.

Dewey J (1938) Experience and Education. Kappa Delta Pi (Reprinted version by Touchstone), New York.

Dourish P (2001) Where the Action Is: The Foundations of Embodied Interaction. MIT Press, Cambridge, MA.

Ermi L, Mäyrä F (2005) Fundamental components of the gameplay experience: Analysing immersion. In: Proceedings of Changing Views: Worlds in Play, DiGRA Conference, Vancouver, Canada.

Experience (2009) In: Merriam-Webster Online Dictionary. http://www.merriam-webster.com/dictionary/experience, Accessed March 2009.

Federoff M (2002) Heuristics and usability guidelines for the creation and evaluation of fun in vide games. Master's Thesis, Indiana University.

Forlizzi J, Battarbee K (2004) Understanding experience in interactive systems. In: Proceedings of the 2004 Conference on Designing Interactive Systems, ACM Press, New York.

Green J, Thorogood N (2004) The Orientations of Qualitative Research. Sage Publications, London.

Hassenzahl M (2003) The thing and I: Understanding the relationship between user and product. In: Blythe MA, Monk AF, Overbeeke K, Wright PC, (eds) Funology: From Usability to Enjoyment. Kluwer Academic Publishers, Netherlands.

Heidegger M (1927) Sein und Zeit translated by José Gaos. Max Niemeyer Verlag, Tübingen.

Herzberg F (1968) One more time: How do you motivate employees? Harvard Business Review 46: 53–62.

Hunicke R, LeBlanc M, Zubek R (2004) MDA: A formal approach to game design and game research. In: Proceedings of AAAI Workshop on Challenges in Game AI.

Juul J (2005) Half–Real: Video Games Between Real Rules and Fictional Worlds. MIT Press, Cambridge, MA.

Kaye JJ (2007) Evaluating experience-focused HCI. In: Extended Abstract of CHI '07, ACM Press, New York.

Koster R (2005) A Theory of Fun for Game Design. Paraglyph Press, Arizona.

Lazzaro N (2004) Why we play games: Together: Four keys to more emotion without story. In: Games Developer Conference.

Light A (2006) Adding method to meaning: A technique for exploring peoples' experience with technology. Behaviour & Information Technology 25: 91–97.

Loewenthal KM (2001) An Introduction to Psychological Tests and Scales. Psychology Press, London.

Mahlke S, Thüring M (2007) Studying antecedents of emotional experiences in interactive contexts. In: Proceedings of CHI 2007, ACM Press, New York.

McCarthy D, Curran S, Byron S (2005) The Complete Guide to Game Development, Art & Design. Ilex, Cambridge.

McCarthy J, Wright P (2004) Technology as Experience. MIT Press, Cambridge, MA.

Nunnally JC, Bernstein IH (1994) Psychometric Theory, 3rd edn. McGraw Hill, New York.

Popper KR (1994) Knowledge and the Body-Mind Problem. In Defence of Interaction. Routledge, London.

Preece J, Rogers Y, Sharp H (2002) Interaction Design – Beyond Human Computer Interaction. John Wiley & Sons, Danvers, MA.

Rollings A, Adams E (2003) On Game Design. New Riders, Berkeley, CA.

Slater M, Wilber S (1997) Framework for immersive virtual environments (FIVE): Speculations on the role of presence in virtual environments. Presence 6: 603–616.

Strauss A, Corbin J (1998) Basics of Qualitative Research: Techniques and Procedures for Developing Grounded Theory, 2nd edn. Sage Publications, London.

Swallow D, Blythe MA, Wright P (2005) Grounding experience: Relating theory and method to evaluate the user experience of smartphones. In: Proceedings of the Conference on European Association of Cognitive Ergonomics, University of Athens.

Sweetser P, Wyeth P (2005) Gameflow: A model for evaluating player enjoyment in games. ACM Computers in Entertainment 3(3): 1–24.

Winograd T, Flores F (1986) Understanding Computers and Cognition. Addison Wesley, Norwood, NJ.

Chapter 5
The Life and Tools of a Games Designer

Emily Brown

Abstract There is a great deal of research exploring the experience of games. However, this research is not necessarily being used in the games industry. This chapter provides a snapshot of the games industry, its people, and the user experience evaluation tools in use. In doing this, we can start to ask what the tools in use are providing and what they are not. Where the tools are weak, we can begin to look at how new tools can help make even more enjoyable games experiences.

Keywords Game industry · Development phases · Lessons learned

5.1 Introduction

There has been a significant shift in the focus of usability research over the past decade. It's no longer just about functionality and efficiency, but about pleasure, and aesthetic. Donald Norman is considering aesthetics (Norman 2002) and Chapman talks of looking at a more holistic approach to design (Chapman 2005). Functionality is no longer our core ambition. We want to deliver experiences.

Games are inherently frivolous. No task is accomplished in the greater universe; the act of playing is for its own sake. This isn't to say that players can't learn anything, just that the motivation for play is somewhat distinct to other platforms. So we start asking questions like the following: What is fun? How do we design for fun? How do we know fun is happening? Research in this area has also become more common; this book is testament.

Researchers are looking into immersion and gaming, constructing and evaluating questionnaires, testing developing theories on immersion and how it is exhibited, how it might be measured, and identified (Jennett et al. 2008). Much work has been devoted to constructing heuristics for game design, going back to Federoff (2002). Developed further by Deservire et al. (2004) and again by Sweester and Wyeth

E. Brown (✉)
Sony Computer Entertainment, London, UK
e-mail: ems_brown@gmail.com

R. Bernhaupt (ed.), *Evaluating User Experience in Games*, Human-Computer Interaction Series, DOI 10.1007/978-1-84882-963-3_5,

(2005). Björk and Holopainen (2005) have composed an inspiring compendium of patterns for game design. Others have looked at physiological measures of emotional response to assess when players are bored or excited (Mandryk and Atkins 2007).

All of these are potentially powerful tools to help evaluate the experience of games. However, it is unclear whether any of these methods are actually being used in the games industry. Have any of these tools been tested in industry? How do they fit with existing processes or the people who use them? To address this issue, this chapter describes the games industry, its people, and methods which are used to evaluate the experiences created.

The ambition is not to dictate how to evaluate experience, but instead to look at which methods are currently in use, and which are not. This will allow us to explore why certain tools are used and how we might enhance the tools currently being used all within the framework of game development.

It is important at this point to define user experience and how it will be discussed in this chapter. In this chapter, it is used to describe the overarching experience that a person has when they use a product. Within this are different facets of experience such as usability, fun, immersion, and aesthetic pleasure. This chapter focuses on usability and fun. Fun is defined as the point at which players will self-report having a fun experience.

Although this chapter does discuss methods developed and used outside the author's experience, the methods discussed are very much one particular example in the industry. What follows is essentially a case study of the author's experience of evaluation methods in the games industry.

The games industry and the people who make games will now be introduced. From there we will look at each of the main stages of game development and the evaluation methods that are taking place. Finally, we can explore the kinds of tools that are not in use and begin to consider ways forward.

5.2 The Industry and the People

As a way of understanding the culture and environment in which game development takes place, we need to look at the landscape of the industry as a whole, as well as the people and their roles. This will allow us to understand the culture and structures that influence the creation of games.

5.2.1 Industry

5.2.1.1 Platforms

The games industry is composed of many different platforms for development: mobile phones, consoles, PCs, and hand-held devices for example. The technology, audience, context, and cost for the consumer as well as developer vary considerably for each platform.

When comparing the Nintendo Wii platform to the PC, you can immediately see distinct contexts. Who plays these games, where are they playing, and are they alone or with other people? More obviously, what controls do they have available to them?

5.2.1.2 Genres

Not only do you have the various platforms to contend with, but there is also the plethora of genres that exist. Puzzle, first-person shooter, adventure, Role-Playing Game (RPG), or Simulation (Sim) games to name a few. Each of these comes with a set of historical rules, some which dictate perspective and game play such as in first-person shooters, others that dictate rule sets and game development, for example in RPGs.

All of these genres have a different impact on the kind of experience that people will have and expect to have. The pace, types of thought processes and challenges that will take place, the scale of the game and time that might need to be invested are all implied in the genre alone.

5.2.1.3 Delivery

The method in which the game is delivered to its audience also needs to be considered. How will users get their content, will it be downloadable or on a disc bought from stores? Will there be periodic updates, or does it remain unchanged after release? Can users create content and if so how and where do they do this? Each of these decisions will impact cost, user expectations and their experience of the product.

The platform, genre, and delivery method are only the beginning of the decision-making process that will shape the game. Sometimes there is little choice in the direction the game will take. If a game is designed for Sony, then it will most likely be a PlayStation product to be played on Sony platforms. The platform the game will be played on impacts the audience the game will attract and the experience that can be created.

5.2.2 The People

It is not just the technology and its structures that make up this industry. The most important element is the people who work in this landscape.

The games industry is notoriously male-dominated, especially on the development side. About 11% of people in the games industry are female (IGDA 2005). The reasons and impact of this on the kinds of experiences created have been debated from all angles. These debates will not be expanded upon here, but it is clearly something we should be aware of. Depending on your position on how software is influenced by those that create it, it may be of integral importance to the kind of experiences we create.

The average age of a game developer is 31, with approximately 5 years industry experience and most likely to have a university education and to be heterosexual and white (IGDA 2005).

5.2.3 *How We Work Together*

Game development is a team affair. Team sizes range from four or five people to a hundred plus. Producers, creative directors, programmers, artists, and designers make up these teams.

These roles are not always singularly defined; artists can work on concepts, characters, or environments. Programmers can work on platforms, audio, and user interfaces. Designers are no different; there are technical designers who have coding ability, level designers who work with 3D modeling tools, and those focused on user interface design. There are designers who focus on details and others who sculpt the broad scope of the project and its ambitions. Whatever the type of designer, it is their responsibility to think about experience. It is down to them to ensure all implementations have been considered from the user perspective. It's up to them to define fun, throughout the project.

It is important here to emphasize that it is not only designers who do this – everyone on the project is committed to creating the best experience possible. However, this exploration is going to focus on designers, because defining the user experience is their core role and part of this role is evaluating whether the desired experience is being achieved.

This is our starting point, a brief outline of the industry, its landscape, and the people who work in it. All of this affects experience from the beginning before anyone has written a concept or drawn a sketch. From here, we can start to look at the detail and how products are evaluated at each stage in the development process.

5.3 Development

The distinct phases of development are concept, pre-production, production, and launch. Throughout these processes, ideas, prototypes, and builds of the product are being generated and evaluated.

This section looks at each stage of development and the methods, both formal and informal, that are used by designers to evaluate their product. As important as it is to know what methods are used, it is just as essential to note what methods are not being used.

5.3.1 *Concept*

This is where it all starts. A team has just completed a project or is getting together for the first time, either way it is officially time to start generating ideas. Of course idea generation is happening throughout development, but for the purposes of this chapter we will look at it as a distinct phase.

The key goal of this stage is to compose a pitch for the concept that will allow the team to gain further resources and eventually see their game released. At this point, everyone is exploring potential directions for the game. Artists are sketching out characters, designers are researching other game experiences and the current state of the industry and where there may be space for a novel concept to fit in. Coders are exploring the technology and tools available. Depending on the scale of the team and the time available, the final pitch may be a one-page PowerPoint with an image and key bullet points. Or it may be a prototype of game play.

Throughout this early stage in development, ideas are being evaluated. Key questions being asked are not just about the potential for fun but also whether there is a workable game mechanic that will provide a developing challenge for the player. How does the product fit with the company's ambitions and their customer base? Can it make a profit, is it a novel proposition?

Many of these questions can be answered fairly well. Companies know the market and what has sold before. The team know whether the idea is a new proposition and what the company ambition is. The fun aspect is somewhat harder to pin down.

So everyone is asking will this be fun? Designers are trying to answer how the concept will be fun. What is the essence of the experience they want players to have? What is the landscape for this experience and how does it compare to existing experiences? Often concepts are defined in terms of their reference experiences, being described as a combination between one game and another. They are also asking how the game provides challenge, how long could the experience last, and is there enough to keep people interested? If not, how could it develop and become more complex as the player interacts? While looking to answer these questions, designers are also starting to think about how best to prototype this experience to find out if there is something that can be built on.

Concepts at this stage can be shot down merely because they are not pitched in the right way, or to the right people, and maybe not at the right time. If the idea passes the interrogation of all the questions above, and someone still believes it can be fun, then it gets a bit more time and opportunity to really evaluate whether it works.

At this stage, you want to get things up and running as quickly as possible. The sooner designers can play with their concept, the sooner they will be better able to evaluate experience. Either you have existing tools from previous products that allow you to get things moving quickly or you have a tech research team that have been playing with things and have some working prototypes to start from. Or sometimes, it's just one person and he/she has to rely on his/her own skills and wits to try and make something. So with this in mind, the two methods that will be discussed here are paper prototyping (which can be used to great effect when there are few resources) and the tech demo (which some games rely upon heavily at this very early stage).

5.3.1.1 Paper Prototyping

Like paper prototyping in other software design fields, the idea is simple – make your product in paper to see how it works (Snyder 2003). What is slightly different in games development is that you are not mocking up screens and flows – you are creating your core game mechanic in paper form. It is possible that all video games could be simulated on paper; however, the type of experience the player would have would not necessarily be comparable. SingStar (SCEE 2004) is a Karaoke game for the PlayStation. Players sing along to the music and their vocal skills are rated. Paper prototyping the game mechanic in this case would not help understand the potential experience in any meaningful way.

On the other hand, a game like SimCity is a different prospect. SimCity (Electronic Arts 2004) allows players to build a city, its roads, and buildings. They decide the layout and where industrial areas will be placed, what departments get funding, and how many fire stations there are. All of their decisions impact the happiness of the SimCity people (e.g., the congestion on the roads). A paper prototype of this game would be able to replicate the core mechanic and allow its evaluation much more easily than with SingStar.

At this stage, the core concept of the game is documented. The rules and components mapped out. From this, the designer can develop their prototype, either by creating and printing cards, pieces, and boards or by using existing boards and the new rules. With the example of SimCity a board can be created, the player can be given a limited amount of money and spend it on tiles to build roads, residential areas, and industrial zones. To simulate the time aspect, an egg timer can be used. Each time the timer empties, the player gets money from investments and the city grows. With this simple starting point, the core workings of the game can be explored. Which elements affect each other and how these are made obvious can be examined. Then slowly layers of complexity can be added to the core.

Once this prototype is at a playable state, the designer can give it to others to play. They have to explain the rules and resolve any confusion or conflict. In doing so, they quickly find any flaws or loop holes that mean players can't win or can cheat intolerably (because sometimes cheating is acceptable as long as it doesn't ruin it for everyone). They find out what makes sense to players (e.g., do they understand how road layouts affect traffic congestion? If not, how does the game teach them this?).

The designer not only learns the weaknesses in the game, but also learns how to teach it. They learn how players can break it with unpredictable actions (Henderson 2006). Whether they learn about the enjoyment of the game is up for debate. They learn what is fun in the paper version; however, the difficulty is then trying to transfer that experience to the digital platform. It is a matter of looking at the type of enjoyment taking place. Is the player enjoying the physical element of the game? Or from another perspective, is there something lacking in the paper version that can be enhanced in the digital version? Answering these questions allows them to continue to refine the concept and understand its strengths and limitations.

5.3.1.2 The Tech Demo

The tech demo is a very different proposition. It may be that the technology is core to the concept and the game play has to be formed around it. To explore how tech demos are used in aiding the evaluation process, this section will look specifically at EyeToy.

EyeToy is a USB camera that connects to the PlayStation and faces the player. It allows players to interact with specific games through motion rather than buttons and controller. As a camera, it has several limitations. For example, its ability to detect motion can be hampered by light conditions, such as a dark room. Not only are there technical constraints due to the environment, but there is also the player to consider. There is a huge gulf between the player and the technology. The interface between them has to be extremely responsive to user action. It has to show the user what is possible and reinforce the right kind of actions. The players have to know what the game is looking for. They need to know if the camera is looking for any movement or a specific kind of movement. Not only do players need to understand what is required of them, but the movement required has to be fun.

To find this out there needs to be something to play with. So the tech demo is the combined test of the robustness of the technology and its potential for fun. These demos can start as a technical concept, such as a button that detects and reacts to the player's motion. Or they can be toy concepts, for example each motion detecting "button" is represented as a ball on screen and they are attracted to player when they move. These can be tested, both for their ability to cope with variable light conditions and for their ability to be fun.

Designers play with the demos and begin to form game mechanics around them. For example, thinking that if the balls were attracted to motion, then some can be made red and some blue and the game is to separate them. Thoughts like this can be explored and the demos enhanced into more fully featured prototypes.

While doing this, designers are starting to decide how to develop the simple tech demos with more fully fledged game mechanics. A majority of the time, they are doing this purely by playing with the demo and imagining the potential experience. Do they have fun while playing with it? Is the experience reminiscent of other games or experiences they have enjoyed? When other team members approach the demo, how do they react? All these aspects contribute to the designers understanding the potential of the experience.

Informal user evaluations can take place at this stage, where members of other teams are invited to play and evaluate the experience. These evaluations allow designers to see through the eyes of a new user. How do they make sense of the technical limitations? If the buttons don't always react as the user expects, how do they rationalize this? From these limited user evaluations, designers can see what actions players can understand, the movements players enjoy making, and which ones frustrate them. They can also see how players react the first time they encounter the demo and the exploration patterns they use. Watching users play with these demos allows designers to start understanding how to communicate the workings of the technology and to consider whether the hurdle is too great for the experience to be fun.

Tech demos are just another way of letting designers explore potential game experiences and try to see the experience through the eyes of the player. If you can show a segment of game play to someone for the first time and see them smile and laugh as they explore it, then that is enough to know whether there is potential for something even greater.

5.3.2 Pre-production

At this point, the product has been granted funding, which equates to more resources and more time. The goal of this stage is to build something that is playable that represents the core experience of the game. The design starts developing greater detail on paper; artists further develop their story boards, character, and level designs. Programmers can start to come to terms with the requirements, what tools might be needed and the framework required. Most importantly, we start to see playable elements of the game. These are the pieces that allow for the further evaluation of the developing experience.

It is at this stage the process that the core idea of the product and the definition of the experience is developed even further. Electronic Arts (EA) call this the "X" (Hight and Novak 2008), other companies use different phrases. The idea remains the same, what is the core of the experience you want to create?

It is also important to continue to define the target user of the game. Often this is not made explicit. Sometimes, it is implicit and all members of the team are aware of the target audience. Occasionally, more formal systems such as personas are used.

Evaluations that take place at the early part of this phase are still very much peer and expert evaluations. Informal heuristics based on the designers' knowledge of previous games are used to question the potential experience. Also, as game elements develop, team members and other people in the office will pass by and encounter them for the first time. These interactions are explored in the same way as the tech demos described earlier. Do people laugh when they interact with the game? What are their first actions when they encounter it? These questions can be answered through these observations. Watching these interactions can give the designers an idea of what experience is being created.

User evaluations can and sometimes do take place at this stage, depending on how developed the product is at this point. However, user evaluations more often happen later in the process and will be discussed later in this chapter; this section will focus on heuristics and personas.

5.3.2.1 Heuristics

Heuristics are simply an aggregation of rules defining key aspects of design. They allow any interface to be interrogated using simple questions. Most heuristics that are used in practice are informal and not used in a rigorous methodical manner. EyeToy is a great example where common themes of evaluation take place. Players are almost always expected to stand while playing, making fatigue a key concern. Levels and mechanics need to allow the user to rest or not demand they are holding their arms above their heads for too long. However, these rules do not necessarily apply to all types of game play or game genres.

Most game genres have historical rules for how they are controlled, in what perspective the camera is oriented, and the types of user interface and interactions available. For example, traditionally first- and third-person shooters have the concept of ammunition, and weapon choice and primary and secondary ammunition. Players collect ammunition as they play, so they do not run out. With this knowledge, designers are able not only to create a baseline expectation that users will have for their game, but also to choose certain rules and break them. This is where these heuristics become incredibly important; without this baseline, designers do not have a reference point defining where their concept is novel when compared to existing products.

These are all part of the knowledge of a designer. These historical rules are called up when required. However, they are rarely, if ever formally and methodically used to evaluate a game concept or developing game.

5.3.2.2 Personas

Personas are archetype users. They represent the target audience of any product. They are best developed in close discussion with market research. When constructed, a few representative users are defined with an age, name, hobbies, job, lifestyle, and the kind of software and hardware they use (Pruitt and Adlin 2006). These archetypes are then the core reference whenever the users' needs and preferences are discussed. In the same way that the "X" focuses the ideology of the game, personas focus the target market.

Only recently have personas become increasingly discussed in games development. Discussions on developer-focused websites such as Gamasutra.com have arisen and developers are becoming more aware of personas as a concept. It seems that as games become more mass market, people who are making games feel less able to define the audience and their likes and dislikes. Historically speaking, gamers made games and they know gamers. As soon as the prospect changes to an audience who are not traditionally gamers, it becomes more difficult for designers to understand their needs. It seems that personas can fulfill this need for understanding nontraditional users and how they would react and enjoy the games being developed.

The power of personas in games is much the same as in their use elsewhere. Throughout the process, they provide a focus for user needs. When new features are suggested or current features prioritized, they are done with reference to the personas. In this way, they allow designers to evaluate their concepts and decisions based on knowledge of the audience. Questions about fun and experience are now addressed in reference to the particular personas created.

The most important factor about personas is that they are a formal definition of the audience. All the questions, mentioned earlier in the chapter, designers are asking about the potential experience are now placed in the context of the personas. Without personas, the types of users imagined when asking these questions change depending on the decision taking place. Personas provide a much more clear line to evaluate against keeping everyone focused on the key audiences.

5.3.3 Production

The product has proved to the business and senior stakeholders that it can achieve the experience that it set out to. Schedules and budget are more clearly defined. All the game content needs to be developed. The art is polished and all bugs eliminated from the code. This is where formal Quality Assurance (QA) takes place and key milestones need to be reached. By this point in development, the team size has grown and the project may already be a year old and have another year or two to go. Throughout this time, the evaluation methods already discussed are still being used, but it is usually at this stage that representative users are also brought in to play the game.

The product's stability is variable: It may have art glitches and buggy code which means it can crash unpredictably. However, more of it is becoming playable. Usability tests with single players or groups playing together take place. Survey data and automated data can be extracted from these sessions. Open betas can also take place, where many people use the product from home and leave their feedback through forums.

5.3.3.1 User Testing

User testing in game development has many forms ranging from small-scale one-on-one sessions using think aloud to large numbers of users and automated systems recording user progress. Whatever the scale of the evaluations, the key aspect is that representative users are playing the game.

Some user evaluations are managed by consultancies where labs are rented, users are recruited, and the development team can observe and receive documents and presentations describing the results. Most often, this will be using a traditional think-aloud technique. Unfortunately, this is an incredibly expensive process that can only really be conducted and repeated by large companies.

When these evaluations take place internally, they can happen in group or one-on-one sessions in modified meeting rooms. A mixture of think-aloud and post-play interviews are used to explore the players' experience. Alternately, large groups of people can be brought in to play and automated systems record their play patterns when and how they fail and the time spent in the different areas of the game.

The information gathered from these sessions is shared with producers and designers working on the product. Videos, notes, and documents are distributed to the team. Designers then need to formulate redesigns that alleviate the problems users encountered. This is not particularly different to the experience of usability assessment in other industries. However, when we start to look at the kind of data being gathered from user evaluations, there are two distinct elements. The first is locating areas where players struggle, become lost, breeze through much faster than expected, or repeatedly press the wrong buttons. This is the usability of the game and links more directly with judging the difficulty gradient, editing level designs tweaking control mechanisms, and structuring tutorials. The second element is the piece that is often not assessed formally and that is whether the players had fun, where they had it, and how much fun it was. This element is gained when designers watch the users play their game.

There seems to be very little, if any, resistance at all to user testing from designers. Currently, only lack of knowledge is really hindering its wider use. This lack of resistance stems from the fact that designers want to know if their game is having the desired emotional impact. The more people they see experiencing the product, the better understanding they have of the way their design impacts experience. The power of user testing is in this key aspect. Seeing is believing, and allowing designers and other team members to see players interacting with their product is extremely powerful. They do not have to blindly trust the user evaluation experts, they can see for themselves.

One of the issues that does arise when receiving results from user evaluations is the fact that it is extremely rare for feedback to come in that the designers have not anticipated themselves. This may in part be due to the broadness of the results that are received from small-scale user evaluations. This does lead us to question whether more detailed large-scale evaluations may be better able to find specific usability flaws.

Microsoft has constructed a tool for user evaluation that combines the ideas of user testing and automated data collection. Each event time stamped and wrapped with data about what context the user was in. On top of this survey, data collected at specified points allow the inclusion of the users' rating of their experience. Combined with a strong visualization tool that can represent the data real time on a map of the game world (Kim et al. 2008), you have an extremely powerful tool.

The examples given when discussing the strengths of user evaluations and the tools that Microsoft have developed are very specific. For example, Kim et al. (2008) talk about the number of deaths for each level of a game and notice one level had a particularly high number of deaths. When drilling into the data, they found where in the level the majority of deaths were taking place. Drilling further, they could find the way players were dying and the exact weapons and characters that did the killing. Finally, this data is linked to in-game video footage of the player's character when they died. This is powerful information, allowing designers to pinpoint areas of game play causing issues. However, these elements seem like tweaks perfecting an already strong experience.

Difficulty testing is another distinct aspect of game development. The difficulty is something that is carefully tweaked throughout the game. As the players become more skilled, they require more challenge but not too much. The evaluation of the difficulty gradient is something that QA does assess. However, their primary focus is software bugs. Also, QA quickly become expert users. Therefore, the value of watching new users experience the game for the first time is incredibly useful to the evaluation of user experience.

5.3.4 Post Launch

After potential years of work, the game is finally released to the public. The press has reviewed it and consumers are buying and playing it. This is the point where designers learn whether the experience they have created gets players' attention. It is also one of the first moments that designers really have time to distance themselves from work and evaluate what they have created.

At this point, there is very little that can be done to alter the experience in a significant way. Patches and updates can be released to fix flaws or periodically enhance or extend the experience, but an overhaul would take a significant amount of time. Depending on the product, any evaluations that take place at this point can have differing impact. An example is with Massively Multiplayer Online Role Play Games (MMORPG). With these games, the core experience takes place online where players explore a virtual world with others. With these games, once they are released the product becomes a service and developers must begin a dialogue with their customer. Whenever developers want to release an update, for example, this has to be communicated. When will it happen, how will it affect game play, will players lose anything, and what do they gain? This is a distinctly different prospect to releasing an offline puzzle game where players buy the game, install it, and would expect nothing from developers except possibly to release a sequel. This means that the impact of any evaluation that takes place at this stage ranges from directly influencing the game while people are still playing to affecting future games the team make.

Sales figures, reviews, and consumer reaction are the main resources available for understanding the impact the game has made. Sales figures are the most powerful; however, they provide little detail on why the game is popular. Are the people who buy the game actually playing it or does it sit on a shelf as a talking point for parties? The two key resources at this stage are reviews and forums. The use of these will be expanded upon here.

5.3.4.1 Reviews

Reviews are a key measure of quality. They are expert evaluations of the experience. Sites, like metacritic.com, that aggregate review scores can be used as independent measures of quality.

Aggregate scores can be used at a corporate level to evaluate the quality of the products being produced by a studio. At a team level, almost every review of their game, especially from respected sites and magazines, is read. Designers can take stock of the decisions they made throughout development and look at how they influenced the experience of their expert reviewers. They can look at themes and key areas that produced positive and negative experiences. It is difficult to take reviews and use them to influence redesign directly. They don't contain enough detail, or the numbers to back up the commentary. However, they do provide insight into some key points and an overall opinion of the game.

5.3.4.2 Online Forums

Forums are the meeting place for your users. They may be created by the development team or evolve informally around a product. At the very least, they allow players to share their experiences and help each other when needed. At their best, they become a powerful communication tool between a developer and their community.

What they can provide depends on whether they are managed by developers or unconnected community sites. Both of these do provide a good idea of the mood of the community playing the game. Volunteered information is often very extreme reactions to the product. This information can often be used as a signpost directing more detailed user tests exploring the issues raised.

When the developers participate in the community, a dialogue can begin where more specific questions can be posed to players. Results of these questionnaires are aggregated and fed back to development. Players speak their minds, developers listen, and players see change. When there are issues such as bugs that cause the players to have negative experiences, developers can communicate and show that they are working on solving problems. This dialogue is invaluable when it comes to supporting online products.

Unfortunately, few formal systems of analysis are used for forum data, especially for the volunteered information. It is just as important to get designers and other team members reading the forums and seeing the impact they have on players as it is to gather quantitative and qualitative data from them. Players can be passionate about the games they play, and seeing this can motivate a team to do more to support them.

5.4 The Future

This chapter has provided a snapshot of the industry, its people, and the process used in the evaluation of user experience. We have talked about paper prototypes, tech demos, informal heuristics, personas, user evaluations, forums, and reviews. However, there are many tools that have not been discussed. For example, physiological measures, eye tracking, formal heuristics, and ethnographic methods and patterns have not been mentioned as tools currently in use. If we take a couple of these, we can start to explore the way in which they could be utilized in the process described in this chapter.

Formal heuristics are rarely, if ever, discussed in game development. But designers are using informal heuristics all the time. There have been several approaches made at compiling heuristics for games. Nokia focused specifically on mobile phone games (Nokia 2006), while others have encompassed all genres and platforms (Desurvire et al. 2004). However, it would be fair to say these works are not common knowledge in the games industry. One way that these could be reconciled is by developing heuristics for a game as it is being developed. This could then become the rule set by which it is evaluated. Exploring how this could be done and the kinds of tools needed to do this could prove interesting.

Patterns are not currently extensively used, despite extremely comprehensive game patterns existing. Again, if we look at the processes that are taking place, where will these most effectively be used? It may be that at the concept stage they could be integrated with the brainstorming, allowing designers to challenge their ideas with historical rules.

Game developers have been creating enjoyable experiences since the early days of video game development and games like PONG (Atari 1972). The industry has evolved, games have become more complex, team sizes have expanded, and so have the numbers of people playing games. During this time, the industry has taken on board user experience evaluation tools, particularly those that provide insight into usability flaws in a game. The most powerful tools offer insight not just into the user experience but into the exact elements influencing the experience.

Although these usability tools are being used, the evaluation of experience in relation to fun is still being done, a majority of the time, without formal tools. Watching players during evaluations and using expertise to gauge the impact of any game elements are still the core methods used. These are successful methods, but if we look at the impact of usability tools, they have been able to support the creation of great games. So, what more can we do to help create even more enjoyable game experiences?

5.5 Conclusion

There is a great deal of experience evaluation that takes place throughout game development. The majority of evaluation is expert based and relies on the knowledge of the designers involved. There are also tools that provide extremely detailed and actionable information about usability. However, there is a great deal of potential to develop new tools and integrate them into the process. To do this, there needs to be more active discussion between academic research and the industry. This chapter tries to bridge that gap and challenges us to explore how new methods and tools can fit into the working life of games development.

References

Atari(1972) PONG, Arcade Machine.
Björk S, Holopainen J (2005) Patterns in Game Design. Charles River Media, Hingham, MA.
Chapman J (2005) Emotionally Durable Design: Objects, Experiences and Empathy. Earthscan, London.
Desurvire H, Caplan M, Toth JA (2004) Using heuristics to evaluate the playability of games. CHI 2004 Extended Abstracts.
Electronic Arts (EA) (2004) SimCity, PC.
Federoff M (2002) Heurisitcs and usability guidelines for the creation and evaluation of FUN in video games. Thesis at the University Graduate School of Indiana University, December 2002 (http://melissafederoff.com/heuristics_usability_games.pdf).
Henderson J(2006) The paper chase: Saving money via paper prototyping. http://www.gamasutra.com/features/20060508/henderson_01.shtml.
Hight J, Novak J (2008) Games Development Essentials: Game Project Management. Thomson Delmar Learning, Clifton Park, NY.
International Game Developers Association (2005). Game developer demographics: An exploration of workforce diversity. http://www.igda.org/diversity/report.php.

Jennett C, Cox AL, Cairns P, Dhoparee S, Epps A, Tijs T, Walton A (2008) Measuring and defining the experience of immersion in games. International Journal of Human Computer Studies 66(9): 641–661.

Kim JH, Gunn DV, Schuh E, Phillips BC, Pagulayan RJ (2008) Tracking real-time user experience (TRUE): A comprehensive instrumentation solution for complex systems. CHI Proceedings 2008, pp. 443–451.

Mandryk RL, Atkins MS (2007) A fuzzy approach for continuously modeling emotion during interaction with play technologies. International Journal of Human-Computer Studies 65(4): 329–334.

Nokia C (2006) Mobile game playability heuristics version 1.0. http://www.forum.nokia.com/info/sw.nokia.com/id/5ed5c7a3-73f3-48ab-8e1e-631286fd26bf/Mobile_Game_Playability_Heuristics_v1_0_en.pdf.html?language=japanese.

Norman DA (2002) Emotion and design: Attractive things work better. Interactions Magazine ix(4): 36–42.

Pruitt J, Adlin T (2006). The persona lifecycle: Keeping people in mind throughout product design. The Morgan Kaufmann Series in Interactive Technologies.

Snyder C (2003) Paper prototyping: The Fast and Easy Way to Design and Refine User Interfaces. Morgan Kaufman Publishers, San Francisco, CA.

Sony Computer Entertainment Europe (SCEE) (2004). SingStar. PlayStation 2.

Sweester P, Wyeth P (2005) GameFlow: A model for evaluating player enjoyment in games. ACM Computers in Entertainment 3(3): 1–24.

Chapter 6
Investigating Experiences and Attitudes Toward Videogames Using a Semantic Differential Methodology

Philippe Lemay and Martin Maheux-Lessard

Abstract There exists a growing concern in the game design community related to the understanding of the multifaceted nature of players' experiences. This chapter addresses this relevant need by focusing on the attitudinal aspect of experiences and presents the differential semantic approach as a relevant and powerful methodology. Given the importance of attitudes orienting the cognitive and behavioral stance toward objects in general, and games in particular, researchers need to acquire the proper conceptual and methodological tools in order to investigate these significant aspects. This methodology allows researchers and designers to probe many aspects and questions related to attitudes toward games such as how do players perceive a game, a game genre, or a particular game episode. This chapter details the methodology, presents empirical results gathered using this approach, and offers fertile considerations regarding how a better understanding of attitudes toward games enlightens the gaming system and may help game designers develop innovative games tailored to their intended audiences.

6.1 Introduction

Over the past decade, videogames have blossomed into a very popular and significant leisure activity for many people. In fact, videogames have now gone mainstream and are aimed at new audiences that traditionally didn't consider videogames for spending their free time. In what can be described as the casual gamers' paradigm, designers are now challenged with the demanding task of creating games that need to be appealing, accessible, and usable to a rather different audience, and this endeavor is quite different from designing games intended for hardcore gamers (Fortugno 2008). How do gamers perceive videogames? How do

P. Lemay (✉)
Ludosys, 486 chemin de l'Église, Fatima, QC, Canada G4T 2N8
e-mail: philippe.lemay@ludosys.com

R. Bernhaupt (ed.), *Evaluating User Experience in Games*, Human-Computer Interaction Series, DOI 10.1007/978-1-84882-963-3_6,
© Springer-Verlag London Limited 2010

their perceptions compare with other leisure activities? How do specific audiences like non-gamers and women feel toward gaming? What do people look for in a leisure activity? Investigating these aspects is very relevant as it can yield interesting data to help designers create innovative games and provide great gaming experience for their target audience.

With the increasing popularity of videogames, a growing number of research initiatives have been undertaken for evaluating players' experiences in games, using different frameworks (Ermi and Mäyrä 2005, Costello 2007, Apter 1991, Hunicke et al. 2004, Lazzaro 2004, Björk and Holopainen 2005) and methodologies (Pagulayan et al. 2003, Mandryk et al 2006, Appelman 2007). These are aimed at a better understanding of the gaming system, i.e., the players, the games, and the resulting interactions and experiences (Salen and Zimmerman 2004). But more research needs to be done in order to provide designers and researchers a solid, coherent, and shared corpus of conceptual and methodological tools to assess the gaming phenomena and assist game development.

In this regard, the aim of this chapter is to present a specific methodology, the semantic differential (SD), which we consider to be helpful to designers and researchers, as it can probe many aspects and questions related to attitudes toward games. The SD methodology was initially developed by Osgood et al. (1957) to investigate attitudes toward concepts and group of objects. Attitudes are a psychological construct defined as "a sustained internal disposition that underlies favorable or unfavorable individual responses towards an object or a class of objects" (translated from Bloch et al. 1991). Attitudes are organized around three fundamental components: the *cognitive* component that includes individual beliefs about an object, the *affective* component that takes into account motivations and other subjective elements, and the *conative* component that relates to behaviors and their underlying intentions (Ajzen 1989, Ajzen et al. 1986, D'Astous et al. 2003). Investigating attitudes toward games is therefore relevant because what people think of a game can influence their purchase intention and thus their participation.

The use of the SD has been documented in many areas such as politics, architecture, environmental design, ergonomics, and various product designs (Mondragon et al. 2005). However, this kind of methodology has never been applied to videogame research. And given the importance of attitudes orienting the cognitive and behavioral stance toward objects in general, and games in particular, such approach offers an appropriate research strategy related to players' experiences and could help designers develop significant insights into their target audiences.

To illustrate the procedure for conducting SD surveys and analyzing the subsequent data, we will present a meaningful case study where attitudes toward different leisure activities, including more specifically videogames, were investigated using the SD methodology. After reading this chapter, one should grasp the fundamental concepts and tools of the methodology and understand what type of information and knowledge could be extracted.

6.2 Experiences and Attitudes

6.2.1 Experiences, the Core Concept of Gaming

The underlying goal of videogames is to generate particular experiences to players engaged in such an activity, and most often fun or pleasurable ones (Pagulayan et al. 2003, Fullerton 2008, Koester 2004). But with the growing complexity of today's videogames – in terms of content, interactions, and technology – one of the main challenges designers and researchers are facing is the defining and understanding of the elements and interactions that create a great gaming experience. And because different audiences are now drawn to games, what constitutes a great gaming experience isn't something standard across all player groups.

Recent attempts to conceptualize the gameplay experience have been very helpful with this matter by highlighting elements that take part in the formation of experiences generated by playing videogames. One of these attempts is the "SCI model" elaborated by Ermi and Mäyrä (2005), which identifies some of the fundamental components of gameplay experiences and their relation to each other. Their model is based on the immersive nature of gameplay experiences in terms of sensations, challenges, and imagination, and is the result of complex interaction processes influenced by factors such as the *game itself* (in terms of game structures, audiovisuality, and interface), the *person-engaged playing* (in terms of individuality, motivations, and experiential dimensions such as cognition, emotions, and behaviors), and the *social context* in which the gaming activity takes place. From this perspective, players do not simply engage in a "ready-to-play" game, but rather take an active part in constructing and interpreting (i.e., giving meaning to) their own gameplay experiences by bringing with them their desires, anticipations, and past experiences.

Another fruitful model for conceptualizing the gaming experience is the model of optimal experiences (or the "flow" model, e.g., Csikszentmihalyi 1990). Flow theory has been borrowed by the videogame research community to illustrate what players – and designers – want to achieve in a game (Salen and Zimmerman 2004, Appelman 2007, Sweetser and Wyeth 2005). Although this model is very helpful in illustrating an array of experiences a player can go through when gaming (based on the level of challenges and skills the player perceives), flow theory can help designers grasp the answer to a fundamental question about their work: "What motivates people to play?"

According to Csikszentmihalyi (1997), people are motivated to engage in leisure activities because of the satisfaction they get out of it. This usually comes through the accomplishment of goals where meaningful skills are developed and acquired. And even if the aim of this chapter is not to discern which goals are worth pursuing, we suggest that some goals supported by traditional videogames don't fit everyone. For example, not everybody agrees that spending half-a-day collecting weapons to beat a fierce boss is a goal worth pursuing, as many might think that engaging in other leisure activities might be a better investment of time and energy (like getting fit or learning to cook). With this regard, attitudinal research in conjunction with the flow model could be useful to better characterize specific audiences like non-gamers and women, for example (Lemay, 2007a).

Another interesting aspect of the flow theory is how it may be related to impacts of leisure on the quality of life of individuals. As stated by Csikszentmihalyi (1990, 1997), even if the most positive experiences in our daily lives tend to occur in a leisure context, all leisure activities don't exhibit the same effects on the quality of experience. In this regard, this author differentiates the effects of passive and active leisure – where active leisure activities such as sports and arts, for example, tend to provide a context much more favorable for personal development and growth than the context provided by passive leisure activities such as watching TV and reading. The intrinsic rewards and feelings of gratification gained by deeply engaging in active leisure is a major factor that contributes to the quality of life in general (Csikszentmihalyi 1990). Should videogames then be considered a passive or an active leisure activity? Empirical data may provide some corresponding insights.

Fortunately, there is a growing awareness toward quality-of-life and well-being issues, upon which the design community in general is reflecting (Press and Cooper 2003). If videogames are capable of generating fun and pleasure, from a logic of *sustainable experiences* (Lemay 2007b), can videogames also lead to *well-being* and furthermore to a better *quality of life*? The relationships between flow theory and leisure activities stir up interesting issues concerning the nature and value of videogames, and flow theory can help conceptualize important aspects of the gaming experience as a whole.

To some extent, the quality-of-life shift in the design of videogames is already underway and the approach toward conceptualizing the gameplay experience in a holistic manner has already granted the gaming industry with numerous successes. Games such as *Wii Fit*, *Guitar Hero*, *Brain Age*, and even *Dance Dance Revolution* all share and integrate elements inspired from active leisure.

6.2.2 Why Attitudes Matter in Leisure Activities Such as Videogames

From a game designer's perspective, knowing what target users think of a certain game genre has always been valuable data when it comes to creating a new game. Focus groups, benchmarks evaluation, and playtests are typical research methods set forth in order to grasp information about player attitudes and preferences (Pagulayan et al 2003, Appelman 2007, Kuniavsky 2003). But since videogames are one among many other leisure activities worth taking part in, probing attitudes about other leisure activities may provide interesting data about perceptions and needs related to games per se.

Conceptually, investigating attitudes toward leisure activities, including videogames, can enrich the understanding of the dynamics of engagement in an activity. This dynamic can be referred to as the causal chain of motivation/participation/satisfaction as suggested by Crandall (1980). Therefore, answers to question such as why people engage in videogames, what motivates them to play, and what satisfaction they get out of it could help conceptualize gameplay experiences in a more profound manner and help designers create more engaging and compelling games from a practical point of view.

From a leisure research perspective, attitudes toward leisure activities are relevant because of their positive effect on participation (Ragheb and Tate 1993). Said in a straightforward fashion, what people think of an activity influences whether they will engage in it or not. But other factors can also influence leisure participation such as availability, affordability, and social acceptance (Argyle 1987).

Similar to other leisure activities, players interpret their engagement in videogames by means of referral to the cultural and social context (Ermi and Mäyrä 2005). Although videogames have grown over time to be a very popular and significant leisure activity, many social concerns have been addressed toward this form of entertainment (Barnett et al. 1997). That alone justifies the need to probe the attitudes of people and groups of people about it.

For the reasons mentioned above, attitudinal research in the videogame domain represents a relevant and significant approach to grasp valuable information about the underlying players – and non-players – experiences. Knowing that attitudes toward a particular game genre or simply toward a general leisure activity can have a distinct impact on engagement, the acquired information could help game designers create more compelling games and help them tackle the challenge of creating user-friendly and quality-of-life-oriented games.

6.3 Case Study

The authors present here how they have used and tested the semantic differential (SD) approach in the videogame domain. How are videogames affectively perceived? How do they compare with other popular leisure such as Internet surfing and communication, watching TV, reading, and playing a musical instrument? While there exists an abundance of literature regarding how people organize their free time and how their leisure activities are construed, playing videogames as an activity has not been described in such a fashion. The aim of the study was to compare the perceptions of videogames with other leisure activities and investigate if we could pinpoint specific positive and negative perceptions.

6.3.1 Research Objectives

Mainly because this kind of approach was never used in this domain and because no other data were available to compare the results, no specific hypotheses were explicated in the research protocol. Data analyses were subsequently performed from a more descriptive stance rather than an inferential one.

The following analyses were planned: the descriptive analysis of the participants, the descriptive analysis of the perception of each leisure activity, the multivariate comparison of the leisure activities, and finally comparisons between our sample subgroups (male *versus* female, videogame players *versus* non-players). From a game design point of view preoccupied by the accessibility of videogames, these last two analyses would provide interesting information about the underlying engagement toward videogames – or the lack thereof – of these subgroups.

6.3.2 Methodological Procedures

Students and employees from the Faculty of Environmental Design of the University of Montreal and other people were invited to answer an online survey through emails, posters, and word-of-mouth contacts; people finishing the survey were asked to freely provide names and email addresses of people susceptible to be interested in the survey participation.

The survey was organized in three parts. The first part stated the research objectives and instructions. The second part consisted of the main section regarding the attitude toward leisure and a section regarding the socio-demographic profile of participants. Finally, the third part warmly thanked the participants for completing the survey.

6.3.3 Choice of Concepts and Adjectives

Semantic differential is a particular approach for probing the connotative meaning of objects, class of objects, or concepts, through the use of a list of bipolar adjectives (Osgood et al. 1957). Pairs of adjectives were chosen according to attitude theories and models as well as knowledge of the game domain. Because this is the first endeavor using the SD methodology in the game domain, no predefined or tested set of adjectives was available. Therefore, an iterative process of corpus delimitation, adjective generation, set discussion, and validation was undertaken.

Many sets of pairs of adjectives were developed throughout the research project, at some point reaching over 500 pairs. Some pairs originated from a multidimensional framework approach to experiences (Lemay 2008, Shedroff 2001, Schmitt 1999), including the sensorial, emotional, cognitive, behavioral, and social dimensions. Some pairs came from leisure literature (Argyle 1987) and were inspired by flow theory (Csikszentmihalyi 1990). After a lengthy period of discussion, refinement, and testing among researchers and pretest volunteers (where criteria of relevance, interest, and non-redundancy led our selection process), a set of 26 pairs of dichotomous adjectives were established and deemed satisfactory for the main survey.

In order to facilitate the analysis, the final set of adjectives was structured around four categories inspired by leisure attitude components (Ragheb and Beard 1982):

1. *global evaluation* of the leisure activities, related to the cognitive dimension of attitudes, such as beliefs, knowledge, virtues, and features and benefits associated to the activities;

2. *experiential nature* of leisure activities, related to how people may experience leisure;
3. *affective evaluation* of activities, related to the affective dimension of attitudes;
4. *miscellaneous evaluation*, related to various aspects of leisure and hors-champ adjectives, as suggested in SD literature (Osgood et al 1957).

The pairs of adjectives consist in the following (translated from French): *Healthy – Unhealthy, Affordable – Costly, Slow – Fast, Developing – Devaluing, Stressful – Relaxing, Easy – Difficult, Demotivating – Motivating, Popular – Unpopular, Exciting – Boring, Funny – Serious, Good – Bad, Distressing – Reassuring, Pleasant – Unpleasant, Clear – Obscure, Useful – Useless, Peaceful – Violent, Passive – Active, Sad – Happy, Social – Antisocial, Disgusting – Attractive, Satisfying – Unsatisfying, Familiar – Strange, Harmful – Beneficial, Instructive – Thought-destroying, Physical – Mental, Calm – Agitated.*

The choice of concepts – in our case, of leisure activities – was based on reviewing the leisure research literature. Beside the inclusion of the *videogames* activities, those activities that were frequent for adults and important in the literature (either for their active or for their passive connotations) were kept in the final choice: *Physical activities, Reading, Watching TV, Practicing a musical instrument, Internet surfing and communicating,* and finally *doing Crosswords/sudokus.*

Regarding the choice of concepts (here, the leisure activities), the number of concepts was kept to a reasonable number with respect to the length of the survey. Because surveys that are too long are often not completed or even not answered firsthand, we tried to keep the total number of questions to approximately 250, leading to a 20–25 min survey (multiplying the number of activities times the number of pairs of adjectives, i.e., $7 \times 26 = 182$, plus the other questions about sociodemographic and patterns of leisure activity use). This would help to minimize the number of incomplete questionnaires during the survey.

6.3.4 The Differential Semantic Questions

Specifically regarding the semantic differential questions, participants had to answer the same kind of questions for each activity, for example, "How do you perceive videogames?" Pairs of adjectives were then presented on both side of a 7-point Likert scale and participants were asked to rate the activity (cf. Fig. 6.1). Number 3 on the left meant that the left adjective was *very representative* of the activity, number 2 on the left meant the left adjective was *representative* of the activity, and number 1 on the left meant the left adjective was *a little bit representative* of the activity. This reasoning applied for the right adjective in a similar way. Number 0 at the center of the scale meant both adjectives were either *not representative* or *equally representative*. Some negatively connotated adjectives were put on the left side of the scale and some were put on the right, in order to minimize one-sided perception of the scales.

Fig. 6.1 Example of the
semantic differential question
sheet

	3	2	1	0	1	2	3	
Healthy	o	o	o	o	o	o	o	Unhealthy
Affordable	o	o	o	o	o	o	o	Costly
Slow	o	o	o	o	o	o	o	Fast
Developing	o	o	o	o	o	o	o	Devaluing
Stressful	o	o	o	o	o	o	o	Relaxing
Easy	o	o	o	o	o	o	o	Difficult
Demotivating	o	o	o	o	o	o	o	Motivating
Popular	o	o	o	o	o	o	o	Unpopular
Exciting	o	o	o	o	o	o	o	Boring
Funny	o	o	o	o	o	o	o	Serious
Good	o	o	o	o	o	o	o	Bad
Distressing	o	o	o	o	o	o	o	Reassuring
Pleasant	o	o	o	o	o	o	o	Unpleasant

6.3.5 Description of Participants (Descriptive Analyses)

From the 105 participants who begun the online survey, 80 completed it during spring 2007. Participants' profiles were as follows: there were slightly more women (44) than men (36). Thirty-seven participants were in the 18–25 years old category, 23 were 26–35 years old, 12 were 36–45 years old, 5 were 46–55 years old, and 3 were 56 years old and over. Fifty participants were students at the time, 27 were employed, and 1 was unemployed; 2 specified the "other" category.

Regarding the participants' use of their free time, the participants' four most frequent leisure activities were reading (92.5%), Internet use (87.5%), watching TV (86.2%), and doing physical activity (78.8%). Playing videogames was an activity that reached 48.8% of the participants. The least frequent leisure activities were doing crosswords/sudokus (32.5%) and practicing a musical instrument (20%).

Delving into the patterns of use of videogames, 24 out of the 39 participants who indicated that they play videogames played less than 5 h a week, while 9 participants played from 5 to 9 h a week, 2 played from 10 to 14 h. Four of them enjoyed videogames for 15 h and more.

6.3.6 Multidimensional Analyses of Attitudes Toward Leisure and Games

Once the global profile of the population sample was performed and the pattern of leisure use was established, the basic semantic profile for each leisure activity and for each pair of adjectives was computed. Medians were used as a descriptive statistic instead of the typical average because answers must be considered as ordinal data, not continuous ones.

How did participants perceive the seven leisure activities? The statistical median for each pair of adjectives and each activity was computed and plotted on graphics. When all seven activities are plotted together, some patterns could be detected, but they are more difficult to perceive. There seems to be a general trend for which most leisure activities were evaluated. Graphically, no activity seems to be perceived radically different from the others. A very few activities have gathered medians of ±3, which means that more than 50% of the participants evaluated the leisure in a strong manner; those activities that gathered such high marks are physical activities, reading, and watching TV.

In order to make sense of a particular activity, it can be plotted individually. Let's use the videogame activity as an example, as shown in Fig. 6.2.

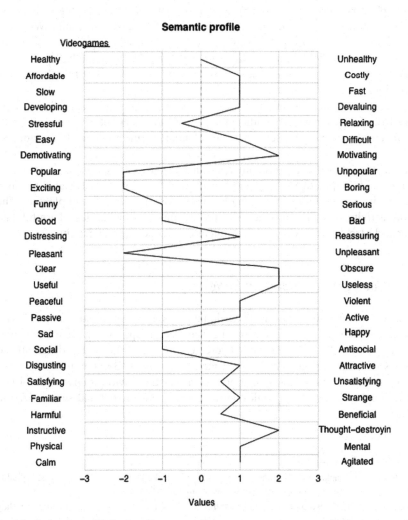

Fig. 6.2 Semantic profile for the videogame activity

Those adjectives whose median is highest (either +2 or –2) are considered as the meaningful ones. The next figure clearly illustrates that videogames were evaluated as: motivating, exciting, pleasant, and popular, but also useless, thought-destroying, and obscure.

Questions arise as if these adjectives that were graphically extracted correspond to statistically meaningful results. Wilcoxon tests[1] were performed comparing empirical medians for each pair of adjectives and each activity in order to pinpoint the statistically significant adjectives; as a metric for this information, those values which differ from the neutral evaluation (0) and the weak perception (–1 or +1) were chosen; stated otherwise, this implies a median inferior or equal to –2, or a median superior or equal to +2. The reference p-value was 0.00027 (i.e., 0.05/(7∗26)), which corresponds to a 0.05 level, with a Bonferroni correction applied because the numerous statistical tests performed on the 7 activities and 26 pairs of adjectives could randomly trigger false positive results. Wilcoxon tests were symmetrically performed on the other side of the pairs of adjectives, for each pair of adjectives and each leisure activity, comparing medians inferior or equal to –2. The reference p-value was also $p < 0.00027$ because of the Bonferroni correction.

Making sense of the resulting tables is easy when the significant adjectives are extracted.[2] The statistically significant adjectives are taken out and put into a table (cf. Table 6.1), showing the leisure on one column and the predefined categories on each row.

From the table it can be summarized that leisure such as physical activities, reading, and the practice of a musical instrument are globally associated to much more positive perceptions, like being healthy, good, developing, and pleasant. The leisure activities having more negative perceptions (such as useless, harmful, and thought-destroying) are videogames, watching TV, and Internet activities.

6.3.7 Comparisons Between Subgroups

Other informative analyses can be undertaken using the rich data gathered with such methodology. The comparisons between subgroups of our population sample are explored here. Because other researches have demonstrated differentiated patterns of game engagement between men and women (Barnett et al. 1997), we wanted to know if the underlying perceptions for these two groups followed this trend. Graphically the two profiles are represented in Fig. 6.3 and summarized in Table 6.2.

---

[1] The R statistical package was used to perform both graphical and numerical procedures; available at www.r-project.org, it is an open-source software similar to Splus.

[2] The exact statistical results are not shown for the two 7×26 tables, for a matter of concision; they are available on request.

Table 6.1 Statistically significant adjectives describing seven leisure activities. Symbol "–" indicates that no adjective was statistically significant for the activity

	General	Affect	Experience	Miscellaneous
Videogames	Useless, thought-destroying	Motivating	Exciting, pleasant	Popular
Physical activities	Useful, good, healthy, instructive	Developing, satisfying, attractive	Exciting, pleasant	Physical, social, calm, sad, peaceful, popular, fast
Reading	Instructive, healthy, good	Developing, attractive	Pleasant, easy	Physical, peaceful, calm, social, sad, affordable
Watching TV	Harmful	–	Pleasant, relaxing, easy	Popular, sad
Practicing a musical instrument	Healthy, instructive, beneficial, good	Attractive, motivating, developing	Pleasant, difficult, relaxing	Physical, social, active, peaceful
Internet	Useless	Attractive, motivating	Easy	Popular, sad, active
Cross-words/ sudokus	Instructive	Motivating	–	Affordable, active, clear

There are similarities between the two genders, but there are quite a few dissimilarities. While both genders perceived videogames as useless, thought-destroying, exciting, popular, and obscure, they differed on affective aspects: men perceived games as motivating and attractive, while women did not find any such things. Also both genders perceived games as exciting, but men thought they were pleasant and women thought they were difficult. On other aspects, women perceived games as costly and fast. These results corroborate data from other sources and may explain why women engage less with games than men (ESA 2008).

The second main finding concerns the comparison of players' and non-players' attitudes toward games. The question we wanted to answer was whether there exist important attitudinal differences between these two groups. Previous studies using this methodology have shown that attitudes differ between people who participate in an activity or interact with an object and those who don't (Cardoso 2007, Bonapace 1999). The comparison yields the following results (cf. Table 6.3) and the graphical representation using the semantic profile (cf. Fig. 6.4).

Results are rather interesting and show the full potential of the methodology. Even if overall the participants perceived videogames as useless, non-players

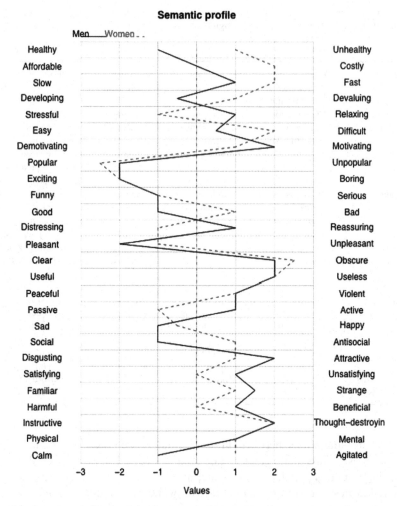

Fig. 6.3 Semantic profile for the videogame activities, comparing men and women (men: *full lines*, women: *dotted lines*)

Table 6.2 Comparison between men and women for the videogame activity. Symbol "–" indicates that no adjective was statistically significant for the subgroup

Dimension	Men	Women	Combined groups
General	Thought-destroying, useless,	Thought-destroying, useless	Thought-destroying, useless
Affect	Motivating, attractive	–	Motivating
Experience	Exciting, pleasant	Stressful, difficult	Exciting, pleasant
Miscellaneous	Popular, obscure	Popular, obscure, costly, fast	Popular, obscure

Table 6.3 Comparison between players and non-players for the videogame activity

Dimension	Players	Non-players	Combined groups
General	Useless	Useless, thought-destroying	Useless, thought-destroying
Affect	Motivating, attractive	–	Motivating
Experience	Exciting, pleasant	Stressful, difficult	Exciting, pleasant
Miscellaneous	Popular, obscure, sad, fast, strange	Popular, obscure, costly	Popular, obscure

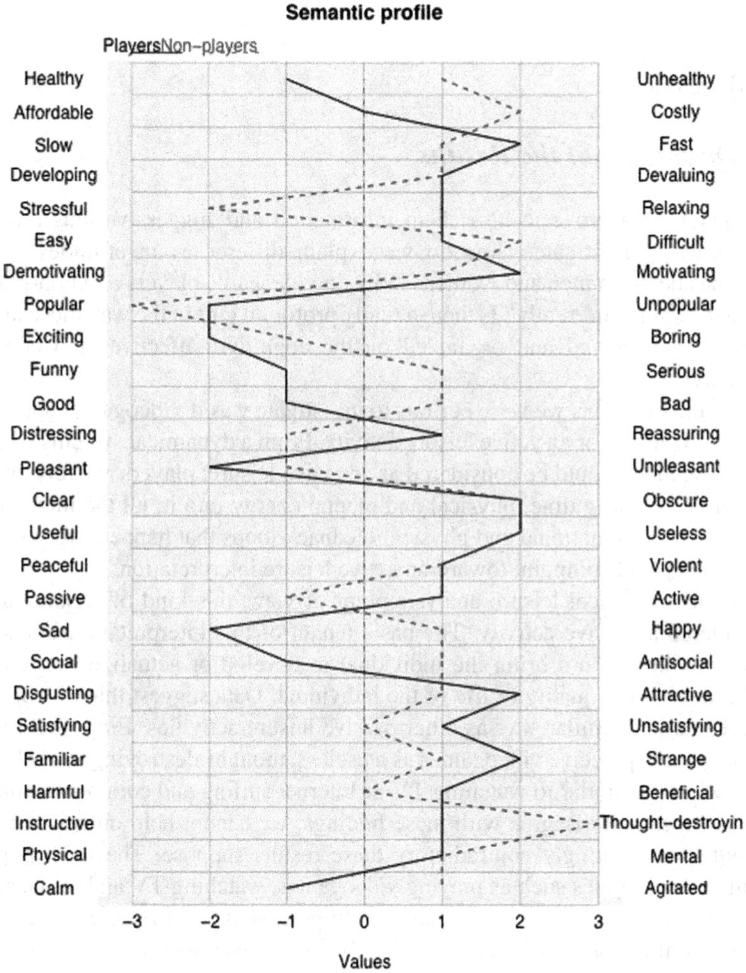

Semantic profile

PlayersNon-players

Healthy	Unhealthy
Affordable	Costly
Slow	Fast
Developing	Devaluing
Stressful	Relaxing
Easy	Difficult
Demotivating	Motivating
Popular	Unpopular
Exciting	Boring
Funny	Serious
Good	Bad
Distressing	Reassuring
Pleasant	Unpleasant
Clear	Obscure
Useful	Useless
Peaceful	Violent
Passive	Active
Sad	Happy
Social	Antisocial
Disgusting	Attractive
Satisfying	Unsatisfying
Familiar	Strange
Harmful	Beneficial
Instructive	Thought-destroyin
Physical	Mental
Calm	Agitated

-3   -2   -1   0   1   2   3

Values

Fig. 6.4 Semantic profile for videogame activities, comparing players and non-players (players: *full lines*, non-players: *dotted lines*)

were even more critical, their attitude toward games being that such activity is thought-destroying. This is rather harsh and probably explains their reluctance to engage in this kind of activity. Other results show that on the affective side, players feel that games are motivating and attractive (that's why they perform such activity), whereas non-players do not have any feeling toward games. While players find this leisure exciting and pleasant (thus having close relationships with flow experiences, e.g., Csikszentmihalyi 1990), non-players see games as stressful and difficult, thus pointing to anxiety experiences according to the flow model. Another result worthy to mention is the fact that non-players perceive games as costly, adding another reason why they do not engage in games.

6.4 Discussion

6.4.1 Discussion of the Results

The gathered data prove to be rich in information and suggest various thoughtful avenues to investigate. How do we explain differences in attitudes toward videogames between men and women? Why do videogame players and non-players perceive the game differently? Is there a really profound gulf in the way these leisure activities are perceived and organized on the cognitive, affective, and conative dimensions?

One of the questions we were curious to investigate was if videogames should be considered a passive or an active leisure activity. From a dynamical systems point of view, videogames should be considered as an active leisure; players actively engage in the game, investing time, physical and mental energy into it; all the interactions that occur, the informational and physical feedback loops that happen every second of the game episode pinpoint toward an active leisure interpretation.

But from a classical leisure analysis point of view, this kind of leisure should be considered a passive activity. The basic tenant of this interpretation holds that passive activities do not bring the individual to develop or actualize himself and do not concur to the quality of life of the individual. Data suggest that videogames are perceived in a similar way as other passive leisure activities. Empirical results show that people perceive videogames as a useless, thought-destroying, and obscure activity, which is similar to watching TV or Internet surfing and communicating.

While we cannot disagree with these findings, we cannot help ourselves thinking about how seemingly contradictory these results suppose. The most popular entertainment activities such as playing videogames, watching TV and movies, and Internet surfing/communicating are negatively perceived, yet they are some of the most sought-after forms of entertainment. But when examined through the lenses of flow theory and leisure practice, these results find a rational explanation. As mentioned by Csikszentmihalyi (1990), engaging in active leisure is something that requires a lot of energy and determination. Therefore, it seems that a lot of people turn toward passive leisure activities as a compromise to occupy their spare time.

Videogames offer a lot of qualities similar to other passive leisure: they are easily available and they don't require much activation energy (one doesn't have to prep for the activity very much or travel to a specific facility); they are affordable and most of all they offer great entertainment value. So from this point of view, it's reasonable to assess that videogames are popular even if to some extent negatively perceived.

6.4.2 Discussion of the Semantic Differential Methodology

The semantic differential methodology has brought about some very interesting findings related to how videogames and other leisure activities are perceived. As such, it has proven itself a relevant methodology for the investigation of attitudes toward leisure such as videogames.

Benefits and limitations of this methodology must nevertheless be expressed. One of these issues relates to the choice of descriptors (pairs of adjectives). Because there is no well-defined or accepted corpus of such adjectives, each research project has to define their own set. On the one hand, this has the advantage of flexibility, allowing researchers to tailor their set to their specific needs; on the other hand, empirical research results are then difficult or even impossible to compare. This alone may slow the adoption of this methodology in the community.

One of the disadvantages of having to elaborate a set of adjectives is that some pairs of adjectives may yield sound and interesting responses, while others may not be useful for the subsequent analyses. For example, adjectives where answers are too much concentrated or too skewed on one side of the scale are difficult to integrate in the analyses; true, they provide meaningful interpretation as how people perceive a particular activity, but the lack of variations is undesirable in statistical analyses, even if the use of ordinal data and medians alleviates problems associated with non-normal distributions. In our results, pairs of adjectives like "distressing–reassuring," "familiar–strange," and "peaceful–violent" were diverging from a normal distribution (using QQplots), but were kept in the analyses.

6.5 Conclusion

This first survey regarding the attitudes toward videogames and other leisure activities using a semantic differential has provided interesting results and has proven the methodology to be relevant for this kind of research endeavor. The methodology is firmly established in other disciplines, online questionnaires are well suited for the data collection, the statistical analyses are well known, and the graphical representations are easily understood and facilitate communication of its content. Attitudes per se are worthy constructs to be investigated, and the associated three-dimensional framework (using the cognitive, affective, and conative dimensions) provides a solid and coherent basis for further investigations in the videogame domain.

We have shown that videogames were in part negatively perceived by this sample, so were watching TV and surfing and communication on the Internet. In this regard, these kinds of leisure activities adhere more closely to a passive leisure interpretation, in the line of leisure science researches. We also found fundamental differences of attitudes between men and women and between videogame players and non-players.

This innovative approach for the game community should be complemented by other researches in order to consolidate its relevance and usefulness. In order to be more widely adopted, the foreseen challenges for this methodology are to elaborate a standardized corpus of adjectives and to test it across various projects (games, types of games, players, etc.) and being much language sensitive, across different cultures. The knowledge then gained could lead to a better appreciation of this ever-popular form of entertainment.

From the empirical results, a few key points are worthy to consider for the design of videogames. First, an effort should be undertaken in order to develop and market games as a constructive form of entertainment, a leisure activity that helps to develop oneself and one's quality of life. The potential benefits on the physical, emotional, cognitive, behavioral (physical), and social levels should be addressed by both design and marketing departments. Beside the useful ludic and entertainment value of videogames, they should strive at least in part to provide the pursuit of individuals' meaningful objectives, where the developed abilities in the games could be transposed in daily life and vice versa. This would have an incidence on how society as a whole perceives this kind of leisure.

References

Ajzen I (1989) Attitude structure and behavior. In: Pratkanis AR, Breckler S, Greenwald AJ (eds) Attitude Structure and Function. Lawrence Erlbaum Associates, Hillsdale.

Ajzen I, Madden TJ (1986) Prediction of goal-directed behavior: Attitudes, intentions, and perceived behavioral control. Journal of Experimental Social Psychology 22(5): 453–474.

Appelman RL (2007) Experiential modes of gameplay. In: Proceedings of DIGRA 2007, Tokyo.

Apter MJ (1991) A structural phenomenology of play. In: Kerr JH, Apter MG (eds) Adult Play: A Reversal Theory Approach. Swets & Zeitlinger, Amsterdam.

Argyle M (1987) The Psychology of Happiness. Menthuen & Co Publishing, New York.

Barnett MA et al. (1997) Late adolescents' experiences with and attitudes towards videogames. Journal of Applied Social Psychology 27(15): 1316–1334.

Björk S, Holopainen J (2005) Patterns in Game Design. Charles River Media, Hingham, MA.

Bloch H et al. (1991) Grand Dictionnaire de la psychologie. Larousse, Paris.

Bonapace L (1999) The ergonomics of pleasure. In: Green WS, Jordan PW (eds) Human Factors in Product Design. Taylor and Francis, London.

Cardoso S (2007) The development of the affective value in the entertaining interaction. In: Proceedings of Kansei Engineering (Managing Emotion & Feeling) for Services and Products 2007, Lund.

Costello B (2007) A pleasure framework. LEONARDO 40(4): 370–371.

Crandall R (1980) Motivations for leisure. Journal of Leisure Research 12(1): 45–54.

Csikszentmihalyi M (1990) Flow: The Psychology of Optimal Experience. Harper and Row, New York.

Csikszentmihalyi M (1997) Finding Flow: The Psychology of Engagement with Everyday Life. Basic Books, New York.

D'Astous A et al. (2003) Comportement du consommateur. Chenelière/McGraw-Hill, Montreal.

Entertainment Software Association (2008) Essential facts about the computer and video game industry. http://www.theesa.com/facts/pdfs/ESA_EF_2008.pdf. Accessed 7 December 2008.

Ermi L, Mäyrä F (2005) Fundamental components of the gameplay experience: Analyzing immersion. DIGRA. http://www.digra.org/dl/db/06276.41516.pdf. Accessed 21 March 2007.

Fortugno N (2008) The strange case of the casual gamer. In: Isbister K, Schaffer N (eds) Game Usability: Advice from the Experts for Advancing the Player Experience. Morgan Kaufmann Publishers, Burlington.

Fullerton T (2008) Game Design Workshop: A Playcentric Approach to Creating Innovative Games, 2nd edn. Morgan Kaufmann Publishers, Burlington.

Hunicke R, LeBlanc M, Zubek R (2004) MDA: A formal approach to game design and game research. Northwestern University. http://www.cs.northwestern.edu/~hunicke/MDA.pdf. Accessed 16 January 2007.

Koester R (2004) Theories of Fun for Game Design. Paraglyph, Scottsdale, AZ.

Kuniavsky M (2003) Observing the User Experience: A Practitioner's Guide to User Research. Morgan Kaufmann Publishers, San Francisco, CA.

Lazzaro N (2004) Why we play games: Four keys to more emotion in player experiences. In: Proceedings of GDC 2004, San Jose. http://www.xeodesign.com/whyweplaygames/xeodesign_whyweplaygames.pdf. Accessed 28 December 2005.

Lemay P (2007a) Developing a pattern language for flow experiences in video games. In: Proceedings of DIGRA 2007, Tokyo.

Lemay P (2007b) Course notes. Jeux, expériences et interactions. Tuesday 11 September 2007. DESS en design de jeux. Université de Montréal.

Lemay P (2008) Game and flow concepts for learning: some considerations. In: McFerrin K, et al. (eds) Proceedings of Society for Information Technology & Teacher Education International Conference 2008, pp. 510–515. Chesapeake, VA: AACE.

Mandryk RL, Atkins MS, Inkpen KM (2006) A continuous and objective evaluation of emotional experience with interactive play environments. In: Proceedings of SIGCHI 2006, Montreal.

Mondragon S, Company P, Vergara M (2005) Semantic differential applied to the evaluation of machine tool design. International Journal of Industrial Ergonomics 35(11): 1021–1029.

Osgood CE, Suci G, Tannenbaum P (1957) The Measurement of Meaning. University of Illinois Press, Urbana, IL.

Pagulayan RJ, Keeker K, Wixon D, Romero RL, Fuller T (2003) User-centered design in games. In: Jacko JA, Sears A (eds) The Human-Computer Interaction Handbook: Fundamentals, Evolving Technologies and Emerging Applications. Human Factors and Ergonomics Society, Hillsdale.

Press M, Cooper R (2003) The Design Experience – The Role of Design and Designers in the Twentieth Century. Ashgate Publishers, Burlington.

Ragheb MG, Beard GB (1982) Measuring leisure attitudes. Journal of Leisure Research 14(2): 155–167.

Ragheb MG, Tate R (1993) A behavioural model of leisure participation, based on leisure attitudes, motivation and satisfaction. Leisure Studies 12(1): 61–70.

Salen K, Zimmerman E (2004) Rules of Play – Game Design Fundamentals. MIT Press, Cambridge.

Schmitt B (1999) Experiential Marketing. The Free Press, New York.

Shedroff N (2001) Experience Design. New Riders Publishing, Indianapolis, IN.

Sweetser P, Wyeth P (2005) GameFlow: A Model for Evaluating Player Enjoyment in Games. ACM Press, New York.

Chapter 7
Video Game Development and User Experience

Graham McAllister and Gareth R. White

Abstract The first step in understanding the user experience needs of the video games industry is to ascertain current practice. The following chapter gives an overview of the game development process and provides background on the time frame and roles involved. We present case studies from three world-class development studios and show how the user experience is currently addressed during a game's creation. The first case study with Disney's Black Rock Studio details the development of their most recent racing game, *Pure*, and describes the usability testing which the developer believes improved the game's Metacritic score by 10%. The second case study with Zoë Mode refers to several of their recent releases, *Rock Revolution*, *You're in the Movies*, and games in the *Eye Toy* series. Special consideration is given to understanding and addressing players in a language appropriate to their background as gamers. The third case study with Relentless Software concentrates on the studio's use of focus group testing and attention to the casual gamer demographic. In addition to showing real-world examples of current practice, this chapter identifies the contribution that HCI can make for user experience methodologies in the games industry. Recommendations are made for generally applying usability techniques earlier in development, and user experience testing later once a playable vertical slice is available. We conclude with some discussion of innovative methodologies and pose the need for a formalised framework for user experience in video game development.

7.1 Introduction

In order to design new methodologies for evaluating the usability and user experience of video games, it is imperative to initially understand two core issues. First, how are video games developed at present, including aspects such as processes and time scales and second, how do studios design and evaluate the user experience?

G. McAllister (✉)
University of Sussex, Brighton, UK
e-mail: g.mcallister@sussex.ac.uk

R. Bernhaupt (ed.), *Evaluating User Experience in Games*, Human-Computer Interaction Series, DOI 10.1007/978-1-84882-963-3_7,
© Springer-Verlag London Limited 2010

This chapter discusses the video game development processes and practices that studios currently use to achieve the best possible user experience. It will present three case studies from game developers Disney Interactive (Black Rock Studio), Zoë Mode, and Relentless Software, all based in Brighton, United Kingdom. Each case study will detail their game development process and also how this integrates with the user experience evaluation. In an attempt to represent a balanced view of state of the art in game development practices, the game studios chosen focus on different game genres and target user groups.

Reader's takeaway:

- Three concrete case studies of how video games are developed at world-leading studios
- Clear understanding of the game development life cycle
- Understanding of industry terminology, laying the foundations for a common language of user experience
- Understanding of industry needs, in terms of what they expect and require from usability and user experience evaluations

In summary, the key contribution that this chapter makes to the games usability community is an understanding of the game development process and how these studios currently involve the end user.

7.2 Previous Work

Although the topic of evaluating video game user experience is gaining more attention from both academia and industry, it is not a particularly new area. One of the earliest papers (Malone 1981) discusses which features of video games make them captivating and enjoyable to play. Today, this discussion still continues, and there is active research in determining which game features to evaluate and which approaches should be used.

Current approaches to evaluating the usability and user experience of video games have centred around themes such as mapping established HCI methods to video games, refining these methods, identifying guidelines and, perhaps most importantly, evaluating the overall player experience. A summary of relevant literature will be discussed below.

7.2.1 Traditional HCI Approaches

Due to the generic nature of the majority of usability methods, researchers have analysed how existing usability methods can be applied to video games (Jørgensen 2004). Others such as Cornett have employed usability methods such as observations, questionnaires, think aloud and task completion rate to determine if they would be successful in identifying usability issues in MMORPGs (Cornett 2004). Without much, if any, modification, there is evidence to support the claim that conventional usability techniques can be successfully applied to video game evaluation.

7.2.2 Refining Traditional Methods

Although established usability methods can be directly applied to games, Medlock and others at Microsoft Game Studios have developed a usability process which is specific to games (Medlock et al. 2002). Their approach is called the Rapid Iterative Testing and Evaluation (RITE) method and although it is very similar to a traditional usability study, there are two key differences. First, the process is highly iterative, meaning that whenever a fault is found and a solution identified, it is immediately corrected and re-tested with the next participant. Second, the usability engineer and design team identify and classify each issue to determine if it can be resolved immediately, or if further data are needed before a solution can be found. This can be thought of as usability "triage".

7.2.3 Heuristics

Nielsen's usability heuristics (Nielsen 2005) have long served as general guidelines for creating usable applications or websites. However, various researchers (Federoff 2002, Desurvire et al. 2004, Schaffer 2008, Laitinen 2006) have constructed sets of heuristics which are specific to video games and compared their effectiveness to Nielsen's. They found that their heuristics are most useful during the early phases of game development. Despite the existence of specific game heuristics, questions remain about their specificity and utility (Schaffer 2008), and feedback from developers suggests that they are too generic to be of much use.

7.2.4 User Experience

According to Clanton, the overall deciding factor of a good game is game play (Clanton 1998). Trying to specify what makes a good game is not a straightforward task, and Larsen has tried to unpack this problem by examining how professional game reviewers rate games (Larsen 2008).

Others have addressed the key criticism of heuristics by wrapping them up in a unified process (Sweetster 2005). This process, which they call GameFlow, can be used to design, evaluate and understand enjoyment in games. Meanwhile, Jennett has conducted a series of experiments to measure and define the immersion in video games (Jennett et al. 2008). The concepts of immersion and flow in games are often related to involvement or enjoyment, but they appear to have subjective and imprecise definitions, thus making them difficult to design for and measure. Furthermore, flow seems to be applicable only to describing competitive gaming, despite other research pointing to the diversity of emotions a player can experience during play (Lazzaro 2004), and indeed the diversity of players and games (Schuurman et al. 2008).

7.2.5 Game Development

Most research in the area measures games towards the end of the development life cycle. Although this may be suitable for fixing small changes on time, it is not sufficient for altering key game mechanics. If new techniques are to be designed, which can evaluate a game during its development cycle as well as the final product, then a better understanding of the development life cycle needs to be obtained.

One reason for the lack of tailored techniques which could be applicable to all stages of game development is that the game development process itself is not known in detail to the HCI community. Federoff's work shadowed a game development team for 5 days and has reported some details of the development process (Federoff 2002). However, the main focus of this research was to construct game heuristics, not report on the development process per se.

The next section discusses the general characteristics of game development including the development life cycle and relevant industry terminology.

7.3 Introduction to the Game Development Life Cycle

In the video game industry, it is nominally accepted that the development life cycle is constructed from the following phases, though in practice those occurring prior to production are often contracted or skipped entirely.

7.3.1 Concept

Game concepts can be initiated either from the publisher, who provides finance, or from the development studio, which is responsible for the day-to-day production of the game. Once a general concept has been agreed between the two parties, a small development team of around five staff may spend 1–2 months producing an initial Game Design Document and visual representations such as still images or a movie to communicate the vision for the game. Additionally, a rough budget and plan is produced, including milestone agreements which define the production commitments of the developer and the corresponding financial commitments of the publisher. This would normally represent a phased or iterative delivery of the product, where only a first-pass of each feature is completed prior to evaluation and feedback from the publisher. Later in the schedule, a second delivery is made, which is a more concrete implementation. Agreements made at this stage are still subject to adjustment at any future point.

7.3.2 Prototyping

During the early stages of development, many different aspects of the game may be prototyped simultaneously and independently. These provide examples of features such as menus, physics and vehicle handling, or could be technical demos such as grass rendering or other components of the game or graphics engine. In order to define a visual benchmark, the art team may construct virtual dioramas, which are models of events that players will experience during the game. Some of these prototypes could be interactive, others could be non-interactive movies demonstrating an example from which the interface for this part of the game could be developed.

This initial phase can take between 3 and 6 months, by the end of which these prototypes and concepts are evaluated, and if the project is given a green light, it moves into pre-production.

7.3.3 Pre-production

Following design approval, the game development team enter the important pre-production phase, during which time fundamental game mechanics are proven and problematic areas are identified. The purpose of this phase is to try out ideas quickly without getting bogged down in issues of final presentation quality, to identify risks and prove the important aspects of the game concept.

7.3.4 Production

During the main production phase, the team will be scaled up to full size and would tend to spend in the order of 12 months producing all of the characters, levels, front-end menus and other components of the game. Often during this stage, the team will produce a "vertical slice", which is a high-quality, 10–15-min demonstration of a small sample of the game.

In addition to the core team of programmers, artists, designers and audio engineers, game developers also include a Quality Assurance (QA) group who are responsible for testing the game. This is essentially functional testing rather than usability or experiential testing. The QA team are keen gamers with a good understanding of the market and what to expect from a high-quality game. As such, in addition to functional bugs which are entered into a database and addressed in a formal process, testers may also identify "playability" issues which are informally discussed with the rest of the development team. Final issues of usability and playability are the responsibility of the producer and designers. QA teams are often only scaled up to full size towards the end of the production phase, through Alpha and Beta.

7.3.5 Alpha – Beta – Gold

Towards the end of production, the game progresses through a series of statuses which indicate how close development is to completion.

In order to achieve Alpha status, all content in the game should be represented, but not necessarily be of final quality. Placeholder content is common, but the game should exist as a coherent whole.

From Alpha, a further 6 months would typically be spent advancing through Beta status until the game is finally available for release, with attention turned to bug fixing and finalising the quality throughout.

By Beta all content and features should effectively be finished, with all but final polishing still to take place. Nothing further will be added to the game, only tweaking and final adjustments. In particular, this phase is focussed on bug fixing. After Beta, the developer and publisher consider the game to be of a shippable quality and submit a Master candidate disc to the format holder (i.e., Microsoft, Nintendo or Sony) for approval.

Each game that is released on any of their consoles has first to be approved by the format holder's own QA team. Strict technical and presentation standards define how all games on the platform should deal with issues of brand recognition as well as certain HCI guidelines. For example, which controller buttons to use for navigating dialogue boxes, the format and content of messages to display to the player while saving games, or where to position important interface elements on the television screen.

The approval process usually takes 2 weeks, but in the event that the submission candidate fails, a further submission will have to be made once the development team have resolved all of the faults. How long this takes depends on the severity of the issues, but once the team have successfully dealt with them, another 5–10 days will be required for the re-submission approval process. Conceivably, further submissions could be required until all issues have been resolved.

Once approval has been given, the publisher uses the Gold Master disc to begin manufacturing and distribution, which takes between 1 and 4 weeks. Typically, a unified release date is agreed upon with all retail outlets, which requires an additional week to ensure stock is delivered from the distributors to all stores in time for simultaneous release. In the United Kingdom, this results in retail outlets releasing games on a Friday.

7.4 Case Studies

This section presents three case studies from world's leading developers Black Rock Studio (part of Disney Interactive), Zoë Mode and Relentless Software. Each studio will discuss their development process, time scales and how they involve end users.

7.4.1 Case Study 1 – Black Rock Studio

Black Rock Studio specialise in developing racing games for Xbox, PlayStation (PS) and PC. Their latest game, *Pure*, was released in September 2008 to critical acclaim. We interviewed Jason Avent, the Game Director of *Pure*, who attributes the high ratings to not only the talent of his team, but also the usability evaluations that were conducted during development.

7.4.1.1 Game Development at Black Rock Studio

Game development at Black Rock Studio typically takes between 18 and 24 months, with a phase breakdown as follows:

– Prototyping (3–6 months)
– Pre-production (6 months+)
– Production (6–12 months)
– Alpha, Beta, submission and release (4–9 months)
– Testing by the format owner (10 days)
– Disc manufacture (2–4 weeks)

The total development time for *Pure* was approximately 20 months, which was at the lower end of the range of each phase. Delivering the product while keeping to the lower end of the range was attributed to the team's experience and their agile development process. Each of these phases will now be explained in more detail.

7.4.1.2 Prototyping

During the prototyping phase, the publisher's marketing team employed a recruitment agency, which produced a detailed online questionnaire about the game concept and distributed it to approximately 100 people within the target demographic. Following the online survey, a focus group study was conducted with three groups of 4–5 participants to discuss the game concept. The study was run in a lounge environment, with two members of staff, one taking notes from behind a one-way mirror and the other sitting with the participants to facilitate the discussion.

The team also decided to build a "Pre-Vis" (pre-visualisation) prototype for one of *Pure's* key features, player-customised vehicles. This took the form of a non-interactive movie showing each part of the bike attaching to a central frame. This was not a technical demo, but rather just a visual benchmark or reference from which the interface for this part of the game could later be developed.

7.4.1.3 Pre-production

Pure had originally been intended to just be an incremental advance on the previous title in the series, but over the course of 7 months the game concept evolved through several different designs. The initial idea was to make the most authentic quad bike racing game on the market, but this was abandoned in favour of a concept tentatively called *ATV Pure*, which avoided realistic sports simulation in favour of informal, social, off-road racing. The final concept, called simply *Pure*, was only settled upon by the time the team were halfway through pre-production. Each of the preceding versions contributed some design features to the final game, but many were prioritised so low that they were never included in the released title. The design strategy for *Pure* was to focus on implementing a few core features to a very high standard, rather than attempting many features to a lesser standard.

By 12 months into the development cycle, the team had fixed their vision for the game and were only addressing issues that supported four key aspects: massive airborne tricks, customisable vehicles, 16-player online games and so-called "FHMs" (which for the purposes of this chapter we will describe as "Flying High" Moments). These FHMs represent the core experience of *Pure*: When the player drives round a corner at high speed, only to realise that what they thought was just a bump in the road turns out to be the edge of a cliff face, leaving them flying thousands of feet up in the air. This is not only a highly exciting part of the game, but also a key mechanic as it allows the player plenty of time to perform tricks in the air, which eventually results in a higher score and other rewards.

These concepts were graphically documented in a number of ways specific to Black Rock, but which have similar implementations in other studios. An important tool for summarising the concept of the game and keeping the team on track is the X-Movie, used by some of the world's largest games publishers such as Electronic Arts. The X-Movie for *Pure* was a video showing a bike rider on an off-road race track jumping high into the air. Black Rock maintained the idea of "X marks the spot" when it came to their "Core Idea Sheets". These were large display boards hung around the team's development area showing the four key game aspects superimposed onto a bull's-eye target. At the centre of the target was the FHM feature, as this was intended to represent the essence of the entire game. It is worth highlighting that this essentially puts the user experience (or excitement), as the single most important criteria for the game.

7.4.1.4 Alpha to Release

For *Pure*, Black Rock did not employ a QA team throughout the entirety of the project, instead they used only one or two testers in the month leading up to Alpha. From Alpha, this was increased to five staff to deal with both the Xbox 360 and PS3 versions of the game (which were simultaneously developed). Furthermore, the QA team were only concerned with addressing functional testing rather than questions of usability or user experience.

7.4.1.5 Post-launch

The publisher's marketing team conducted studies after the game had been released and sold most of its units. The purpose of these studies was to identify what consumers liked or did not like about the game and what made them purchase it. Similar themes were discussed with consumers who did not purchase the game.

After release of the game, some informal analysis was conducted on official reviews and user comments on forums. Avent asserts that with the exception of some aspects of the garage, few usability issues were mentioned in game reviews. Most users' comments related to features that were intentionally excluded by the team for practical reasons (such as the excessive technical overhead of including replays and split-screen multiplayer).

7.4.1.6 Understanding the User

Pure was the first title on which Black Rock employed usability tests. They began running tests with company staff, careful to choose people who were not in the development team. They then expanded to recruit other people who worked in the same building as them, but who were not part of their own company. Finally, the most substantial tests began with members of the public, recruited directly from the streets and local universities. In total, around 100 participants were involved over the course of 4 months, of which the final month was only concerned with quantitative analysis of the game's difficulty level and any issues that would prevent players from completing the game. The only requirements for recruitment were that participants were 14–24 years old, male, and owned at least one of the current generations of console, i.e. they were likely candidates to make a purchase. Tests were run in-house, in regular office space separated from the development teams. Up to eight players would be present simultaneously, with one supervisor for every two to three players. One of the supervisors was responsible for taking notes, and no video data were captured as this was considered too difficult to analyse due to the very large volumes produced.

Black Rock conducted "blind testing", meaning that testers had never played the game before, and several different categories of testing were devised:

– Free flow: This is an unguided test where the player is encouraged to play the game however they wish. This is particularly useful for giving an impression of how much fun the game is, because as soon as the game becomes boring they would be inclined to stop playing.
– Narrow specific: In this mode, the player would only play a single level and they might play it multiple times in order to measure their improvement with familiarity. This appears to be similar to vertical prototype testing employed in usability evaluations.
– Broad specific: Similar to the narrow specific test, but playing over many levels. This seems similar to horizontal prototype testing in usability evaluations.

Most of the development team also had visibility of the playtests, but generally it was only designers who observed the sessions. Avent reflects that it may have been helpful for more programmers and artists to also have been involved with observation earlier on.

Despite the absence of video data, one of the programmers in the team had implemented "instrumentation" for the usability tests. This is the process of recording quantitative data directly from the games console that describes the timings of events during the game session. This can be used to measure specific events such as lap times or how long it took to restart a game. Similar techniques have been employed by other studios such as Valve and Microsoft (Valve 2008, Thompson 2007).

At the start of a game, *Pure* does not present the player with the traditional selections of Easy, Medium and Hard difficulty levels, but rather dynamically adjusts the AI vehicles to suit the players' performance while they play. During the final 2 weeks of testing, the Black Rock team focused only on balancing this dynamic difficulty system. The team were able to approximate a learning or performance curve by comparing the players' finishing position after their initial and subsequent playthroughs of a given track. By tweaking the dynamic balance system, they were able to adjust this difficulty curve to keep players challenged and engaged enough to replay races and improve their performance.

Avent strongly believes that these tests were crucially important in order to ensure a Metacritic score of 85% and that without them he felt that the game would have been reviewed at around 75% instead. This is a strong recommendation for even simplistic and lo-fi usability testing.

However, reflecting on the quality of results, Avent does recognise some of the limitations with a principally quantitative approach. In particular, he comments that even with a large dataset, results could be misleading or misinterpreted. For example, if the data show that players consistently come last in a race, one response may be to reduce the AI vehicles' performance to be more in line with that observed from the players. However, this may be inappropriate if the real cause lies not with the AI over performing per se, but perhaps with bugs in the vehicle physics system which bias in favour of computational rather than human control.

In order to identify such cases, Avent recognises that qualitative approaches would be beneficial and this is where more effort will be focused in the future. He hopes that future projects will take the agile development model even further, incorporating user testing throughout the development life cycle, including during prototyping and pre-production.

Furthermore, usability testing could begin as soon as the team produce lo-fidelity prototypes. For example, an HTML mock-up of a front-end menu, a 2D interactive demo of vehicle handling and a white box of a level where the visuals are of the minimum possible standard in order to test game play (i.e., typically without colour and with purely blocky, geometric shapes). Indeed, while only a small amount of usability testing was carried out from the vertical slice, Avent believes that the team should be conducting at least one test per week from that point onwards, with two to three playtests per week by the time Alpha has been reached.

During *Pure*'s development, the key team member to be formally concerned about usability was Jason Avent, the Game Director. While individuals in the design team specialised in difficulty and tracks, Avent talks about the possibility of hiring an HCI specialist in the future, who would be the team's user experience expert by the time a vertical slice is produced. Eventually, he imagines multiple usability designers for different aspects of the game, one to specialise in track design, others for difficulty curve, vehicles or avatar design (for more on this topic see

Isbister 2006.) While these may seem highly specific, the team already speak about a nomenclature for the design of tracks, a "track language" involved in the dialogue between game and player. An example of good communication in track language would be a vivid distinction between areas the player can drive on and areas they cannot. This "language" must be clear and "readable" to the player, otherwise their mental model of the game will be inaccurate. Of course, there are occasions when communication in this language is intentionally obfuscated, for example where there are secret shortcuts that should be indicated in a much more subtle way. Avent hopes that for future projects semiotic codes can be defined for each of these areas of game design.

7.4.1.7 *Pure* Development Summary

Off-road racing game for Xbox 360, PS3 and PC
Target demographic: young, male console owners
60–70 staff
Agile development model
20-month development lifecycle
5 functional testers from Alpha
100 playtesters
Custom quantitative usability analysis
Usability studies increased Metacritic score by 10%

7.4.2 Case Study 2 – Zoë Mode

In 2007, Zoë Mode rebranded itself as a casual games developer, with a mission to become the world's leader in music, party and social games. In general, the company tends not to design for a specific age group, but rather hopes to create games that anyone can pick up and play easily. Such a broad target can present obvious challenges, such as a development team who are largely in their 20s and 30s trying to design for consumers who could be 6–60 years old.

We spoke to Martin Newing, Executive Producer, Karl Fitzhugh, Design Director and Dan Chequer, Lead Designer about the studio's recent games including *You're in the Movies*, *Rock Revolution* and a number of titles in the *EyeToy* and *SingStar* series of games.

7.4.2.1 Understanding the User

The studio head, Ed Daly, was the core driver for involving usability and quality control in the studio's development process, though a number of usability techniques came to Zoë Mode from outside the company, and Microsoft were a particularly strong influence. Despite Codemasters being the publisher, Microsoft were involved in the testing of *You're in the Movies* as the game ran on their Xbox 360 platform. Fitzhugh comments that the quantification of results was particularly useful for the team, with Microsoft presenting data in the form X out of Y participants found this aspect of the game problematic. Twelve groups of four participants were involved during the course of a week. Recognising that this is a small sample size, particularly given the intention to sell the game to millions of consumers, Fitzhugh would like to involve more people but does reflect on the difficulty of analysing a much greater volume of data. In particular, he comments that participant selection is critical, so while the kind of ad hoc testing they have performed with friends and families can be productive, formal testing should be of a much higher standard.

Some focus testing was also conducted with *EyeToy Play Sports*. Sessions were led and run by the publisher, Sony, at a location in London rather than in the developer's studio. Newing is keen to point out, as have others in our case studies, that publisher interest in this kind of testing is very welcome but currently uncommon. Furthermore, Newing is also aware that focus group testing can be misleading if the sample size is too small to draw general conclusions or so wide that the results suggest the game be reduced to the lowest common denominator. Chequer is also anxious about individual participants controlling focus group discussions by exerting their influence on other participants who may have valuable feedback which is never revealed. This is a concern for all focus group studies, however, we would argue that good moderation should be able to overcome this challenge and draw out all issues that any of the participants may have.

As with other studios in this series of case studies, Zoë Mode points out the problems of presenting pre-release games to focus groups. In particular, Newing relates an anecdote about showing an early version of the game to personal friends and family who were simply too distracted by the poor quality of early artwork to want to play the game.

Zoë Mode's latest release, *Rock Revolution*, incorporated observational playtesting as a key part of the development process. Chequer argues that running these studies was essential for Jam Mode, a more free-form music making part of the game. Although the team already had some ideas about aspects that needed to be changed, observing real players struggle gave them the impetus to actually make the changes before release. Indeed, the bulk of revisions came from focus group and playtesting, with Chequer mentioning two issues in particular: help text to explain what on-screen buttons do and further encouragement for first-time players to just get in and start making music. Despite *Rock Revolution* being a challenging project with some poor reviews, and only one iteration for testing, the team were pleased that a GameSpot preview praised the game's Studio, in which Jam Mode takes place, saying "The most fun we found is in the jam session".

7.4.2.2 Game Language

Discussing the value of observing playtests, Newing and Chequer reflect on how easy it is for developers to overlook the simplest of things which can impede novice players from even starting to play. Like the other studios in this study, the team are now aware of the problems associated with using traditional terminology for games that are intended to appeal to a broader demographic.

Newing referred to the distinction between "Challenge Mode" and "Story Mode", which are clear labels for the team who've discussed and created these different play modes, but for the player who's just interested in playing for the first time they can be a source of uncertainty. Newing goes on to discuss the difference between the traditional "Easy", "Medium" and "Hard" difficulty levels, commenting that typically these offer effectively the same game with more or less and harder or weaker enemies. Critiquing the terminology of difficulty further, Newing also refers to *Brothers In Arms – Hell's Highway*, which offers "Casual", "Veteran" and an unlockable setting, "Authentic". However, the descriptive text for even the casual setting gives the impression that it is a challenging setting even for experienced players. The alternative he proposes is, rather than varying the number and strength of the opposition, to vary the game mechanics. This way, the easiest levels would accommodate only a simple subset of possible mechanics which could be opened up to the player at harder levels. A case in point is the Nintendo 64's *Golden Eye* where higher difficulty levels provided extra challenges by adding more demanding success criteria. Levels could be completed by beginners, but on the more advanced settings players would be required to complete additional goals.

The *EyeToy* series of games gave Zoë Mode a particular challenge due to their unique input mechanism. Players interact with these games primarily through their real-world movements which are seen by a camera attached to the console. For gamers and non-gamers alike, this is a novel mode of interaction which introduces the potential for many problems. Chequer remembers one particular scenario where the player was in-game, then the game cut to a non-interactive animation before returning to interactive play. During the observational sessions, it became clear that the players did not understand the difference between the interactive and non-interactive sections and were unclear when their physical movements in front of the camera would have an effect or not.

Fitzhugh likewise discusses some of the challenges of *You're in the Movies* and communicating technical instructions to the player. For this game, there is a calibration process which requires the player to evaluate whether the game has successfully identified and separated the camera's image of the player from the background of the room they're playing in. The developers refer to this process as "segmentation", a technical term that comes from the field of image processing – a concept and term that's almost certainly alien to players of this casual game. Despite using everyday language both in voiceover and on-screen texts, the team had to iterate through several different phrases during focus testing, for example "have you been successfully cut out from the background?" Unfortunately, even this apparently straightforward question was inappropriate for the audience who were concentrating more on the fact that they appeared on-screen than on attending to the game's needs of identifying whether its algorithm had been successful or not. Finally, the team settled on the presentation of images showing examples of what successful and unsuccessful results would look like, which is effectively a tutorial or training session for the player. This is particularly significant for casual games which are intended to be played by anyone, and especially people unwilling to invest much time and effort in learning how to effectively use them.

7.4.2.3 Game Complexity and Accessibility

Note that in the games industry, the term "accessibility" usually does not refer to disability as is often the case in the HCI community, but rather any player's initial contact with a game, and especially so for casual games (see also Desurvire and Wiberg 2008). Throughout our text here, we keep to this meaning.

Newing is keen to point out that while games should be open to play without having to read through complex instructions or manuals, having a degree of hidden depth behind the scenes is still important for the longevity of the title. Chequer sums up the issues by stating that games should try to avoid any issues that would block the player from play and should also provide interesting secondary systems and mechanics for advanced players. Fitzhugh goes on to point out the success of games like *Guitar Hero* which offer notoriously challenging difficulty levels for the most experienced players, but which also appeal to beginners on easy levels.

Chequer reflects that in retrospect some of the minigames in *EyeToy Play 3* required too much learning through trial and error before players could really experience them. In contrast, *EyeToy Play Sports*, which featured 101 minigames, lacked some of the depth but perhaps was more accessible to beginners. Finding the middle ground is where the art of balancing comes in, and we would suggest that usability and user experience testing provides a number of approaches to facilitate this.

Chequer points out that the most accessible games in the Wii are relatively instinctive and easy for beginners to play. This can be observed in *Wii Sports* where most of the games are based directly on real-life actions that non-gamers are familiar with, such as swinging your arm for tennis, and which serve to give the impression of a transparent interface. The boxing minigame, however, is significantly less accessible due to its more abstract input mechanism which responds less well to natural movements.

Another example of accessibility is navigation flow through menus. Proficient gamers are used to a certain set of conventions for menu screens, such as where to find controller options, etc. but observing non-expert players can reveal that this is a learnt association that may be at odds with the assumptions novice players bring with them.

7.4.2.4 Usability Tests

During 2005, Sony employed a usability company to run tests for *EyeToy Play 3* with children and families, which were observed by Chequer and others from the team. The results of the sessions were encouraging for the team both as a morale boost to show real players having fun with their work and as a keen insight into some big design flaws they hadn't considered before. Unfortunately, these sessions occurred late in development as the game approached Beta and so the team didn't have sufficient time to address some of the more significant issues. Newing mentions that the quality of reports from these sessions was very high, providing recommendations for the team in a non-prescriptive way. For the focus group sessions, reports also provided background on individual participants and interpretations for events during play as well as a description of the overall mood. Finally, the large amount of video data gathered was invaluable for demonstrating and resolving problems with the game.

7.4.2.5 Changing Demographic

Chequer comments on the development of the industry as a whole and points out that in earlier times the market was predominantly made of a small core of people who were experienced players, of which the game developers themselves were part. In those times, it was relatively easy for developers to make games they liked and be more confident that they would appeal to the market, as the team represented that market (for more discussion of the background and effect of these "cultures of production", see Dovey and Kennedy 2006). Now with a broader market and games that are particularly intended to be played by less experienced players, the distance between the developers and market means that fewer assumptions can be made and more attention has to be paid to testing. Chequer describes observing his own mother playing a game (see also the "mum-factor" in the Relentless case-study), who wanted to stop playing but wasn't familiar with the convention that the "Start" button not only starts games but also stops them. These kinds of conventions can clearly be confusing to the casual audience who may need additional assistance and explanation.

7.4.2.6 Studio-Wide Quality Review

Currently, Zoë Mode do not have an official mandate to conduct usability studies, though a new initiative in the company does incorporate usability techniques as part of their new studio-wide quality review, which also includes focus group testing and their standard postmortem of the development process itself. This is a relatively new initiative which was begun only a year ago, and which itself is currently under review. Under this process, qualitative comments about the development process are collated and summarised, then anonymously reported back to the team. Previously, only senior management were involved in the process of deciding whether a game was of sufficient quality to ship, but a new model for this process additionally involves members of the team. These include senior staff such as the discipline leads, but some people from other teams in the company are also brought in for a fresh perspective. Newing points out that internal reviews can be problematic, whereas bringing in external reviewers helps to provide fresh, impartial and unbiased assessment. We would agree and further recommend considering feedback from players *external to the game development industry*.

7.4.2.7 Postmortem

Games finished in the previous 2–3 years have run postmortems, but not in a standardised manner that would allow the team to quantify and compare their successes and failures with previous projects. The definition of a standardised postmortem template is one of the goals of the quality review process. Typically, Zoë Mode's previous postmortems have been conducted 1–3 months after each game has been finished, and only circulated internally after 3–6 months, by which time some of the team may have moved on and others may have simply forgotten important issues that arose during the 1–2 years development period.

The ability to quantify data is also considered important by the Zoë Mode team. For instance, the games industry is prone to underestimating the amount of time required for tools and technology production, so in that sense the same sort of issues commonly cause the same sort of scheduling problems. However, due to the R&D and creative endeavour involved, the specific instances of these problems are hard to estimate in advance. By taking an approach similar to that used in agile software development, comparing the amount of time initially estimated for a given task and the amount of time actually required, overall trends become apparent that could be used to plan future projects. Fitzhugh states that quantifiable measurements should allow the postmortem to identify three to five specific goals that should be addressed in the next project and provide conditions by which to measure success.

7.4.2.8 Summary

Casual game developer
Casual (non-technical/non-traditional) terminology
12 months from pitch to release
QA for functional bugtesting
12 groups of four participants for playtesting
Video data invaluable
Usability and focus group testing around Beta
Can anticipate future need for in-house usability expert
Postmortem circulated 3–6 months after release

7.4.3 Case Study 3 – Relentless Software

Relentless are an independently owned developer, working exclusively for Sony Computer Entertainment, manufacturers of the PlayStation series of games consoles.

Following the release of Relentless' first title, *DJ Decks and FX* for the PS2 in 2004, the creation of the *Buzz!* franchise began when Sony approached Relentless with the proposal to develop a music-based game. As a result, *Buzz! The Music Quiz* was released in October 2005. Their most recent title, *Buzz! Quiz TV*, was released in July 2008 and is a continuation of the *Buzz!* series. Casper Field, Senior Producer, discussed with us the process of designing a new game and where user experience currently fits into their development strategy.

7.4.3.1 Internal Testing

In addition to the core team of programmers, artists, designers and audio engineers, Relentless have a QA group who are responsible for testing the game throughout production. This is essentially functional testing rather than usability or experiential testing. As an example, Field comments that network functionality is a perennial problem and that their testers try to identify scenarios under which the current implementation will fail – such as how to handle a matchmaking case where one party loses connectivity.

Relentless have no formal procedures for dealing with these concerns, particularly towards the beginning of a project, rather relying on the skill of the producer to recognise what the audience want. Later on, when the game is of a sufficient standard that people external to the team are brought in for focus group testing, the producer's earlier decisions are put to the test.

7.4.3.2 Understanding Users

In addition to internal and external QA, the producers at Relentless decided to employ external focus group testing for *Buzz! Quiz TV*. This study was conducted during February 2008, 8 months prior to the game's eventual retail release date, which Field describes as being approximate 75% of the way through production. Based on data from previous games in the series, Sony's marketing team had identified three demographic groups, from which the focus group test company sourced four individuals each, totalling 12 participants:

1. Social players (mid-20 s, the "post-pub crew")
2. Family players (mother, two children and family friend)
3. Gamers (students, late teens)

Field devised 64 questions for the focus test, which were grouped into the following 8 categories,

– Instructions in the intro sequence (4 questions)
– Using the game's menus (12 questions)
– News page (4 questions)
– First impressions (16 questions)
– The overall experience (14 questions)
– Enjoyment (5 questions)
– User-created quizzes (5 questions)
– Future purchases (4 questions)

Each participant rated their response on a 4-point Likert scale, with an additional non-numerical code for no data. The responses were analysed as ordinal data and metrics were produced per question and per participant. In addition to this numeric analysis, mean responses were also presented back to the development team in bar graph form, whose value axis ranged from 1.00 to 4.00.

Focus group testing in the games industry is generally approached with a degree of trepidation. Most developers are sceptical about the quality of the processes, participants, their feedback and interpretation of data. Subsequently, it can be hard to get buy-in from the development team, and most importantly from the senior members who have the authority to make decisions relating to them. Field's answer is to prove the quality of these issues to the major stakeholders in the team. For example, during their recent testing sessions the lead programmer and artist were actively involved, visited the testing site and gave their feedback about the research questions the study was intended to address.

Field praised the work of the focus group company and, despite commenting that it was an expensive process, would consider doubling the number of participants for their next game. In particular, he pointed out that all of the participants were already aware of *Buzz!*, so an additional control group who had never played before would be beneficial.

The identification of demographic groups does guide the development process, and Field points out the importance of understanding the context and manner in which the game will likely be played. Throughout the development life cycle, the team try to bear in mind what Field calls "the mum-factor"; an informal persona-based approach where they try to imagine their own mothers holding the controllers and enjoying playing the game. Similarly, they have a "drunk factor" scenario, for groups of gamers who come home to play after a drinking session at the pub. Similar to Zoë Mode, it is acknowledged that the Relentless development team do not represent the typical consumer and that features which individual developers might enjoy are not necessarily appropriate to include in the final game.

This attention to players permeates the whole design process to the extent that the designers try to use a more conversational language when addressing players, such as avoiding conventional game terms like "Loading". This terminology could potentially alienate players for whom *Buzz!* might be their first video game experience, so the team prefer to speak to the players informally with phrases like "How would you like to play this game?" instead of the terse but typical "Select Mode".

7.4.3.3 Post-Launch

Not unlike the technique of instrumentation discussed earlier in the Black Rock case study, *Buzz! Quiz TV* captures data which allow the team to identify what, how and when the game is played. However, rather than being captured and used only internally with pre-release versions of the game, Relentless capture telemetry data remotely from players of the final, released game as they play in their own homes. Sony's legal department understandably limits what kind of data can be collected, but clearly this still continually produces a vast quantity of data, and Field comments that this does make it difficult to filter and analyse.

Relentless also analysed the 50 or so reviews available after the game shipped in an attempt to identify problematic issues and incorporate this feedback into future developments. This process involved a frequency analysis of comments about specific individual areas such as menus systems and the user interface, but Field is more interested in whether reviewers understood the game generally. Additionally, not all reviews are treated with the same significance. For the *Buzz!* series, reviews from casual or mainstream media like The Sun newspaper in the United Kingdom are considered more important than niche or hardcore gaming publications. However, once again the issue of historical context is pertinent – as *Buzz! The Music Quiz* was released during the early part of the PS3's life cycle, the market is more likely to be early adopters who have paid more to purchase the console and who have different interests and concerns than the more casual or mainstream market that typically adopts a platform later in its life cycle when the price point has reduced. As such, they are more likely to read website reviews and comment in online forums, so these sites are of more importance than they might be for future games released later in the console's life.

7.4.3.4 Relentless Software Typical Development Summary

12 months production
3 months Alpha – Release
Functional QA
Target demographic: social, family and gamers
Everyday language in games
Focus group test conducted 75% through development
Three groups of four focus group test participants
Content analysis of reviews

7.5 Discussion

The single most important issue that has emerged from the case studies is that the studios are testing too late in the life cycle (sometimes as late as Beta). This means that any feedback they obtain from usability studies is unlikely to make it into the final game.

Fitzhugh discussed some of the problems with testing, in particular highlighting the apparent paradox of when to test. Testing later on in the life cycle ensures that the game is more representative of the final product, and hence improves the validity of test results, but from a production point of view this is the worst time to find out about problems. Newing also comments on the scope of testing and mentions that for both *Rock Revolution* and *You're in the Movies*, only parts of the game were tested due to constraints on time and budget. We would suggest that a productive solution would be to embrace testing as part of an agile development process, whereby discrete aspects of the game are tested individually during prototyping, vertical slice and throughout the remainder of development. To that end, by the time of release all aspects of the game should have been tested individually and in coordination as a whole – with the usual proviso that the finished game may have a tighter scope or size than originally intended in order to ensure that quality is maintained.

All studios agreed that they should be testing sooner, and approaches such as EA's method of using focus groups early on to decide on key game concepts could easily be integrated into the development plan.

The vertical slice could be used as an approximate measure for dividing usability testing from user experience testing. All studios acknowledge that testing a game's overall user experience can only be measured once all the components are in place (final artwork, audio, game mechanics, etc.), and the earliest that this can be achieved is at the vertical slice. During interview, Zoë Mode mentioned that they were considering writing mock reviews before a game is released, and we feel that the vertical slice is a useful point at which reasonably representative and valuable data could be generated early in the lifecycle.

If everything after the vertical slice is user experience oriented, then before that milestone the focus should be on usability issues. This would typically mean issues such as user interface layout, game controls or menu navigation.

However, the usability/user experience divide around the vertical slice is not so clear cut. Usability issues will still need to be evaluated after this point (such as game flow and pace), and it is possible to evaluate user experience before the vertical slice (such as game concept focus group test at the start of a project).

7.6 Future Challenges

Player enjoyment is currently understood by observing or asking participants for their reactions to a game. One of the key future challenges is to capture, measure and understand a player's body data. Signals such as heart rate (ECG), skin conductance (GSR), facial muscle tension (EMG) or eye tracking may become integrated into commercial game usability evaluations in the future. Indeed, studios such as Valve have already expressed that bio-data could help them to better understand the game play experience (Newell 2008).

Extensive academic research has been conducted on psychophysiological metrics (Mandryk 2005, FUGA 2006) and excellent tools and techniques for the capturing and analysis of such data are available (Nacke et al. 2008). However, the focus of these research projects has been on using biofeedback for automatic adaptation of game AI, rather than as a tool with which to iterate on the design of games prior to release. Furthermore, such studies tend to analyse very short periods of game play with small numbers of participants. It remains to be demonstrated whether such approaches can scale to be applicable for games that may be played by millions of diverse players and whether such techniques could be used for representative longitudinal studies of potentially many tens of hours.

In addition to gathering data from the player's body, the studios in our case studies have already begun to automatically capture player performance data directly from the game (such as *Pure's* dynamic difficulty system). This makes it straightforward to capture an enormous amount of quantifiable metrics, making comparison across a large number of players easier.

This chapter has presented three case studies on how world-class games are currently developed. Although studios are keen to integrate usability evaluations into their life cycle, they are not certain how this can best be achieved. As such, one of the main barriers to conducting usability evaluations is the lack of a formal process that studios can follow. However, traditional usability has a similar issue where there is no strict process that can be followed, rather there are a toolbox of methods that exist which practitioners can use when needed. Future work may involve moving towards a general framework of game usability, which would detail not only the usability techniques which can be used, but also where in the life cycle they should be ideally applied.

Acknowledgements The authors would like to thank interviewees Casper Field, Jason Avent, Martin Newing, Dan Chequer and Karl Fitzhugh, and additional feedback from Thaddaeus Frogley.

References

Clanton C (1998) An interpreted demonstration of computer game design, CHI '98 Conference Summary on Human Factors in Computing Systems.

Cornett S (2004). The usability of massively multiplayer online roleplaying games: Designing for new users. In: Proceedings of SIGCHI Conference Human Factors in Computing Systems, pp. 703–710. ACM, New York. doi:10.1145/985692.985781.

Desurvire H, Caplan M, Toth JA (2004). Using heuristics to evaluate the playability of games. CHI '04 Extended Abstracts on Human Factors in Computing Systems. doi:10.1145/985921.986102.

Desurvire H, Wiberg C (2008). Master of the game: Assessing approachability in future game design. CHI '08 Extended Abstracts on Human Factors in Computing Systems.

Dovey J, Kennedy HW (2006) Game Cultures: Computer Games as New Media. Open University Press, Maidenhead.

Federoff M (2002) Heuristics and guidelines for the creation and evaluation of fun in video games. Indiana University.

FUGA (2006) Fun of gaming. http://project.hkkk.fi/fuga/. Accessed 13th December 2008.

Isbister K (2006) Better Game Characters by Design. Morgan Kauffman, San Francisco, CA.

Jennett C, Cox AL, Cairns P (2008) Being in the game. Proceedings of the Philosophy of Computer Games 2008, Potsdam University Press, pp. 210–227.

Jørgensen AH (2004) Marrying HCI/Usability and computer games: A preliminary look. Proceedings of NordiCHI 2004. doi:10.1145/1028014.1028078.

Laitinen S (2006) Do usability expert evaluation and test provide novel and useful data for game development? Journal of Usability Studies 2(1): 64–75.

Larsen JM (2008) Evaluating user experience – How game reviewers do it. CHI Workshop.

Lazzaro N (2004) Why we play games: Four keys to more emotion without story. Game Developers Conference.

Malone T (1981) Heuristics for designing enjoyable user interfaces: Lessons from computer games. Proceedings of the Conference on Human Factors in Computer Systems, pp. 63–68.

Mandryk RL (2005) Modeling user emotion in interactive play environments: A fuzzy physiological approach. Ph.D. Dissertation, Simon Fraser University, Burnaby, Canada.

Medlock MC, Wixon D, Terrano M, Romero R, Fulton B (2002). Using the RITE method to improve products: A definition and a case study. Usability Professionals Association, Orlando FL.

Nacke L, Lindley C, Stellmach S (2008) Log who's playing: Psychophysiological game analysis made easy through event logging. In: Proceedings of 2nd International Conference Fun and Games 2008, Eindhoven, The Netherlands.

Newell G (2008) Gabe Newell writes for edge. Edge online. http://www.edge-online.com/blogs/gabe-newell-writes-edge. Accessed 27th March 2009.

Nielsen J (2005) Heuristics for user interface design. http://www.useit.com/papers/heuristic/heuristic_list.html. Accessed 13th December 2008.

Schaffer N (2008) Heuristic evaluation of games. In: Isbister K, Schaffer N (eds) Game Usability. Morgan Kaufmann, Burlington, MA.

Schuurman D, De Moor K, De Marez L, Van Looy J (2008) Fanboys, competers, escapists and time-killers: A typology based on gamers' motivations for playing video games. Proceedings of the 3rd International Conference on Digital Interactive Media in Entertainment and Arts, ACM, pp. 46–50.

Sweetster P, Wyeth P (2005) GameFlow: A model for evaluating player enjoyment in games. ACM Computers in Entertainment 3(3): 1–24.

Thompson C (2007) Halo 3: How microsoft labs invented a new science of play. Wired Magazine 15(9). http://www.wired.com/gaming/virtualworlds/magazine/15-09/ff_halo. Accessed 13th December 2008.

Valve (2008) Game and player statistics. http://www.steampowered.com/v/index.php?area=stats. Accessed 13th December 2008.

Part III
User Experience – Decomposed

Chapter 8
User Experience Design for Inexperienced Gamers: GAP – Game Approachability Principles

Heather Desurvire and Charlotte Wiberg

Abstract Game Approachability Principles (GAP) is proposed as a set of useful guidelines for game designers to create better tutorials and first learning levels – especially for the casual gamer. Developing better first learning levels can be a key step to ease the casual gamer into play proactively – at the conceptual design phase - before it is too costly or cumbersome to restructure the tutorials, as would be the case later in the development cycle. Thus, Game Approachability, in the context of game development, is defined as making games initially more friendly, fun, and accessible for those players who have the desire to play, yet do not always follow through to actually playing the game. GAP has evolved through a series of stages assessing accessibility[1] as a stand-alone, heuristic-based approach versus one-on-one usability testing. Outcomes suggest potential for GAP as (1) effective Heuristic Evaluation, (2) adjunct to Usability Testing, and (3) proactive checklist of principles in beginning conceptual and first learning level tutorial design to increase Game Approachability – for all levels of gamers.

8.1 Introduction

User experience (UX) has become one of the most central concepts in the research of interaction design. In general, it focuses on the high-quality use of some kind of interactive technology (cf. Forlizzi and Battarbee 2004, Hassenzahl and Tractinsky 2006, Hassenzahl et al. 2006, McCarthy and Wright 2004). User Experience design in the context of computer games is likewise highly relevant. User Experience in this context includes aspects such as Flow (cf. Csikszentmihalyi 2008) as well as a narrower concept specifically for use in gaming – GameFlow (Sweetser and

---

H. Desurvire (✉)
Behavioristics Inc., Marina del Rey, CA, USA
e-mail: heather3@gte.net

[1] NB Approachability and Accessibility are used interchangeably throughout this chapter

---

R. Bernhaupt (ed.), *Evaluating User Experience in Games*, Human-Computer
Interaction Series, DOI 10.1007/978-1-84882-963-3_8,
© Springer-Verlag London Limited 2010

Wyeth 2005, Jegers 2007). The latter aspect was further developed into frameworks of normative principles for evaluation and design (ibid). The approach of normative lists, for example as a list of heuristics, is highly influenced by early works in usability research. It is noteworthy that the first published article of usability and heuristics in the field of Human Computer Interaction (HCI) was about Computer Games and Learning (Malone 1982). However, perhaps the most famous work here was the design of the method of Heuristic Evaluation by Nielsen (1993).

Today, game design includes a focus on traditional usability such as creating clear terminology and a non-intrusive, easy-to-use user interface, as well as the game play aspects such as fun and immersion. A small number of studies have been published that address usability-related issues in gaming. Other principles specific to games include pace and adequate challenge, i.e., offering a game that is neither too difficult nor too easy (cf. Desurvire et al. 2004, Desurvire and Chen 2006, Federoff 2002, 2003, Korhonen and Koivisto 2006). The boundaries between what is addressed as "usability" and what is labeled UX are to some extent blurred. It is clear that the UX for games includes principles beyond usability that make games fun, immersive, challenging, and, frankly, addictive, such as collections found in the 400 Project (Falstein and Barwood), Heuristics for Evaluating Playability (HEP), and Principles of Game Playability (PLAY) (Desurvire et al. 2004).

Recently, video game designers and publishers have been shifting their focus from meeting the desires of hardcore gamers, to serving the less savvy and sophisticated casual gamer. The trend is clear – the crowd of gamers is becoming more heterogeneous. The focus is no longer only on hardcore gamers. There is a distinct shift toward a world where the general player is an inexperienced or casual gamer. Additionally, with the advent of new game mechanics and genre-breaking game play, teaching gamers to play this new style of game becomes a major concern for designers. Players are fickle and easily distracted. They are also easily bored, resulting in their abandoning of the game. In this chapter, the focus is on the initial stages of the UX of games, which is the first time someone learns how to play the game. The players at the initial stages of the game need to learn the tools of the game in order to perceive that they have the possibility to master it. While they are learning these tools, the players must be sufficiently motivated, whether it is through game play challenge, story, emotional connection with the character, pressure from their peers, or all of these. The game needs to unfold for the user in a way that he or she understands well enough to continue to explore the game, without giving away too much, while also motivating the player to investigate and continue to play. This concept is called Game Approachability.

With the strong emphasis expected in the future on casual and/or inexperienced players, the concept of Game Approachability is fast becoming as crucial an aspect of gaming fun and entertainment as "engagement" has been historically. Casual or inexperienced gamers, as their name implies, frequently lack extensive prior game play experience. The casual game player's more occasional or periodic exposure to games, in contrast to their hardcore counterparts, often means that casual gamers require more guidance in playing video games. This, in turn, suggests a challenge to support the casual gamer in getting started with game play without divulging the secrets of the game itself – that is, to provide the tools to play games so casual game players have the potential to be confident in their mastering of the game as well. Therefore, the needs of casual gamers who are now being included in the mix of targeted people for whom games are designed, requires specific methodology and approaches in game design.

There are currently no standardized normative lists or set of principles for creating useful and well-designed tutorials or first learning levels in games. Typically, game designers create the first level and tutorials last, basing them on how the game has developed. Further, the designs are often poorly conceptualized because of scheduling practices that put them at the end of an already rushed design schedule. Even if there is enough time, designers have no clear guidelines or principles, and there are typically prolonged feedback loops between designers and the detailed results of user research, making it too late to make substantial changes for ideal designs for fun and learning.

In order to find guidance when it comes to learning, research from the pedagogical field is introduced. There is a substantial body of research from interactive learning found in learning theories in psychology and education (cf. Bandura 1994, 1977, Bruer 2000, Gee 2003, 2004). The principles for Game Approachability were developed from, and subsequently validated by, the research findings in these fields as well as good game design principles. This chapter covers the purpose of the most related work in these fields in order to show how the theoretical ground of the GAP list was developed.

The objective of this chapter is to present the findings reached in the development of an inspection method for evaluating and improving the level of Game Approachability. This term is defined as the level of helpfulness in a computer game for new and inexperienced players to be able to initiate and continue to play the game. This issue is highly relevant to the game industry. A large number of inexperienced gamers need to be enticed into entering and exploring a game. In order to get these new player groups to experience a game as fun, entertaining, and enjoyable, they need a gentle push over the threshold into the game. Hence, the problem is to help new players just enough without giving away too much of the plot.

8.2 Game Approachability

Inexperienced gamers are likely to start and continue to play games if these games are more easily approachable. That is, the game needs a high level of Game Approachability. So far, research on Game Approachability has been derived from educational research and includes aspects such as Social Learning Theory, Self-efficacy, and Cognitive Learning Theory. There are many systems and artifacts where approachability is highlighted as central, such as online learning, productivity software, and hardware. However, games have not been one of them. We need to ask ourselves how approachability research can apply to games and what needs to be revised and redesigned in concepts and methods? How will these methods help designers include better approachability to their games? In the following section, some related work is discussed in order to contextualize the work presented in this chapter.

8.2.1 Learning as a Means to Approachability

There is no global theory of learning. Learning can be understood in numerous ways. However, some learning theories could be applicable to game design. Theories of learning often highlight aspects such as motivation, helping behaviors, ensuring the tools become second nature, and engagement, which are central for gaming. While these ideas have been applied in educational settings to improve student learning, they can also provide a starting point for describing how game design can improve the accessibility of games for casual gamers.

Some applicable theories are (1) Social Learning Theory (cf. Bandera 1977), which emphasizes the importance of observation and modeling in the learning process; (2) Cognitive Learning Theory (cf. Bruer 2000), which emphasizes the active construction of knowledge and is most commonly associated with the ideas of Piaget; (3) Self-Efficacy is another term used in education and learning (Ormond 1999, Bandura 1994) and refers to people's beliefs about their own capabilities or their beliefs about their ability to reach a goal; and (4) John Paul Gee's research in the current educational field uses good game design to develop principles for designing educational materials and curriculum that are both motivating and fun for students (Gee 2003, 2004). The following are a subset of the elements identified by Gee that are applicable to accessibility: (1) Identity, (2) Co-Design, (3) Customization, (4) Manipulation and Perception, (5) Information On Demand And In Time, (6) Sandbox, and (7) System Thinking (for a more thorough description of the points discussed above, see earlier publications (cf. Desurvire 2007, Desurvire and Wiberg 2008)).

With the knowledge that there are Usability and Game Design Principles, there is a need to identify and utilize approachability principles in order to round out the gaming UX for use as both evaluation and design purposes. There is a need, therefore, to identify and validate the approachability principles for games.

8.3 Design of the Study: Comparison of Empirical Usability Evaluation and Heuristic Evaluation by GAP

The most common way of identifying the areas of games that need to be improved is through game usability testing. Usability testing has been found to be quite successful in improving the design of games, via relying on observing the players' experience. The need to design games in a way that makes them more accessible to casual gamers has also added to the need to define and utilize a set of principles for conceptualizing the design, as well as to utilize usability research to refine the design.

The learning of skills and techniques in a video game is similar to the way that people learn anything else. It follows, therefore, that learning theories must be considered when determining how to design games in such a way that players learn the needed skills while they are having fun. In this research, a set of principles and heuristics has been developed that describe the types of activities necessary to promote learning within a game. Usability testing is enhanced with the use of these heuristics when evaluating issues of accessibility within a game. Heuristics can also be used as a checklist during refinement of game design. In addition, and most important, the accessibility principles can be used to design a good tutorial from the onset of game design. In many cases, lack of accessibility results in the failure of a game, which occasionally leads to the failure of studios that would otherwise have produced successful games.

The current study compares the results from Usability Testing as a benchmark of all usability methods with an evaluation performed using the approachability principles to identify what types of issues each method found in the same games. Both the GAP heuristic evaluator and the usability evaluator had the same knowledge of the games. Did both Usability Testing and the Heuristic Evaluation identify the same issues in the games? Did one method find more accessibility issues or playability and usability issues than the other? How do the different methods complement each other?

8.3.1 The Games

This study includes data from four games to identify the differences and similarities between a Heuristic Evaluation based on Game Approachability Principles (GAP) and usability testing. In order to obtain a breadth of popular game styles and consoles, we studied two games still in development, a shooter and a strategy game, both for the Xbox 360 console. The other two games were racing games also still in the development stage, one that was played using a Nintendo Wii and one that was played using a PlayStation3.[2] The beginning, learning stages of the games were studied, since it is their goal to provide easy access to learning how to play the game, while having fun, and most important, being excited about and addicted to continuing to play.

8.3.2 Heuristic Evaluation Based on GAP

The principles in the GAP list were developed from previous research and based on current literature in relation to learning (Bandura 1977, 1994, Gee 2003, 2004, Ormond 1999). Usability/playability evaluation was performed using the Heuristic

---

[2]The names of the games cannot be revealed due to confidentiality agreements

Evaluation, focusing on how each accessibility heuristic was supported or violated, and then defining the issue. Another usability/playability researcher performed Usability Testing in a one-on-one, think-aloud method, identifying any usability/ playability and approachability issues. The following is the list of GAP utilized in both methods of evaluation.

8.3.2.1 The GAP List

1. Amount and Type of Practice

   – Game allows opportunities for sufficient practice of new skills/tools

2. Amount and Type of Demonstration

   – Game play modeled in more than one way

3. Reinforcement

   – Game provides feedback of player's actions

4. Self-Efficacy

   – Player competent with learned skills and tools after initial training

5. Scaffolding – Failure prevention where help is at first general then more specific as needed

   – Help provided as needed within the game

6. Gee: In control: co-identify, manipulation, perception, and Sandbox

   – Player identifies with game character
   – Player could affect the game world
   – Results of feedback appropriate

7. HEP- and PLAY-Based Guidelines (Desurvire et al. 2004, Desurvire and Chen 2006, Desurvire and Wiberg 2009)

   – Good game design guidelines in the categories of Game Usability, Game Mechanics, Game Story, and Game Play. This comprises areas such as players not being penalized repetitively for the same failure, defining the right challenge and balance, varying activities, and pacing during the game to minimize fatigue or boredom.
   – Player able to succeed at meeting goals

8. Goals of Game Clear

   – Player able to succeed at meeting goals
   – Coolness and entertainment
   – Game attracts player's interest
   – Game retains player's interest

9. Information On Demand and In Time, System Thinking

   – Actions and skills learned are useful throughout game

10. Self-Mastery

   – Player learned new skills and tools to play the game

8.3.3 Empirical Usability Evaluation

After completion of Heuristic Evaluation and Empirical usability/playability laboratory testing with the four games, the results were compared. Heuristic Evaluation was analyzed first, followed by the empirical Usability Testing sessions. During the empirical usability evaluation of the four games, 32 players engaged in usability/playability sessions. For one game, eight players were observed, for another game 12 players were observed, and for two of the games, six players were observed.[3] The majority of the players were male, with only two players being female. All were between the ages of 8 and 35. Forty-nine percent of the players were considered casual players, 25% were considered moderate players, and the rest were considered hardcore players. Each session was organized as a one-on-one, think-aloud evaluation session, in an environment similar to the one where they would actually play the game. Participants were given instructions to begin the game and asked to think "out loud" during the session, except when it interrupted their game play. They were asked several probing questions while using the game prototype. The players were then thanked, debriefed, and asked to fill out a satisfaction questionnaire. The evaluator recorded a log of the players' actions, comments, failures, and missteps and then coded each of these as a positive player experience or a negative player experience. A positive experience was defined as anything that increased their pleasure, immersion, and/or the challenge of the game. A negative experience was defined as any situation where the player was bored, frustrated, or wanted to quit the game. The probing questions and the players' comments were used to verify any assumptions made by the evaluator. GAP was utilized during the sessions by the evaluator as a checklist to assist in identifying and categorizing accessibility issues observed. After the sessions were complete, any issues that were considered hindrances to learning how to play the game and having fun were identified, analyzed, and documented.

8.3.4 Comparison of Results

After both the Heuristic Evaluation and the Usability Testing were completed, the results were compared to identify what types of issues each method found in the

---

[3] An uneven sample size was necessary due to the needs of the game development and was accounted for in the analysis, since this is formative research a small sample size is typical.

same games. The issues found for each evaluation were categorized either as an accessibility/approachability issue or as a playability/usability issue. As noted earlier, the terms accessibility and approachability are used interchangeably depending upon which of two communities one inhabits. In academia, the term accessibility would be associated with disabilities of one kind or another and therefore the use of the term approachability. The gaming community is more familiar with the term accessibility. The accessibility issues were then categorized as one or more of the accessibility heuristics. The accessibility issues in the games were compared to see what issues the Heuristic Evaluation found that usability did not, what issues usability testing found that the Heuristic Evaluation did not, and what issues both methods found. In addition, the GAP Heuristic Evaluation and the Usability Testing results were compared to determine the number of accessibility issues identified in each, as well as the overall number of issues found by both methods. Finally, the descriptions of the issues identified by both methods were compared to determine any similarities or differences in the granularity of each method's description of the issues.

8.4 Results of the Heuristic Evaluation by GAP Heuristic Counts

The GAP Heuristic Evaluation identified a higher percentage of accessibility issues as well as more types of accessibility issues than the Usability Testing, while the Usability Testing found more issues relating to playability/usability. For the four games, the Heuristic Evaluation identified 90 issues, 48% (or 43 issues) relating to accessibility and 52% (or 47 issues) relating to playability/usability (see Table 8.1). The Usability Testing found 207 issues in total, 11% (or 22 issues) relating to accessibility and 89% (or 185 issues) that were issues of playability/usability. In addition, the Heuristic Evaluation found more types of accessibility issues than in the usability study. The issues found in the Heuristic Evaluation incorporated ideas across six categories of accessibility heuristics, as compared to four categories in the usability study.

The following quotations and screenshots provide examples for the types of accessibility issues found only in the Usability Testing, only in the Heuristic Evaluation, and those shared in both the Usability Testing and the Heuristic Evaluation.

8.4.1 Examples of Approachability Found in Data

8.4.1.1 GAP as Heuristic Evaluation Not Found in Usability Testing

The GAP principle of Amount and type of demonstration occurred twice in the Heuristic Evaluation and not at all in the Usability Testing. An example of this Amount and Type of Demonstration was identified in the Shooter game, where the player was unable to win against the Artificial Intelligence (AI) opponent, even when not making any mistakes. The players did not recognize they could get extra

Table 8.1 Accessibility heuristics identified

Principle	Usability testing	Heuristic evaluation
Amount of practice: player provided with opportunities to practice new skills so as to commit skills to memory	–	5
Amount and type of demonstration: player given opportunity to model correct behavior and skills	–	2
Demonstrate actions and reinforcement: player able to demonstrate and practice new actions without severe consequences. Player knows what actions to take	2	7
Self-efficacy: player able to succeed at playing game after training period, i.e., first level or tutorial	–	3
Gee: Identity: player identifies with character	–	9
Co-design: player affects the game world		
Customization: player able to use preferred style		
Manipulation and perception: player given increased capabilities/tools to use		
Information on demand and in time: player has access to answers regarding: the game whenever needed and when first coming across new material		
Sandbox: player feels rewards and punishments for game play action were appropriate		
Information presented on demand and in time, system thinking: actions and skills learned were important for playing the game not just for a single event in the game	1	–
Scaffolding-failure prevention: player provided with help to meet goals of game	1	–
Build on prior knowledge: games similar to others in same genre allowing new skills to be built on previous knowledge	–	–
HEP and PLAY: player able to succeed at game's goals and found their expectations fulfilled	17	12
Entertainment and coolness: player was entertained and enjoyed playing the game	–	–
Self-mastery: player able to master game using skills and tools provided	–	–
Total	22	43

points by doing combination moves, required in order to win, as these were not obvious from playing the game. Having AI Non-Player Characters doing these moves would demonstrate to the player that this is both possible and an option. Furthermore, demonstrating the controller buttons and thumbsticks using a controller image and an increased health meter would demonstrate exactly how to do this. Usability Testing did not find this GAP principle.

Finding that Self-efficacy was a violated GAP principle found via Heuristic Evaluation, but not Usability Testing has implications for using GAP in design. Since this is an issue that was found when called out by using GAP as a checklist in the Heuristic Evaluation, but not found in Usability Testing, alludes to it being a more subtle issue not easily discovered from players' comments and from observing their experience. Self-efficacy was found to be violated, for example, when the evaluator determined the players would be expected to know how to perform several button combinations, along with timing in competing against challenging AI opponents in the Shooter game. In the Racing game (see Fig. 8.1), the evaluator determined the players would not know certain moves, such as a special 180 that would help them beat the AI opponents. Without these moves, they would be unlikely to continue to try to win without considerable motivation to continue. They would likely not feel confident they could continue and that would undoubtedly cause the players to feel incapable of making it through the first level. The rest of the levels would therefore be too difficult. There is a considerable likelihood this player would be one to drop out of playing this game. Increasing Self-efficacy would give the players confidence that they would be able to continue and be successful. This would require giving the player some of the basic GAP principles, such as Demonstration, Practice, Reinforcement, Scaffolding, and Sandbox. The specifics would depend on the type of issue identified. In this case, the player needed to have the fighting techniques Demonstrated, then have a chance to Practice, be given Reinforcement (positive feedback), and Scaffolding help if they could not kill all the opponents before the end of the level, since the first level needs to be a successful experience. This has implications for initial concept design, since the designers could plan for Self-efficacy and have the design refined based on real-user testing (Usability Testing).

Fig. 8.1 GAP: Self-Efficacy found in Heuristic Evaluation in racing game

Fig. 8.2 GAP: Gee: Sandbox without consequence, lack of Sandbox in Shooter game

The GAP Gee (Identify, Co-Design, Customization, Manipulation, Information On Demand and in Time, Sandbox) was found in Heuristic Evaluation, but not with the Usability Testing. Observing the users playing the beginning learning levels, it was identified that there was a need for the GAP Gee: Sandbox without consequence. In the Shooter game, players were taught how to use a combination of buttons for attacking their enemies. They were taught three new moves and then were required to use these attacks in game play. Due to the Heuristic Evaluation, players would need to practice any new moves successfully and would otherwise likely lose their characters' lives. Many players would not have enough time to play and master the new skills without consequences, as per the approachability principle Gee: Sandbox without consequence. When the players have the time to practice, they can combine the new skills in an open play format without the risk of losing. When they have learned these skills via the Sandbox, the players would continue to first level with preparation, and thus be able to fairly defend themselves (see Fig. 8.2).

The GAP Heuristic Evaluation assisted the evaluator to notice and design for the consequence of not having enough practice via a Sandbox, thus adding a Sandbox.

8.4.1.2 GAP Found in Usability Testing Not Found in GAP Heuristic Evaluation

Usability Testing found issues related to GAP Scaffolding not found in the GAP Heuristic Evaluation. The GAP Scaffolding was found to be missing when the player was supposed to cut some chains down from a fort in order to release a

Fig. 8.3 Example of GAP, scaffolding needed in Shooter game via *usability testing*

bridge; the player was stuck (see Fig. 8.3). They did not know what to do in this learning level and could not continue the game. Had this occurred in a real-world play session life, the player would likely quit the game. Scaffolding was violated, and had it been added, would have assisted the player in continuing the game. Scaffolding would be useful because, if the player still did not understand after being offered a small parcel of assistance, other and more varied parcels would be offered. Usability Testing offered this insight, since the players were stuck without this information.

Issues that were found only in Usability Testing and not in the GAP Heuristic Evaluation were more HEP and PLAY guidelines. Since Usability Testing has the advantage of real players thinking aloud their experiences in real time, the evaluator had the advantage of players' comments of their experience: "I think the tutorial is way too long. I want to be playing the game, but instead I'm doing the tutorial. I thought the stuff in the beginning was useful, but now it just seems like too much and I am not having that much fun."

This led to the identification of the GAP – HEP and PLAY, where the guidelines recommend that players have a fun and successful experience in the first 10–20 minutes. The Heuristic Evaluation did not find this. Ideally, the key for the tutorial based on GAP is a design where the player is learning the tools, while this learning is masked by their having fun through game play challenge and story motivation. This has implications for designing using GAP as a checklist of the conceptual tutorial design. However, seeing where the actual users are having a fun and successful experience seems to only be validated with real players; otherwise, it is simply a guess.

Information on demand and in time in system thinking from GAP was one that was found from Usability Testing in the Shooter game, but not in the Heuristic Evaluation. When there were instructions offered in both text and audio, the evaluator observed players still missed this information. They were on to another area of the game. Since players missed the necessary information when it was presented, they then did not have the ability to repeat the instructions to learn what they had missed. As one player said, "the instructions need to be clearer and you should have the ability to repeat instructions. It just seems like they tell you the instructions once and if you miss it you are lost". (Fig. 8.4) In addition, this instruction was teaching a skill that would be required for later play in the game. In other words, system thinking meant what the player learned would have consequences to the player's game tools later in the game. If there were repeatable and pauseable instructions, the player would then have the ability to receive the instruction when they needed it, rather than when it was offered. In addition, later on when the player may need the instruction again, they could locate this assistance. In this Shooter game, the objectives text actually disappeared after the instruction was given. It would be better for the text to stay on the screen until the players were successful and well onto the next area of the game. Having this list accessible at all times, via a button leading to a table of contents help screen, for example, would allow the players access later in the game if they should forget the instruction. Alternatively or in addition, employing the basic GAP such as Demonstration, Practice, and Sandbox would help reinforce this new skill for later use (System Thinking). This GAP was missed in the Heuristic Evaluation, as it was likely the evaluator could not predict that the skill had not been taught and offered on demand and in time. This is a good example of where the designers can make their best guess, Usability Testing will validate this

Fig. 8.4 GAP information on demand and in time, system thinking in Shooter game

principle. The GAP offered a structure for the evaluators to categorize what was missing, which will lead to potential solutions.

This explanation provides implications for both design and evaluation, since GAP can offer designers the conscious design principle that information ideally is taught on demand and in time for skills required to play the game (system thinking) and refined via Usability Testing. Heuristic Evaluation would identify this as a potential issue, but could only be validated with real representative players.

8.4.1.3 GAP Found in Both Usability Testing and Heuristic Evaluation

From both the GAP Heuristic Evaluation and Usability Testing, the GAP – HEP and PLAY were both found. There were many issues found in both methods, (17 in Usability Testing and 12 in Heuristic Evaluation). This is not surprising, since HEP and PLAY issues are related to fun and playability. These do not directly have anything to do with learning and approachability, but learning must be fun and successful. These are issues that are the focus of game usability/playability, which both methods are focused upon. The difference is that Heuristic Evaluation can identify these issues, but Usability Testing validates these with real players. The violated issues that were identified under GAP – HEP and PLAY in both Usability Testing and Heuristic Evaluation in the games were the following:

a. The first 10–20 minutes of play was fun and successful.
b. Players should not be penalized repetitively or for the same failure.
c. Varying activities and pacing during the game in order to minimize fatigue or boredom.
d. The game provides clear goals; overriding goals are presented early, and short-term goals throughout game play.
e. The skills needed to attain goals were taught early enough to play or use later, or right before the new skill was needed.
f. The game gave rewards that immersed the player more deeply in the game by increasing their capabilities or capacity to do things in the game.

8.4.2 Level of Detail

In addition to differences in the number of accessibility/playability issues identified by each method, there was also a difference in the level of detail that each method provided concerning the identified issues. The Usability Testing referred more to specific areas of the games where problems occurred, providing a count of the number of players that had difficulty at certain areas of the game, as well as quotations from players that indicated frustration. Conversely, the Heuristic Evaluation identified areas where a player was not given the means to master a skill set, whether by motivation to follow through, or by the actual teaching given and practicing allowed. This evaluation then indicated other areas in the game that might give players trouble since they had not learned the needed skill. This is most likely a result of Usability

Testing describing problems as they are seen while Heuristic Evaluations are predicting problems players are likely to have. The high number of HEP and PLAY issues identified by Usability Testing may also be a result of this difference (see Table 8.1). For Usability Testing, each area that a player had difficulty in was identified as an issue, such as unclear goals, and thus each separate area would be counted as an issue. For the Heuristic Evaluation, the problem was counted once but then noted that players would continue to have problems with a certain skill set because it had not been learned at the time the designers intended.

8.5 Conclusion

Our results indicated that the usability one-on-one testing and the GAP Heuristic Evaluation of the games provided information that supplemented each other. The GAP principles were useful in evaluating the game design and offering suggestions to the designers based on the principles and the associated issues found. GAP provides a structure for organizing approachability issues, so that designers can have an understanding of what is lacking, and thus what is necessary to create an optimal learning level that is also fun. The GAP Heuristic Evaluation alone provided more information about Game Approachability while the Usability Testing provided more information about playability/usability of the games. GAP with Usability Testing can be perhaps best thought of a way to validate and refine assumptions made in the initial GAP Heuristic Evaluation, with real players. This was evident especially with the GAP Scaffolding and Information on demand and in time. GAP used for Heuristic Evaluation is likely to identify more approachability issues, since that is the focus of the evaluation, whereas the Usability Testing focuses on not just approachability, but usability/playability issues that may supersede the approachability focus. Alternatively, the Usability Testing is able to provide a level of detail that is not possible in the Heuristic Evaluation, such as specific quotations from the players that validate real experience, rather than predicted experience. It is important to note that the evaluation is performed with live players and, as we know, human behavior can never be accurately predicted. More important for approachability, GAP offers the promise and ability to be proactive when used by the developers in creating a design that includes these principles prior to the design being finalized. This in fact may be one of the most valuable uses of GAP, since the conceptual design sets the foundation. If a design is used based on GAP, then it provides a built-in structure for learning while having fun. Heuristic Evaluation using the same language and structure in GAP allows a refinement, and Usability Testing with GAP uses a finer level of evaluation since real users are involved.

Further, since GAP is a novel approach to Usability Testing, evaluators may be more likely to focus on more traditional usability issues, as opposed to approachability ones. With more practice and experience with GAP, evaluators are likely to uncover more issues upon further use when testing real players. Still, Heuristic Evaluation, used as an adjunct and alternative inspection method, allows a way to uncover some issues that may be similar to evaluating real users, and some that are beyond what is found with real users. GAP also would be a viable structure for game designers to utilize for conceptualizing and setting a good beginning level design that is based on what we know about how humans learn and also have fun.

In summary, the suggested best use of GAP and Usability Testing is to utilize GAP as a checklist to design and refine a good tutorial and entry game level. The Usability Testing can then be utilized to refine the design, and GAP as a Heuristic Evaluation can be used as an adjunct to Usability Testing between research iterations. Thus, taken together, both methods of research can help make video games more accessible to casual players. The GAP list offers a checklist for the conceptual design for approachability, while usability/playability one-on-one evaluation offers both validation and correction to the design for approachability.

8.6 Future Work

The GAP checklist has already been utilized for conceptual design with several game companies worldwide, resulting in tutorials and first entry levels that are notably improved beyond what they would be without the checklist. Utilizing Usability Testing as a refinement of the conceptual design for approachability has been found to be important in both validation and refinement of the design with real users (for which there is *no substitute*). In the process of using GAP on game tutorials and first design levels, there are several refinements and additions that could be made to GAP that could improve its usefulness for design teams. We have developed a three-step process or checklist that has been found to be quite useful. It is a tutorial design process that includes GAP for ensuring that players are having fun while learning the first level. Future work would focus on a case study, and validation of this checklist to be utilized by game designers and game evaluators to create optimal beginning game levels.

References

Bandura A (1977) Social Learning Theory. General Learning Press, New York.
Bandura A (1994) Self-efficacy. In: Ramachandran VC (ed) Encyclopedia of Human Behavior, 4th vol. Academic Press, New York.
Bruer J (2000) Schools for Thought. MIT Press, Cambridge, MA.
Csikszentmihalyi M (2008) Flow: The Psychology of Optimal Experience. Harper Perennial Modern Classics, New York.
Desurvire H (2007) List of core and approachability principles for good game design. LA CHI Association Meeting Presentation.
Desurvire H, Caplan M, Toth JA (2004) Using heuristics to evaluate the playability of games. In: CHI '04 Extended Abstracts on Human Factors in Computing Systems (Vienna, Austria, 24–29 April 2004). CHI '04. ACM, New York, pp. 1509–1512.
Desurvire H, Chen B (2006) 48 Differences between good and bad video games: Game playability principles (PLAY) for designing highly ranked video games. Behavioristics.com LA CHI Association meeting Presentation.

Desurvire H, Wiberg C (2008) Master of the game: Assessing approachability in future game design. In: CHI '08 Extended Abstracts on Human Factors. ACM, New York.

Desurvire H, Wiberg C (2009) Game usability heuristics (PLAY) for evaluating and designing better games: The next iteration. In: Proceedings of HCI'09 International Conference, San Diego, CA, July.

Falstein N, Barwood H (2006) The 400 project.http://theinspiracy.com/Current%20Rules%20 Master%20List.htm.

Federoff M (2002) Heuristics and usability guidelines for the creation and evaluation of FUN in video games. Thesis, University Graduate School of Indiana University, IN.

Federoff M (2003) User testing for games: Getting better data earlier. Game Developer Magazine June'03: 35–40.

Forlizzi J, Battarbee K (2004) Understanding experience in interactive systems. In: Proceedings of the 5th Conference on Designing Interactive Systems: Processes, Practices, Methods and Techniques, (Cambridge, MA, 1–4 August 2004). DIS '04, ACM, New York, pp. 261–268.

Gee JP (2003) What Video Games Have to Teach Us About Learning and Literacy. Palgrave Macmillan, New York.

Gee JP (2004) Learning by design: Good video games as learning machines. Interactive Educational Multimedia 8: 15–23. http://greav.ub.edu/iem/index.php?journal=iem&page= article&op=view&path[]=55&path[]=74.

Hassenzahl M, Law E, Hvannberg ET (2006) User experience – Towards a unified view. In: Proceedings of the 2nd COST294-MAUSE International Open Workshop UX WS NordiCHI'06COST294-MAUSE. http://141.115.28.2/cost294/upload/ 408.pdf MAUSE: 1–3.

Hassenzahl M, Tractinsky N (2006) User Experience – A research agenda. Behaviour & Information Technology 25(2): 91–97. DOI: 10.1080/01449290500330331.

Jegers K (2007) Pervasive game flow: Understanding player enjoyment in pervasive gaming. ACM Computers in Entertainment 5(1). DOI=http://doi.acm.org/10.1145/1236224. 1236238.

Korhonen H, Koivisto EM (2006) Playability heuristics for mobile games. In: Proceedings of the 8th Conference on Human-Computer Interaction with Mobile Devices and Services (Helsinki, Finland) MobileHCI '06, 159: 9–16.

Malone TW (1982) Heuristics for designing enjoyable user interfaces: Lessons from computer games. In: Thomas JC, Schneider ML (eds) Human Factors in Computing Systems. Ablex Publishing Corporation, Norwood, NJ.

McCarthy J, Wright PC (2004) Technology as Experience. MIT Press, Cambridge, MA.

Nielsen J (1993) Usability Engineering. Morgan Kaufmann Publishing Inc., San Francisco, CA.

Ormond JE (1999) Human Learning, 3rd edn. Prentice-Hall, Upper Saddle River, NJ.

Sweetser P, Wyeth P (2005) GameFlow: A model for evaluating player enjoyment in games. ACM Computers in Entertainment 3(3). DOI=http://doi.acm.org/10.1145/1077246. 1077253.

Chapter 9
Digital Games, the Aftermath: Qualitative Insights into Postgame Experiences

Karolien Poels, Wijnand IJsselsteijn, Yvonne de Kort, and Bart Van Iersel

Abstract To date, most research on user experiences in digital games has focused on what happens during game play. In this chapter, we conceptualize the phenomenon of postgame experiences, that is, experiences gamers have once they stopped playing. We propose and tackle two types of postgame experiences: short-term postgame experiences that arise immediately after game play and long-term postgame experiences that occur after repeatedly and intensively playing a particular game or game genre. We present two focus group studies that offered qualitative insights into which postgame experiences are at play, to what extent, and under which conditions. The chapter concludes with a discussion and recommendations for future research.

9.1 Introduction

Everybody who has ever played a digital game or has watched other people play will undoubtedly agree that digital games have the potential to trigger a wide variety of experiences and emotions. Examples are the joy or pride when you beat your friend in a game of virtual tennis, the suspense you feel when fighting in a First Person Shooter Game, or the experience of being immersed in the story of a Role Playing Game. These *in-game experiences* are mostly the focus of studies on user experiences in games (Brown and Cairns 2004, Ermi and Mäyrä 2005, Jennet et al. 2008). However, it is reasonable to ask whether game-related player experiences do occur only while gaming and consequently stop when the player turns off the gaming device? Or whether they linger and even transfer into real life? And what kind of experiences occur once the player has stopped gaming? These are all important questions when conceptualizing and evaluating the full picture of user experience

K. Poels (✉)
MIOS Research Group, Department of Communication Studies,
University of Antwerp, Belgium
e-mail: karolien.poels@ua.ac.be

R. Bernhaupt (ed.), *Evaluating User Experience in Games*, Human-Computer
Interaction Series, DOI 10.1007/978-1-84882-963-3_9,
© Springer-Verlag London Limited 2010

in games. This chapter provides qualitative insights into the concept of *postgame experiences* or experiences that relate to the game play but typically occur after play.

Academic research on postgame experiences is still very limited. Until now, studies that did investigate experiences or behavior after game play have mainly focused on the effect of playing games on other, mostly nongame-related behavior (Buckley and Anderson 2006). More specifically, some studies have focused on the positive effects of gaming such as heightened attention to visual cues (Green and Bavelier 2003) or bonding with friends (Selnow 1984, Colwell et al. 1995). In comparison, ample studies have investigated negative aftereffects of playing digital games. For example, the interplay between playing violent games and aggressive behavior (Carnagey and Anderson 2005) or desensitizing from real-life violence (Carnagey et al. 2007). These studies have largely neglected actual postgame experiences. Nevertheless, postgame experiences could potentially moderate after game effects. For example, intensive team play with online co-players could bring to bear a sense of affiliation with those people (i.e., a postgame experience), which could then stimulate real-life bonds with those online friends (i.e., a postgame effect). Postgame experiences could also moderate negative game effects. For example, leaving a game with a feeling of frustration could trigger aggressive thoughts or feelings of hostility, irrespective of violent game content.

Given the lack of academic research on postgame experiences, this chapter aims at setting a first step toward the conceptualization of what gamers experience after game play. In the next sections, we first identify potential postgame experiences, inspired by academic literature on players' motivations and in game experiences and also partly based on basic human perception theory. We propose and tackle two types of postgame experiences; those that immediately occur after one has stopped playing, these are *short-term postgame experiences*. The relief after passing through a difficult level, the warm feeling of having spent time with friends through online gaming, and guilty feelings after having gamed too long and as such neglected other people or responsibilities are examples of short-term postgame experiences. Besides these direct and short-lived experiential effects, repeatedly and intensively playing a particular game or game genre could also induce postgame experiences affecting gamers' perceptions, emotions, and cognitions on a longer term. We call these *long-term postgame experiences*. Examples could be the direct association of real-life objects with game elements, or the integration of typical game slang into everyday language.

We present two focus group studies that explored which specific postgame experiences are at play, to what extent, and under which conditions. The first focus group study, involving various types of gamers, aimed at getting firsthand verbalizations of how gamers feel immediately after they stopped gaming. As such, this first study primarily explored the existence and occurrence of short-term postgame experiences, directly related to a specific game session. The second focus group study then further probed on long-term postgame experiences that result from repeatedly playing a specific game or game genre for a substantial period of time. We conclude this chapter with a discussion and recommendations for future research.

9.2 The Conceptualization of Postgame Experiences

This conceptualization proposes a set of postgame experiences that emerge from specific in-game or game-related experiences. We suggest how potential postgame experiences can emerge.

9.2.1 Postgame Experiences Related to Game Enjoyment

Playing digital games is an increasingly popular form of media entertainment. One of the core elements of entertainment is enjoyment (Vorderer et al. 2004, Vorderer et al. 2006). In other words, people play games because it is fun (Colwell 2007, Poels et al. 2007). Consequently, we assume that after a game session people will be generally *satisfied* and *feel good* because they have enjoyed the activity they were engaging in.

Given the fact that most people repeatedly engage in playing digital games, we might expect that they do not anticipate negative postgame experiences. Nevertheless, if playing games is comparable to watching television, it might be reasonable to assume that excessive game play has negative aftereffects. Kubey and Csikszentmihalyi (2002) have argued that excessively watching television offers short-term pleasure and satisfaction (i.e., a positive orienting response) but induces negative aftereffects such as loss of concentration, bad moods, and dizziness. People with low self-control or people who are depleted, in particular, tend to prefer temptations that induce short-term pleasure in favor of long-term self-interest. As such, ironically, people start watching television and keep on watching for a long period because they know they will feel bad after viewing. They ultimately end up feeling really bad after they eventually stop and do not only feel uncomfortable about the amount of time spent, but also suffer from mental and physical consequences of excessive TV viewing. If this reasoning applies to gaming, playing digital games could be satisfying in the short run, but heavy players might end up feeling *tired*, *depleted*, or *dizzy* after long sessions of game play. Given the tempting allure of short-term enjoyment, this uncomfortable postgame experience will, however, not prevent them from not playing the next day.

9.2.2 Postgame Experiences Related to Game Immersion

Besides enjoyment, another important motivation to start playing digital games is to vent daily stress and to withdraw from daily worries. This is often referred to as the escape motivation (Colwell 2007, Yee 2006). If this motivation is fulfilled successfully, a play session should induce *stress relief* and *relaxation*, especially after the actual game play has ended. Along with the escape motivation comes the motivation to immerse in a fantasy world (Brown and Cairns 2004, Yee 2006). We assume that when people get extremely immersed in a fantasy world, or fully identify with their game character, they experience the game environment with all their senses, creating a game-specific mind-set. Consequently, players might experience *difficulties to return to the real world* once they stopped gaming. These difficulties can be short lived and directly related to a particular play session. For example, *feeling confused, or introvert* after a game session, or having difficulties with sleeping or switching the mind-set. This experience could presumably also occur on the long term, particularly for habitual players who repeatedly experience difficulties related to switching between the game world and their real life. In extreme cases, this could lead to serious *withdrawal symptoms* (Griffiths and Davies 2005).

9.2.3 Postgame Experiences Related to Game Flow

The experience of flow is often discussed within a gaming context (Sherry 2004, Sweetser and Wyeth 2005). A state of flow typically involves high levels of cognitive absorption or deep concentration. One of the characteristics of cognitive absorption is that it makes people lose track of time (Csikszentmihalyi 1990). As such, *time goes by faster than expected* (Agarwal and Karahanna 2000). Since playing games has the potential to get people fully drawn into a fantasy world, or to really soak them into challenging tasks and activities, people lose track of time and, inevitably, end up spending more time than they actually planned at playing games. However, for most people, time is a scarce good. By consequence, they are forced to divide their precious time between work, family, and leisure. If playing digital games, as a leisure activity, absorbs a substantial amount of time, more than intended, it can cause people to forego other activities that involve expectations or responsibilities, like spending time with their family, studying, or carrying out household activities. We assume that people will often only realize this after they stopped gaming, causing negative postgame experiences such as *shame, regret, guilt,* or a general *bad mood*. In extreme circumstances, spending nightly hours at playing digital games might lead to *sleep deprivation* which is known to affect mood as well as cognitive and motor performance (Pilcher and Huffcutt 1996).

9.2.4 Postgame Experiences Related to Social Gaming

A motivation that is often neglected is the social motivation to play digital games. Nevertheless, an increasing number of digital games include possibilities for social interactions both within the game world and in the real and tangible world of the gamer. As such, playing digital games is often as much about the social interaction per se as it is about the interaction with the game content (de Kort et al. 2007). The social nature of gaming and the social experiences during game play can presumably lead to a set of social experiences after gaming, both positive and negative in valence. As already stated, playing games with friends can increase *bonding* and enrich friendships (Selnow 1984, Colwell et al. 1995). This game effect could probably stem from the experience of warmth or connectedness both during and after game play. Further, cooperation in an online world (e.g., being a member of a World of Warcraft guild) can bring about *a sense of affiliation or belonging*. Moreover, being affiliated to an online guild or clan comes with certain responsibilities and engagement toward the clan. Possibly, in the long run, this could put the gamer under *pressure*, leading to negative experiences such as *stress, guilt*, and *frustration*. This could, for example, occur if a person repeatedly experiences that he or she has not the time to invest as much as he or she likes in the clan. Or, seen from the other side, players can experience deep *disappointment* when an affiliated member does not fulfill his/her commitment toward the group.

9.2.5 Postgame Experiences Related to Embodied Gaming

Recently, embodied gaming (e.g., Nintendo Wii, Playstation Eye Toy) has become very popular. This type of game play distinguishes itself from traditional digital games in the sense that people's actual body movements are a part of the game play. Similar to other physical activities like playing sports, these bodily efforts during play have the potential to induce a set of experiences after the game session has ended, for example, *release of tension, relaxation*, and *satisfaction*, but on the backside also *exhaustion, tiredness*, and *sore muscles*.

9.2.6 Postgame Experiences After Repeated Exposure to a Game Environment

Most above-mentioned postgame experiences occur directly after a gamer has stopped playing and can thus be considered as short-term postgame experiences. Additionally, we envisage experiences that occur after repeated exposure to a game environment. These long-term postgame experiences presumably originate from the way people perceive and process their environment. To explain this, we rely on basic human perception theory (Boring 1930, Rock 1983). When processing their environment, people use prior knowledge to recognize objects, words, or sounds (i.e., top-down processing). The prior knowledge that is used as a reference point can be shaped by any perceptual stimulation that is repeated frequently and over long periods of time. Consequently, this prior knowledge biases our perception by creating a perceptual set, or a mental predisposition to perceive a stimulus in a certain way (Boring 1930, Bruner and Potter 1964). Perceptual sets make people perceive and interpret stimuli in a way that is relevant for themselves. For example, a model hunter will perceive tall, slim girls on the street as potential top models, whereas a dietician might perceive those girls as suffering from an eating disorder. Both perceptions and interpretations stem from their prior knowledge and subsequent perceptual sets.

If we apply this reasoning to digital gaming as one particular kind of perceptual stimulation, we could assume that for habitual players of digital games, real-world perceptions, cognitions, and actions will be partly structured by their repeated exposure to the game environment. This means, habitual players use their knowledge from the game environment when perceiving and interpreting real-life environmental stimuli. We expect that long-term postgame experiences can be established through this process. These postgame experiences can relate to all kinds of environmental stimuli, such as objects, situations, sounds, and words. Moreover, their impact can presumably affect various affective, cognitive, and behavioral processes. Examples could be seen in the context of objects in the real world that are associated with objects from the game world, sounds or songs heard in real life that trigger lively memories of a game world, and language and expressions used in the game world that show up in everyday vocabulary. We expect the concrete manifestation of these long-term postgame experiences to depend on the type of game or game genre one is repeatedly engaging in. This means, frequent players of First Person Shooter games will probably experience different things, make other associations, and use other game-related slang, compared to habitual players of Massively Multiplayer Online Role Playing Games (MMORPGs). To the best of our knowledge, there has not yet any research been carried out to investigate the existence and conditions of these specific kinds of postgame experiences. In this chapter, we present a focus group study that was specifically designed to explore concrete manifestations of long-term postgame experiences.

9.3 Focus Group Explorations

The focus group method is a qualitative research tool that is frequently used in social sciences to explore people's meanings, ways of understanding, and experiences of a complex phenomenon (Lunt and Livingstone 1996). Since there is not yet much documented about postgame experiences, the current focus group studies aimed at exploring the nature, the diversity, and the occurrence of particular postgame experiences. Given various individual differences with respect to play styles or motivations to play games (Yee 2006, Bartle 1996), we further wanted to provide in-depth, contextual, and motivational insights into the specific experiences of different types of gamers. We present two focus group studies: one directed at short-term experiences and the other probing long-term postgame experiences.

9.3.1 Exploring Short-Term Postgame Experiences

We defined short-term postgame experiences as experiences that occur immediately and directly related to a specific game session. The main objective of this study was to explore firsthand verbalizations of how gamers feel or what they experience directly after they stopped gaming.

9.3.1.1 Participants and Procedure

We organized six focus groups with gamers. The composition of the focus groups differed according to several variables such as game frequency, age, and occupational status. Two focus groups (FG1 and FG2) included infrequent gamers (i.e., people who game at least once a month), two focus groups (FG3 and FG4) consisted of frequent gamers (i.e., people who game at least once a week), and two focus groups (FG5 and FG6) were a mix of frequent and infrequent gamers. Participants' ages ranged from 19 to 37 years. In FG1, participants were five undergraduate students of which two were female. FG2 consisted of three male participants, also undergraduates. FG3 had four male participants and was a mix of undergraduate and graduate students. FG4 had four participants; these were people over 30 years of age, all with a full-time job. Participants from FG5 were four working people in their late twenties/early thirties, two of them were female. All three participants from FG6 were female undergraduate students. The focus groups were led by a moderator and an assistant moderator.

Each focus group began with an introductory round in which the moderator and the assistant moderator presented themselves and gave a brief description of the main goal of the focus group. More concretely, they explained that the focus group was about digital games and player experience. Participants were further told that they could freely talk about how they experience digital gaming. Then, participants presented themselves, giving their name, game frequency, and the type of games they usually played. The actual focus group discussion was clustered around three core questions by means of a semi-structured questionnaire. The three core questions were fixed but additional questions could be posed, probing for clarification or more in-depth insights. The three core questions were (1) On what occasions do you typically start gaming? (probing both motivations and opportunities for game play), (2) what do you experience or feel *while* gaming? (i.e., in-game experiences), and (3) what do you experience or how do you feel *after* gaming? (i.e., postgame experiences). In this chapter, we only discuss the third question about postgame experiences. For a detailed description of the remainder of this focus group study, we refer to Poels et al. (2007).

Each focus group took about 90 min in total and approximately one-third of the discussion time was devoted to the question concerning postgame experiences. Participants were rewarded 10 € for their participation. All focus group interviews were recorded and transcribed. Citations we report in the results section are all translated from Dutch.

9.3.1.2 Results

Given the exploratory nature of this focus group study and the newness of the topic, we did not employ a formal coding scheme to analyze our results. This result section is structured according to the different experiences that we proposed in the theoretical part of this chapter.

Participants generally reported *positive feelings* after game play.

> I always feel better after a session of game play. I have had some fun, so that's nice. (Female participant, 23 years)

They frequently mentioned feelings like satisfaction, release of stress, relief, and getting into a good mood.

> If, after an intensive game session, I have completed a level or an important goal in the game, I feel really relieved and satisfied. (Male participant, 31 years)
>
> If my boyfriend and me have been very busy with work or household activities, we often take a 15 minutes break and play with the Wii for a while. We do a round of boxing for example. That really gives you relief, you can vent all your "aggression". (Female participant, 29 years)

However, most participants admitted that *time goes by faster than expected.*

> I often start gaming on Saturday, right after I wake up, around 10 in the morning. It often happens that my wife gets back from work at six in the evening and that I am still there in my boxer shorts, without having eaten anything during that day. For me, it feels like only half an hour has passed. (Male participant, FG4, 34 years)
>
> When I was a kid my parents determined how long I could play by placing an alarm clock next to my console. I always thought that they sabotaged that alarm clock, that it went much faster than the "real time". I never believed that an hour had already passed. (Female participant, 23 years)

When probing whether spending a lot of time, often more than intended, to playing digital games led to feelings of *regret* or *satisfaction*, the answers varied according to personal and situational factors. The more frequent gamers were quite unanimous; they generally did not see gaming as a waste of time and often reported the feeling of having done something really useful.

> Watching TV is much more of a waste of time, because it is a passive activity. Playing games is an active activity. Compare it to playing sports: you don't regret playing sports either. Similar to that, I never regret playing games. (Male participant, 28 years)

The postgame experiences of *guilt* and *regret* clearly depended on the situation in which people played the game. More concretely, guilt, regret, or a general *bad mood* were greater if the game play had restrained them from doing more urgent or more useful activities. This typically has to do with dividing scarce time between work, family, and leisure.

> Regret depends on the things you had to neglect while playing. If it was another leisure activity like going out for a drink, then I don't mind. If you had to neglect things like mowing the lawn, or spending time with my wife and kids, then I do regret having played that long. (Male participant, 34 years)
>
> ...Only if you have been gaming for quite a long time and you did not achieve anything, I often regret having spent so much time on it. Especially when I have more urgent things to do. (Male participant, FG3, 29 years)
>
> I often feel bad if I wasted my time playing a game. However, if it is a lazy Saturday afternoon and you have nothing better to do it doesn't matter. Then I even find it useful to play a game. (Female participant, FG1, 21 years)

Interestingly, some participants reported that they often *anticipated* these negative experiences. For example, one participant explicitly stated that he only quits gaming when he is in a favorable position. This way, he reported, he always has a good feeling after gaming. Another participant said he would not start gaming when he had more urgent things to do. Yet another mentioned only playing short games in order to prevent that he would spend his whole evening playing games, and feel guilty afterward.

Playing digital games is often very engaging and cognitively demanding. You need to focus on the game play, get acquainted with specific game rules, and also think strategically. Some participants did recognize that they get completely soaked in the game and that makes them *feel a bit weird* afterward. It usually takes them some time to adapt to the real world.

> I game to chill. However, afterwards I always need some time to recover, I cannot directly fall asleep for example. (Male participant, FG5, 30 years)

Further, games that make use of an embodied controller can induce postgame experiences of a physical nature. Several participants, who regularly play embodied games, mentioned becoming *physically exhausted* or *having sore muscles*.

> I often try to get rid of my aggression by playing a couple of Wii games. I often really feel exhausted afterwards, and the next day, I have sore muscles. (Female participant, 23 years)

Some participants mentioned that a lot of postgame experiences we were probing at were not really unique to playing digital games, but rather an effect of entertainment or leisure activities in general. For example, after playing sports, experiences such as satisfaction, feeling energized, or physical tiredness do also occur. Along the same line, reading a book or watching a movie can really soak people into a fantasy world and leave them disoriented or making them feel like they have returned from a *journey* as well.

> I can become energized after intensively running as well. However, sometimes gaming is easier, because you don't need to leave the house. (Female participant, 29 years)
>
> Books can also completely soak me into a story. After reading, this does not directly goes out of my mind. It's quite similar to what some games do to me. (Male participant, 32 years)

To summarize, gamers did generally report positive postgame experiences. After probing, negative experience also came to surface. The postgame experiences surfaced through this focus group study are largely in line with the conceptualizations we made earlier this chapter. However, the short-term satisfaction followed by long-term depletion, we described for a TV context [14], did not surface through our focus groups. Gamers did, however, report that they were aware of the potential negative after feelings and they frequently mentioned to anticipate these experiences. Further, some postgame experiences are experiences that typically come with engaging (entertainment) activities in general and, consequently, are not unique to playing games.

9.3.2 Exploring Long-Term Postgame Experiences

We defined long-term postgame experiences as experiences that originate from repeated exposure to a game environment. The aim of the second focus group study was to explore the existence and concrete manifestation of these postgame experiences and to get insights into the extent to which habitual players experience the real world based on inferences that stem from the game world. Further, we wanted to learn more about how these long-term postgame experiences relate to game frequency and game style.

9.3.2.1 Participants and Procedure

The second focus group study included two group discussions with habitual players of MMORPGs. We define habitual gamers as gamers who – on average – play digital games for more than 3 h a day. We specifically targeted this group of gamers, since this study aimed at probing long-term postgame experiences, induced by repeated immersion into a particular game or game genre. The first focus group consisted of three male participants, all students, aged between 18 and 23. They all played MMORPGs (e.g., Lord of The Rings Online, EVE online, World of Warcraft) on a daily basis (3–8 h a day). Participants of the second focus group were four male players, two students (age 22 and 23), one job seeker (age 31), and one full-time employed (age 45). All four were habitual players of digital games (3–7 h a day). One of them solely played World of Warcraft, the other two played MMORPGs, but played other game genres as well.

Each focus group began with an introductory round in which the moderator presented himself, followed by a brief description of the main goal of the focus groups. Next, participants presented themselves, giving their name, game frequency, and the type of games they usually played. The actual focus group discussion was clustered around four potential long-term experiences, we expected for habitual players of MMORPGs. These experiences formed the core topics, and thus the basis for the discussion. Concretely, the four core topics were (1) association of game elements with environmental stimuli in the real world; (2) sounds and music that trigger lively memories about games or game elements; (3) elements of the game showing up in daydreams, fantasy, and dreams; and (4) the use of words and expressions from the game into real-life conversations. Moreover, participants were encouraged to come up with other experiences when these came to mind. Special attention was given to probing whether these experiences are intensified, and are thus more salient, after each game session.

All participants took part on a voluntary basis and were not paid for their participation. Each focus group took about 90 min. All focus group interviews were recorded and transcribed. Citations we report in the results section are all translated from Dutch.

9.3.2.2 Results

For reasons similar to the first focus group study, we opted for a nonformal, explorative analysis of the results. We were mainly interested in the nature and the concrete manifestation of different long-term postgame experiences. This result section is structured according to the four core topics that were probed during the focus group discussion.

With respect to *associations of game elements with "real-life" stimuli*, participants reported several examples of how objects, people, and situations in real life bring about associations with game objects.

> Sometimes, I see something in real life and relate it back to the game. For instance, signposts I noticed on the university campus. Those reminded me of World of Warcraft, where you have similar signposts, for example, Stormwind that way and Ironforge that way. (Male participant, 22 years)
>
> I used to play Halo2 in which you have a wall where someone screams "Boggers, heading over the rooftop". Always when I see a wall, within two big building, this sentence comes to my mind. (Male participant, 21 years)
>
> A while ago, I was going out with a group of friends with whom I play WoW. We were at a concert and there were children playing with a toy bow and arrow. We immediately said to each other: "Hey, there are the hunters!". (Male participant, 31 years)
>
> One night, while going out, me and my friend wanted to grab some food. Though, most food tents were already closed. We were going from the one closed tent to the other and joking to each other what an irritating *fetch quest* this was. (Male participant, 22 years)

Participants also mentioned experiences stemming from hearing particular *music*, both directly and indirectly related to the game, transforming to and creating experiences in real life. For example, when they hear music of a game they enjoyed playing, this immediately triggers lively memories of that game and even makes them want to start playing the game. Or songs they used to listen to while they were playing a particular game instantly remind them of that game.

> When I hear songs that I often play in the background while I am playing WoW, then I immediately start thinking about the game and how fun it is to play WoW. (Male participant, 21 years)
>
> I have certain music I can no longer listen to, because it reminds me of a game I used to play a lot (i.e., Diablo II). When I hear those songs, I just have to play Diablo II again. And then I'm busy for another year, haha. (Male participants, 23 years)
>
> When I was playing Castlevania, I downloaded the game music for my MP3 player. It then sometimes happened that I listened to that music while walking through the streets, fantasizing that skeletons and other creatures from Castlevania would appear in the streets. (Male participant, 21 years)

This last quotation also relates to the next topic, which is *daydreaming and fantasizing* about the game world. Most participants admitted that they often daydream about what tactics to use in their upcoming game sessions. Interestingly, some participants reported that they often fantasize what would happen if specific game elements would also exist in real life.

> I often daydream about my gear, what I can still improve about my character's equipment. (Male participant, 22 years)

> If our train is delayed, I often think: I wish I had a Hearthstone; a WoW object that transports you to a specific location in no time. (Male participant, 23 years)

Most participants also recognized *game elements showing up in dreams*. The specific content of game-related dreams differed from one participant to the other. Some reported dreaming about the social aspects of the game, or dreaming about people from the game in the form of their game characters. Others described dreaming about specific quests or actions that happened in the game.

> I don't dream about raids in the game, but I do dream about social aspects from the game. I sometimes see people from the game pop up in my dreams in the form of their game characters. (Male participant, 31 years)
> Sometimes, in my dreams, in see my game character killing certain monsters in a certain area, trying to get certain items. Or, when I lost in a player vs. player battle, I dream of winning by doing things differently. (Male participant, 21 years)

Language and expressions used in the game did also seem to show up in the everyday vocabulary and thinking processes of our participants.

> I sometimes use WoW words when talking to my kids. For example, if they ask: "dad, can I get some money", I say: "Gold? Eh, money". Or, if someone does something really stupid, I use the word "noob", a word that is often used in MMORPGs to refer to someone who does not know the rules. (Male participant, 45 years)
> For many small things you think in the terminology of the game. For example, someone accidentally drops something, you think aloud "WTF!" (= what the f∗ck!). Such things happen to me quite often, but I try to only use them when talking to people from whom I know they are gamers as well. (Male participant, 31 years)

Most participants agreed that the above-mentioned experiences seemed to happen more often immediately after game play, or in periods in which they game very intensively (e.g., during holidays). In some circumstances, this led to *difficulties in stepping back to the real world*.

> If I have gamed very intensively, I notice that I start using game related words and expression more often. (Male participant, 23 years)
> During holidays I play a lot more than during school periods. If I then return to school, it takes me a while to adapt to daily routine, to directly interact with people again. (Male participant, 23 years)

Also, these long-term experiences seem to build up gradually and become more activated when playing a particular game for a long period of time. Some participants even reported that they completely internalize the game world as a part of "their life." It became a part of their identity.

> Playing games has had an influence on my personality, my vocabulary, and on the way I perceive the world. This is not a short term process, it is a process of years and it will probably still last for years. (Male participant, 22 years)

Interestingly, some participants mentioned that they started interpreting particular real-world situations, influenced by how these situations do occur in games. As such, what happens in the game world cultivates expectancies of what might happen in similar situations in real life.

If I see a dark alley, I –unconsciously– try to avoid that. Or dark and dirty bathrooms, I don't like those. (Male participant, 21 years)

To conclude, postgame experiences surfaced through this focus group study provided clear examples of how, for habitual players of MMORPGs, the game world influences real-world perceptions, emotions, cognitions, and behavior. This supports our conceptualization of long-term postgame experiences, we made earlier in this chapter.

9.4 Discussion and Conclusion

This chapter introduced and conceptualized the concept of postgame experiences and explored firsthand descriptions of postgame experiences surfaced through focus groups. Results from these focus groups show that a large variety of postgame experiences exist, both on the short and long term, both positive and negative ones. Moreover, experiences that participants from our focus groups described largely followed our initial conceptualization, which was based on academic literature on players' motivation and in-game experiences and on theories from other fields of research such as perception theory and media psychology. To the best of our knowledge, this is the first chapter that highlights postgame experiences. We took the first step in approaching the concept of postgame experiences in an exploratory way by using a qualitative research method. The current study – inevitably – holds some limitations that need to be addressed in future research. We outline some suggestions below.

The current study did only include focus groups as one single method to study potential postgame experiences. Although this is an appropriate method for first explorations in this area, future studies should include other measures and methods. We are planning to design and conduct a large-scale survey aimed at consolidating the different types of postgame experiences and determining the potential impact of a number of play style factors, such as play frequency and duration. Also, future studies should investigate the occurrence of postgame experiences in a more continuous and long-term manner, for example by using the diary method.

Our second focus group showed that long-term postgame experiences are at play for habitual players. The main limitation of this study was that it only included habitual players of MMORPGs as one specific game genre. As such, the experiences described by our participants can be specific for this type of games. Future studies are needed to explore long-term postgame experiences induced by other popular game genres such as First Person Shooters, Race games, Simulation games, etc. Additionally, it would be interesting to see how the nature and the occurrence of long-term postgame experiences differ between casual and habitual gamers.

Besides future research suggestions that arise from the limitation of our own study, results from the current study also give rise to some new research questions. More specifically, the current studies showed that several postgame experiences are probably not really unique to gaming. Our focus groups already revealed that some experiences, like relief and relaxation, do also apply to other leisure activities. It would be interesting to investigate which general motivational factors cause such experiences and which postgame experiences are uniquely related to gaming and which are not. As such, it should be considered in what respect playing games is similar to other leisure activities and what characteristics uniquely apply to digital games.

Another interesting point came out of the second study. Participants in our second study did mention interpretations of real-world situations (e.g., a dark alley) being influenced by what typically happens in such situations inside a game environment (i.e., avoid the alley, because there will be danger). This might suggest that cultivation effects can be induced by playing digital games. The central premise of cultivation studies is that heavy users of a particular medium (e.g., television, movies) are more likely to perceive the real world in ways that reflect the world represented in that medium (Van Mierlo and Van den Bulck 2004). Studies on cultivation effects within games are still limited (Van Mierlo and Van den Bulck 2004, Williams 2006). We think, however, that this area deserves further explorations, especially given the increase in realism and elaborate narratives embedded in current games.

As stated in the introduction, most research on user experience in games has focused on in-game experiences. This chapter showed that user experiences do not stop after the game session has ended. Futures studies should investigate how in-game experiences and postgame experiences correlate and depend on background variables such as gender, play style, type of game played, and general personality traits. Clarification of these relationships can make important contributions to the interplay of gaming motivations, game experiences, and other game-related factors (e.g., game content, game design, and commercial game success) and nongame-related behavior (e.g., [anti]social behavior, personality development, and coordination skills).

To summarize, postgame experiences do occur when engaging in playing digital games. We proposed a diverse set of postgame experiences and explored firsthand experiences through focus groups with different types of gamers. We hope our study can inspire researchers within the domain of user experience in digital games. We call for research that further addresses how postgame experiences relate to other aspects associated with digital game play.

Acknowledgments We gratefully acknowledge financial support from the European Commission's Framework 6 IST program. In particular, the work reported here has been supported by the FUGA project (part of the IST – New and Emerging Science and Technology program) and the Games@Large project (part of the IST – Networked Audio-Visual Systems and Home Platforms program).

References

Agarwal R, Karahanna E (2000) Time flies when you're having fun: Cognitive absorption and beliefs about information technology usage. MIS Quarterly 24(4): 665–694.
Bartle R (1996) Hearts, clubs, diamonds, spades: Players who suit MUDs. The Journal of Virtual Environments 1(1). www.brandeis.edu/pubs/jove/HTML/v1/bartle.html . Accessed 7 November 2008.
Boring EG (1930) A new ambiguous figure. American Journal of Psychology 42: 444.

Brown E, Cairns P (2004) A grounded investigation of game immersion. ACM CHI 2004, pp. 1297–1300.

Bruner J, Potter M (1964) Interference in visual recognition. Science 144(3617): 424–425.

Buckley KE, Anderson CA (2006) A theoretical model of the effects and consequences of playing videogames. In: Vorderer P, Bryant J (eds) Playing Video Games: Motives, Responses, and Consequences. Lawrence Erlbaum Associates, Mahwah, NJ.

Carnagey NL, Anderson CA (2005) The effects of reward and punishment in violent video games on aggressive affect, cognition, and behavior. Psychological Science 16: 882–889.

Carnagey NL, Anderson CA, Bushman BJ (2007) The effect of video game violence on desensitization to real-life violence. Journal of Experimental Social Psychology 43: 489–496.

Colwell J (2007) Needs met through computer game play among adolescents. Personality and Individual Differences 43: 2072–2082.

Colwell J, Grady C, Rhaiti S (1995) Computer games, self-esteem, and gratification of needs in adolescents. Journal of Community & Applied Social Psychology 5: 195–206.

Csikszentmihalyi M (1990) Flow. The Psychology of Optimal Experience. Harper & Row, New York.

de Kort YAW, IJsselsteijn WA, Poels K (2007) Digital games as social presence technology: Development of the social presence in gaming questionnaire (SPGQ). In: Proceedings of 10th Annual International Workshop Presence, Barcelona, Spain, pp. 195–203.

Ermi L, Mäyrä F (2005) Fundamental components of the gameplay experience: Analysing immersion. de Castell S, Jenson J (eds) Changing Views: Worlds in Play. In Selected Papers of the 2005 Digital Games Research Association's Second International Conference.

Green CS, Bavelier D (2003) Action video games modifies visual selective attention. Nature 423: 534–537.

Griffiths M, Davies M (2005) Does video game addiction exist? In: Raessens J, Goldstein J (eds) Handbook of Computer Game Studies. MIT Press, Cambridge, MA.

Jennet C, Cox AL, Cairns P et al. (2008) Measuring and defining the experience of immersion in games. International Journal of Human-Computer Studies 66(9): 641–661.

Kubey R, Csikszentmihalyi M (2002) Television addiction is not a mere metaphor. Scientific American 286(2): 62–68.

Lunt P, Livingstone S (1996) Rethinking the focus group in media and communications research. Journal of Communication 46(2): 79–98.

Pilcher J, Huffcutt A (1996) Effects of sleep deprivation on performance: A meta-analysis. Sleep 19(4): 318–326.

Poels K, de Kort YAW, IJsselsteijn WA (2007) "It is always a lot of fun!" Exploring dimensions of digital game experience using focus group methodology. In: Proceedings of Annual FuturePlay Conference, Toronto, Canada, pp. 83–89.

Rock I (1983) The Logic of Perception. MIT press, Cambridge, MA.

Selnow GW (1984) Playing video games: The electronic friend. Journal of Communication 34: 148–156.

Sherry J (2004) Flow and media enjoyment. Communication Theory 4: 328–347.

Sweetser P, Wyeth P (2005) GameFlow: A model for evaluating player enjoyment in games. ACM Computers in Entertainment 3(3): 1–24.

Van Mierlo J, Van den Bulck J (2004) Benchmarking the cultivation approach to video game effects: A comparison of the correlates of TV viewing and game play. Journal of Adolescence 27: 97–111.

Vorderer P, Bryant J, Pieper K, Weber R (2006) Playing video games as entertainment. In: Vorderer P, Bryant J (eds) Playing Video Games: Motives, Responses, and Consequences. Lawrence Erlbaum Associates, Mahwah, NJ.

Vorderer P, Klimmt C, Ritterfield U (2004) Enjoyment: At the heart of entertainment. Communication Theory 14(4): 388–408.

Williams D (2006) Virtual cultivation: Online worlds, offline perceptions. Journal of Communication 56: 69–87.

Yee N (2006) Motivations for play in online games. CyberPsychology & Behavior 9(6): 772–775.

Chapter 10
Evaluating User Experience Factors Using Experiments: Expressive Artificial Faces Embedded in Contexts

Michael Lankes, Regina Bernhaupt, and Manfred Tscheligi

Abstract There is an ongoing debate on what kind of factors contribute to the general positive user experience while playing a game. The following chapter introduces an experimental setting to measure user experience aroused by facial expression of embodied conversational agents (ECAs). The experimental setup enables to measure the implications of ECAs in three contextual settings called "still," "animated," and "interaction." Within the experiment, artificially generated facial expressions are combined with emotion-eliciting situations and are presented via different presentation platforms. Stimuli (facial expressions/emotion-eliciting situations) are assembled in either consonant (for example, facial expression: "joy," emotion-eliciting situation: "joy") or dissonant (for example, facial expression: "joy," emotion-eliciting situation: "anger") constellations. The contextual setting called "interaction" is derived from the video games domain, granting an interactive experience of a given emotional situation. The aim of the study is to establish a comparative experimental framework to analyze subjects' user experience on emotional stimuli in different context dimensions. This comparative experimental framework utilizes theoretical models of emotion theory along with approaches from human–computer interaction to close a gap in the intersection of affective computing and research on facial expressions. Results showed that the interaction situation is rated as providing a better user experience, independent of showing consonant or dissonant contextual descriptions. The "still" setting is given a higher user experience rating than the "animated" setting.

10.1 Introduction

Various methods and new methodological developments have been proposed to evaluate user experience in application domains ranging from user experience evaluation of mobile phones (Roto and Rautava 2008) to user experience for interactive

M. Lankes (✉)
Upper Austria University of Applied Sciences, Hagenberg, Austria
e-mail: michael.lankes@fh-hagenberg.at

R. Bernhaupt (ed.), *Evaluating User Experience in Games*, Human-Computer
Interaction Series, DOI 10.1007/978-1-84882-963-3_10,

TV (Bernhaupt et al. 2008b) and several others (e.g. Law et al. 2007). Most of them did not take into consideration recent developments in the area of gaming, such as game play between thousands of players, multiplayer audio channels and the use of novel input devices to encourage physical activity (Bernhaupt et al. 2008a).

Digital games constitute a tremendously varied set of applications, with a wide range of associated player experiences, defying a one-size-fits-all approach to their conceptualization and measurement. One of the main challenges facing the gaming research community is a lack of a coherent and fine-grained set of methods and tools that enable the measurement of entertainment experiences in a sensitive, reliable, and valid manner. Taking a factor-structure approach to characterize user experiences, terms like fun, flow, and playability are most often used to explain user experience in game design. However, there is an open discussion to include other factors which might have relevance for games. Emotion is often cited as a key element of user experience (e.g., Hassenzahl and Tractinsky 2006).

On the other hand, the quality of the display of emotions portrayed by embodied conversational agents (ECAs) is perceived as a necessity to improve the user experience (Lee and Marsella 2006). The following chapter is looking in detail on the relation of user experience and emotions that are expressed by ECAs. It shall provide some insights concerning the relation between emotions displayed in a game (through the characters) in conjunction with emotion-eliciting situations in regard to the user experience. Results of this study are a first step in a series of experiments investigating the relationship between user experience and interaction with embodied conversational agents.

The chapter is organized as follows: Based on an overview on currently used models in emotion theory, the usage of emotional (factor) models in games is explained and how the modeling of nonplayer characters (NPCs) – a field of application of ECAs – is representing these emotional (factor) models. It shall be investigated how the display of emotions (still, animated, or interactive) in various contexts (either with a consonant or with a dissonant context description) is affecting the user experience (measured with a questionnaire). The section on the experimental study describes in detail three prestudies for selecting stimuli and material followed by the main study on the relation of displaying emotion in games via ECAs and perceived user experience. The conclusion shows how the findings can be used in game development in terms of designing positive user experiences.

10.2 Related Work

Incorporating emotional expressions for nonplayer characters in games is seen as an appropriate way to improve the gamers' experiences. The research area of emotions is a central topic in human–computer interaction and is approached from various perspectives. Subsequently, some of these perspectives, and their relation to current developments in user experience research, are presented. First, we look at how emotions can be integrated, seen either as part of the computing system or as part of the overall user experience. Second, we look on how emotions can be measured, and third, we present some related work on how emotions are integrated into ECAs and how we measure the user experiencing in regard to the emotional expressions performed by ECAs in conjunction with emotion-eliciting situations.

10.2.1 General Description on Emotion

The implementation of emotional factors in systems received an increased interest by the human–computer interaction (HCI) community as researchers within this field aim to develop machines that are focused on human needs (Branco 2003). Emotions play a crucial role in our everyday life with computers (Crane et al. 2007) and have a significant impact on user experience as they influence actions, expectations, and future evaluations (Picard 1997). Technological advancements enable machines to perceive, interpret, express, and respond to emotional information. Traditionally, emotional factors were neglected as designers focused on usability aspects and developed systems with the aim to increase efficiency of required tasks (Picard et al. 2002). Although it might be argued that machines should be treated as mere tools that do not (or should not) require any emotions, results of Reeves and Nass (2003) showed that people tend to exhibit social and emotional behaviors toward machines. Picard et al. (2002) also note that interaction with machines is emotional even if the system was not designed to incorporate emotional aspects. Users should be enabled to utilize familiar communication mechanisms when interacting with computational systems. The human–machine interaction process should be designed to resemble human interpersonal interactions, in order to rely on skills obtained from human–human communication. Systems get easier to use if the interaction between human–machine is similar to human–human interaction (Bernhaupt et al. 2007a).

When dealing with the various objectives within HCI research in the field of emotion, we can choose from a tremendous amount of research approaches. Mahlke (2005) provides a taxonomy dividing emotion in HCI into affective computing and emotional design. The concept of affective computing postulates to develop systems that are able to perceive the emotional state of the user, interpret the affective state, adapt to the user's state, and generate an expressed emotion (Minge 2005). Emotional design claims that emotion is considered as an important factor of the user's experience with interactive systems and it is aimed to incorporate emotional aspects in the interactive system design process (Norman 2002). From the perspective of User Experience (UX) research, emotions are investigated to understand their role as antecedent, as a consequence and a mediator of technology use (Hassenzahl and Tractinsky 2006). Researchers in the field of user experience evaluation thus try to concentrate on integrating emotional processes of the user experience into the evaluation procedure of the interactive systems.

Our experiment addresses the factor emotion concerning user experience by raising the questions how emotional stimuli (facial expressions by ECAs and emotion-eliciting situations) in interactive system affect the (more general) user experience?

Concerning the factor emotion, there are two major research foci: the assessment of emotional dispositions aroused by games and the incorporation of emotion into the game world (see the following two sections).

10.2.2 Games and User Experience

Several tools are available to investigate the factor emotion: the Self Assessment Mannequin (SAM) (Fischer et al. 2002), Emoticons (Desmet and Hekkert 2002), or Affective Grid (Russell and Fernandez-Dols 1997) are just a few examples. Until now, no commonly accepted method for measuring emotions is available. Ravaja and colleagues (2006) presented 37 subjects different types of computer games (Tetris, James Bond, Nightfire, and others). To measure emotional response patterns they employed categorical (fear, joy, etc.) and dimensional measurement methods (arousal and valence dimensions). They conclude that different types of games elicit different types of emotional dispositions. Furthermore, the researchers believe that developers will increase the commercial success of a game by incorporating emotional aspects while testing different computer game concepts. Pleasant emotional episodes during game play are deemed to be an indicator to provide positive (and desirable) user experience (Ermi and Mäyrä 2005).

To understand the overall user experience, we decided to focus on a general perception instead of only looking at the elicited emotion. User experience in games is evaluated using a large variety of approaches ranging from questionnaires to physical measurements (Mandryk et al. 2006). As we wanted to have a simple and flexible to use measurement, we decided to measure user experience with the AttrakDiff questionnaire (www.attrakdiff.de) that has been used in various studies to investigate pragmatic and hedonic quality of users interacting with a system.

The AttrakDiff questionnaire was developed to measure implications of attractiveness of a product. Users indicate their impression of a given product by bipolar terms that reflect four dimensions. The first dimensions, the pragmatic quality (PQ), describes traditional usability aspects, while the dimension Hedonic Quality-Stimulation (HQ-S) refers to the need of people for further development concerning themselves. By supporting this aspect, products can offer new insights and interesting experiences. Hedonic Quality-Identification (HQ-I) allows to measure the amount of identification a user has toward a product. Pragmatic and hedonic dimensions are independent from each other and share a balanced impact on the overall judgment. The two aspects contribute equally to the overall judgment of the situation/product and is referred to as hedonic quality (HQ). Attractiveness (ATT) resembles an overall judgment based on the perceived quality.

10.2.3 Embodied Conversational Agents

According to Bartneck (2000), computer games were one of the first applications that incorporated interactive virtual characters. One main driving force in the games industry is innovation in computer technology, which enables the development of more visually elaborated game entities (here: characters). As video game systems have become more powerful from a technical point of perspective, the gaming community has demanded games that push the technical capabilities of the platforms (Pruett 2008). At the beginning of video game, history game elements were displayed as very abstract and simple forms, while nowadays players are confronted with rather highly realistic virtual actors inhabiting complex virtual worlds. A lot of effort is put in the creation of NPCs by game companies. NPCs can include capabilities of verbal and nonverbal communication and may aid the player in a gaming situation. Players may encounter NPCs as enemies that try to interfere to reach game goals, or as characters that serve them as tutors or supporters. Isbister introduces in her book "Better Game Characters by Design" (Isbister 2006) a classification of NPCs based on their social roles within the game.

NPCs can be seen as a field of application regarding ECAs. In general terms, an embodied agent can be understood as a specific type of agent whose behaviors are executed by some type of perceivable digital representation (Bailenson 2008). Lieberman (1997) describes agents, in contrast to traditional interfaces, as any program that serves as an assistant or helper to aid users during the interaction process. Bates (1994) adds emotional aspects when defining embodied agents. Nonverbal signals form an essential part in the communication process, which incorporate the portraying of emotional dispositions via facial expressions, gestures, voice, etc. With the implementation of emotional aspects, agents are more attractive to users because they communicate in ways we are used to (Elliott and Brzezinski 1998). Agents containing knowledge about the conversational process and capabilities to perceive and express emotional signals can be summarized under the term ECAs. They are characters that visually incorporate, or embody, knowledge about the conversational process (Prendinger and Ishizuka 2004). ECAs are virtual humans able to perform conversations with humans by both understanding and producing speech and nonverbal signals (Cassell 2008). They form a type of multimodal interface where the modalities are the natural communication channels of human conversation. The visual representation of ECAs of interacting is intrinsic to its function, meaning that visual information (for example, display of facial expressions) is crucial in the process (Bickmore and Cassell 2001). Nonverbal channels are necessary for both conveying information and regulating the communication process (Bickmore and Cassell 2001). They can be utilized to provide social cues as attentiveness, positive affect, and attraction. For investigating the affect of displayed emotions on the users (players) experience, the definition by Mancini et al. (2004, p. 1) shall serve as the basis: "ECAs are virtual embodied representations of humans that communicate multimodal with the user (or other agents) through voice, facial expression, gaze, gesture, and body movement."

10.2.4 Facial Expressions Performed by Embodied Conversational Agents

Emotion theory offers a variety of approaches including perspectives of social constructivism, cognition, or theories based on the work of William James or Charles

Darwin (Cornelius 1996). The "Darwinian approach" focuses on facial expressions and propagates a limited number of basic, fundamental, or discrete emotions that are directly linked to the motivational system (Scherer et al. 2004). Followers of this tradition assume that specific eliciting conditions would automatically trigger a pattern of reactions such as peripheral physiological responses. It is postulated that mechanisms of emotion mixing or blending occur, which lead to a great variability of facial expressions. Russell and Fernandez-Dols (1997) summarized the discrete emotion approach to outline basic assumptions. First, there is a small set of basic (or fundamental) emotions that are genetically determined and discrete. Each of these emotional states is composed of behavioral patterns like the portrayal of specific facial expressions. The encoding and decoding of emotional signals developed based on adoption processes. States that are not linked to facial signals are not considered as basic emotions. Evidence is present for the basic emotions happiness, surprise, anger, contempt (some uncertainty), disgust, sadness, and fear. These emotions are recognized by all humans (innate) independent from their cultural background. Emotions that share nonfundamental states are considered to be blends (mixtures) of basic emotions. Cultural restrictions may inhibit or mask certain behavioral patterns called display rules.

Based on these assumptions, Ekman and Friesen (1972) developed Facial Action Coding System (FACS). It serves as a high-level description of motions by feature points (Jaimes and Sebe 2007). Each facial muscle is assigned a numeric value that is modified when muscles move. Thus, facial expressions could be synthesized by relating to FACS codes. FACS allows measuring facial expressions objectively, which enables the synthesis of specific expressions by applying the required FACS codes. Movement of individual facial muscles sections lead to observable alternations within the overall appearance of the face.

Fernandez-Dols and Carroll (1997) emphasized the importance of context, claiming that the perception of emotional signals is significantly influenced by situational factors and vice versa. Wallbott (1990) also supports this position by noting that subjects were confronted with isolated stimuli to indicate their perception of the presented emotion. He propagated the explicit incorporation of context-related information in the investigation of facial expression. Without context, subjects are forced to simulate (or construct) the missing information, which inevitably will lead to invalid research results. According to Wallbott (1990), three factors are relevant when judging the emotional quality: the stimulus (for example, photos showing facial expressions), the background (or context), and the emotional disposition of the observer. Contextual aspects are not only embedded in emotions, but also the cause for emotional dispositions. Context in facial expression can be subdivided into a situation-related context (modification of the current emotion), a comparative context (the relation of one nonverbal communication channel between others), the static context (captured via photos), and the dynamic context (involved channels in a given time frame).

To summarize the findings of Wallbott (1990), person-related aspects (here: facial expressions) have more influence on emotion judgments than situational components. However, the analyzed data revealed that (although visual stimuli are dominating the perception) descriptions of emotion-eliciting situations will gain importance if the constellation of stimuli is dissonant. Furthermore, subjects employ different strategies when being confronted with different types of stimuli constellations. Person-related aspects do not completely dominate situational factors, as they are always integrated into the judgment of emotional stimuli. An important factor that determines the importance of components is the type of presentation medium. The increase of visualization in regard to situational aspects leads to a shift of dominance. The more visualized a situation is presented, the more it will influence the judgment on emotion. Wallbott (1990) assumes that dynamic stimuli material (descriptions of emotion-eliciting situations) in "still" settings (presentation of facial expressions via film clips) grants more clear information on a given situation than static presentations (presentation of facial expressions via photos).

The following proposal for evaluating UX in the context of ECAs will build on these findings as it tries to extend the framework by employing a new (interactive) presentation medium. The relative importance of information channels shall not be addressed, but a novel experimental setting to investigate the perceived user experience in regard to facial expressions and their relation to contextual aspects shall be presented. The introduced theoretical considerations on emotion should serve as a foundation, as well as to provide some insights into this multidimensional research topic. It should have been pointed out that situational aspects have to be considered when investigating the perception of facial expressions as they determine the quality of the interpretation process.

10.3 Evaluation

The goal of this experiment was to understand the influence of emotional facial expressions of ECAs and descriptions of emotion-eliciting situations in three inter-action conditions (still, animated, or interactive) on the user experience. We see user experience as a concept that is best described as a property of the human interacting with the game. The overall user experience during game play is consisting of some key components. Emotions are the most prominent component together with immersion, playability, or flow. As we only wanted to understand how changes in the emotional expression of an ECA and emotion-eliciting situations might influence the general perception, we decided to focus on a general measurement of user experience, based on the AttrakDiff questionnaire.

10.3.1 Methodological Considerations

To investigate user experience in games, a set of methods has been developed. Following traditional HCI approaches of classifying evaluation, methods can be grouped in expert- and user-oriented evaluations (Dix et al. 2004), other classifications are based on development cycles or more social science-oriented approaches (Bernhaupt et al. 2007b). How emotional expressions of ECAs and emotion-eliciting situations affect the user experience in a game can be evaluated using several of these methods. But what the relationship between these methodologies is stays rather unclear.

To understand the influence of emotional expressions of ECAs and the influence of emotion-eliciting situations on UX, a more rigid approach is necessary. An experiment (including three prestudies) was set up to investigate the relationship between emotional expressions of ECAs and emotion-eliciting situations in interactive settings compared to still and animated settings.

The main study investigates how a given emotional facial expression and an emotion-eliciting situation combined in either a consonant (for example, facial expression: "joy," emotion-eliciting situation: "joy") or a dissonant (for example, facial expression: "joy," emotion-eliciting situation: "anger") constellations presented in either a still, animated or an interactive format is influencing the overall user experience. The goal was to investigate the influences on the overall user experience to understand how the design of ECAs influences the game play.

10.3.2 Prestudy 1: Evaluation of Emotion-Eliciting Situations

The goal of prestudy 1 was to identify and validate emotion-eliciting situations. The purpose was to identify emotion-eliciting situations with "pure" emotions (weak or no presence of other emotions) and high intensity that will be utilized in the main study. As emotion descriptions set up by the researchers influence heavily the outcome (Wallbott 1990, p. 37), a categorized and standardized emotion-eliciting situation experienced in real life was used. Projects (for example, Summerfield and Green 1986, Scherer et al. 2004) were carried out for years in different cultures to identify emotion-eliciting situations that are culturally independent from their meaning. The "International Survey on Emotion Antecedents And Reactions" (ISEAR) database (ISEAR 2008), which was made freely available for researchers interested in this field, contains data files and explanations for a major cross-culturally comparative study on the cognitive antecedents of emotion (based on appraisal notions) and the reaction patterns reported for seven basic emotions (joy, fear, anger, sadness, disgust, shame, and guilt) by close to 3000 respondents in 37 countries.

We used 200 randomly chosen database entries as a basis and then removed descriptions that did not refer to the emotion categories of Summerfield and Green (1986). Within prestudy 1, the applicable descriptions were filtered using three criteria. Criterion 1 identify the dominating emotions by analyzing the intensity of all six basic emotions. The second criterion should reveal the presence of "pure" (one emotion present) and "blended" (mixture of emotions) emotions, as the questionnaire allowed multiple choice answers. Only pure emotions are considered applicable to the main experiment. The purpose of criterion 3 is to filter out pure emotions that have a fairly low intensity. Descriptions that are employed in the main experiment have to fulfill all three criteria.

Table 10.1 Selection of stimulus material based on prestudy 1, criterion 1. The mean values are shown for each emotion type

Stimulus	Joy	Fear	Anger	Sadness	Disgust	Surprise	Dominance
Aa1	5.76	0.76	0.00	0.10	0.06	1.26	Joy
Aa4	7.10	0.00	0.00	0.00	0.00	0.17	Joy
Ab1	6.16	0.00	0.00	0.00	0.00	0.93	Joy
Ab3	7.20	0.00	0.00	0.00	0.00	0.26	Joy
Bb1	0.00	0.86	0.26	4.76	0.06	1.73	Sadness
Bb2	0.00	0.13	1.13	7.33	0.00	0.43	Sadness
Bb3	0.00	0.33	0.63	7.50	0.00	0.80	Sadness
Bb4	0.00	0.03	0.66	7.26	0.00	0.33	Sadness
Ca4	0.06	3.40	0.00	0.80	0.23	1.86	Fear
Cb1	0.30	4.90	0.26	0.00	0.00	0.10	Fear
Cb3	0.00	6.66	0.86	0.13	0.13	1.33	Fear
Da1	0.00	0.03	5.46	0.63	0.00	1.16	Anger
Da2	0.20	0.00	3.83	0.93	0.96	1.00	Anger
Da4	0.00	0.33	6.40	0.76	0.06	120	Anger
Db1	0.00	0.03	6.20	0.93	0.00	1.13	Anger
Db4	0.00	0.00	6.73	0.80	1.66	0.70	Anger

Thirty participants (15 male, 15 female) aged 22 to 61 took part in the study. To validate the experimental descriptions based on the three criteria, a simple questionnaire was used. Participants rated the evoked emotion (joy, fear, anger, sadness, disgust, and surprise) and the dominance for each description (scale from 0 to 8 [emotion not present at all, emotion intensively present]).

Based on the ratings of the participants, 11 descriptions are applicable for the main experiment. For criteria 1, the dominating emotion was analyzed (see Table 10.1), followed by criteria 3 selecting only emotion-eliciting situations that were rated on average higher than 4.75 (on the scale from 0 to 8) and finally excluding blended emotions (ratings of two emotions that were higher than 2 on average). Based on these criteria, finally 11 situations were showing pure emotions. For the following prestudies, we used two situations for each of the four emotions from the category of Summerfield and Green (1986): sadness, joy, anger, and fear. Table 10.2 shows these eight situations that were used in the following steps of the experiment.

10.3.3 Prestudy 2: Evaluation of Artificial Facial Expressions

It proved to be a difficult undertaking to find appropriate stimuli material mainly due to license or quality issues of available virtual actors. Since no appropriate stimuli material was at hand, it was decided to create the actors and facial expressions. Constructing six ECAs performing four basic emotions along with a neutral one leads to a total number of 30 stimuli images.

Table 10.2 Descriptions selected based on prestudy 1

Stimuli	Description
Aa4	My girlfriend was arriving back from overseas and I picked her up from the airport. She finally appeared from customs and we came into contact again
Ab3	I went back home after a long trip and met beloved people and close friends
Bb3	A close friend was involved in an accident and passed away instantly. He had gone to buy a new car and had asked me to wait at his house so that I could see his new car
Bb4	I hear about the death of somebody I liked very much and I was not present either to see that person or to try to share my emotions with other friends
Cb1	At about midnight I had to go by bike through the city alone. On the whole it was a distance of several kilometers. A car followed me through the streets. Only when I went into a one-way street the car disappeared
Cb3	I was living with my brother and one day he went away on business. I was left alone to look after the house and the property. At night, thieves came and wanted to break into the house
Da1	I had arranged with a friend to go with him to the city by car. We had arranged a place where to meet. I was a bit late and my friend had left already. I had no money to go by train. It was very important for me to go to the city
Db1	The headmaster of the job appointment committee in charge explained me that teacher (of the opposite gender) was more suitable for a particular post. I had more years of service than the male/female

After selecting the emotion-eliciting situations in prestudy 1, it was necessary to construct and investigate facial expressions performed by the constructed ECAs. The stimuli should be presented to subjects without any additional information and should communicate one of the four chosen basic emotions (joy, fear, anger, and sadness). The constructed expressions should convey pure emotions with a rather high intensity. As in the previous study, participants of prestudy 2 rated stimuli by answering via a multiple-choice questionnaire containing the six basic emotions and were rating the emotional intensity on a scale from 0 to 8 (emotion not present at all, emotion intensively present).

In contrast to prestudy 1, the questionnaire was not printed out on paper, but was shown via an LCD display to match the presentation as close as possible in regard to the main experiment. Therefore, a tablet PC was utilized in order to resemble study 1 as close as possible and to grant a certain amount of mobility. With the aid of the lime survey or application (Lime 2008), an online questionnaire tool, the questionnaire was set up and images were implemented along with emotion type and intensity scales. The application also enabled the scrambling of picture order. The evaluation of facial expressions is carried out by applying the three criteria from prestudy 2. This step was necessary to verify if constructed facial expressions are perceived as intended.

Thirty participants took part in prestudy 2 (16 male, 14 female), age ranging from 20 to 63. The filling out of the questionnaire via the tablet PC took about 15–20 minutes. Material was selected based on the same criteria as in prestudy 1. All stimuli were perceived as intended (criterion 1: most intensive emotion), the rates for perceiving blended emotions followed the reported recognition rates of emotions

Fig. 10.1 Female and male ECAs showing the emotions joy, sadness, anger, and a neutral face

in faces (Ekman and Friesen 1972). For criterion 3, the intensity of the emotion was over 4.75 for all presented stimuli. The constructed material thus fulfilled the intended purpose. Figure 10.1 shows examples of female and male ECAs showing different emotions.

10.3.4 Prestudy 3: Evaluation of Settings and Text Fragments

Prestudy 3 deals with the assessment of virtual settings mainly utilized in interactive condition of the main experiment. The virtual settings should indicate the physical context in which emotion-eliciting situations are embedded. The step of creating virtual settings is necessary as conversations in real life take place in physical contexts.

The introduction of a physical context layer may cause unwanted artifacts. The interpretation of facial expressions and emotion-eliciting situations may be influenced by the color of settings. The work of Suk (2006), who investigated emotional responses to color to analyze the relationship between color attribute and emotional dimensions (dimensional approach), helped to overcome this issue. He found out that emotional responses to color vary more strongly with regard to tone than to hue categories. The overall color of settings and its lightness are slightly toned down to avoid affective-related influence. The blue prints for the construction of virtual settings are derived from the situations of study 1. Most descriptions of prestudy 1 indicate a physical context by containing words such as "airport," "home," or "town." We thus constructed eight contextual settings, one airport setting, two town settings, and five home settings for the eight emotion-eliciting situations. Eight settings were available as text (for the still images), and eight virtual settings were additionally constructed for the interactive setting of the main experiment.

Similar to study 1, the fragments of emotion-eliciting situations should be judged by presenting the six basic emotions, and intensity was rated on a scale from 1 to 8. Thirty participants (14 male, 16 female) aged 22 to 57 took part in the evaluation. The evaluation of text fragments and virtual settings led to a total number of 16 stimuli (eight images of virtual settings plus eight split up emotion-eliciting situations). As in prestudy 2, the questionnaire presents stimuli via an LCD display to match the presentation as close as possible in regard to the main experiment.

Table 10.3 presents the emotion ratings for the eight text fragments describing the context of the eight emotion-eliciting situations (see again Table 10.2) and the rating of the emotional judgment of the eight virtual scenarios (which should not influence the experiment, thus ratings should be below 2.00 on average).

10.3.5 Experiment: Facial Expression and User Experience

The goal of the main experiment was to evaluate the impact emotion-eliciting situations and facial expressions on the overall user experience. We manipulated two conditions: condition one was the influence of a consonant/dissonant contextual descriptions. Condition two was the influence of either a "still" situation (frame), the "animated" (animation clips) situation, or the "interactive" situation (game environment).

The following hypotheses are related to the general research question on how emotional facial expressions of ECAs and emotion-eliciting situations influence the user experience:

- (H1) The overall user experience in the interactive situation is rated higher than the user experience in animation scenario and the still scenario.
- (H2) The animation scenario in terms of user experience is rated higher than the still scenario.
- (H3) The perceived user experience will be the higher for consonant settings than for settings with dissonant stimuli.

The experiment is based on 576 possible stimuli. Four consonant scenarios presenting the four selected basic emotions (joy, fear, anger, and sadness) and 12 dissonant settings, each performed by one out of six possible virtual actors, embedded in eight different emotion-eliciting situations. Since the experimental setup consists

Table 10.3 Ratings of the stimuli for the emotion-eliciting situations and ratings for the virtual settings showing that the design does not influence the emotion elicitation

Stimulus	Joy	Fear	Anger	Sadness	Disgust	Surprise
T_Aa4	6.87	0.40	0.17	0.03	0.70	0.00
T_Ab3	6.73	0.17	0.20	0.40	1.33	0.20
T_Bb3	0.80	0.90	0.63	6.57	1.37	0.30
T_Bb4	0.17	1.03	1.37	6.93	1.37	0.33
T_Cb1	0.13	5.97	1.23	0.23	0.87	0.27
T_Cb3	0.10	0.47	5.80	1.27	1.63	0.00
T_Da1	0.10	0.47	5.80	1.27	1.63	0.00
T_Db1	0.03	0.40	6.83	1.50	1.53	0.83

Stimulus	Joy	Fear	Anger	Sadness	Disgust	Surprise
V_Aa4	0.53	0.80	0.17	0.63	0.43	0.13
V_Ab3	1.30	0.23	0.23	0.23	0.63	0.37
V_Bb3	1.03	0.27	0.07	0.10	0.53	0.10
V_Bb4	0.37	1.17	0.20	0.33	0.27	0.17
V_Cb1	1.30	0.23	0.10	0.17	0.77	0.13
V_Cb3	1.67	0.20	0.17	0.07	0.80	0.10
V_Da1	1.10	0.03	0.23	0.03	0.37	0.03
V_Db1	1.57	0.47	0.23	0.10	1.23	0.27

of three different scenarios, 192 constellations have to be multiplied by 3, resulting in 576 stimuli. Out of these 576, six scenarios are randomly chosen for each subject. Subjects have to indicate the perceived user experience via the AttrakDiff (Hassenzahl et al. 2003) questionnaire.

In order to avoid material effects caused by repeated measurements, items of the AttrakDiff were randomized result in six different versions of the AttrakDiff questionnaire. Furthermore, each participant received the six generated Attrakdiff questionnaires in a randomized order when providing information on their impression concerning user experience factors.

For the experiment, each participant was presented three scenarios (still/ animated/interactive) two times (one consonant/one discrepant). Each ECA appeared only one time for each participant. Repetition of consonant and dissonant emotion constellations was avoided and none of the emotion-eliciting situations was repeated for a participant.

Concerning scenario 1 (still), a picture was shown containing a facial expression performed by a virtual actor (evaluated in prestudy 2), along with descriptions of the emotion-eliciting situations (evaluated in prestudy 1). An image of a virtual setting, referenced to the emotion-eliciting situation, is also displayed in the background. After subjects indicated that they were finished with their observations, the experimenter handed out the AttrakDiff questionnaires.

Scenario 2 was structured similar to scenario 1, as facial expressions are presented along with emotion-eliciting situations. In contrast to scenario 1, the faces of virtual actors were animated by performing eye-blinking animations, slight head rotations, and minor changes of emotion intensity to grant a vivid impression. The emotion-eliciting situations were presented in three information chunks (see study 3) along with an animated background showing one of the eight virtual settings. The animation of background contained short clips with camera tilts. Each sequence played in looped cycles and lasted 20 seconds. The animation is stopped when participants finished their observation task during the experiment.

Scenario 3 involved the assessment of user experience in an interactive setting. At the beginning of the experiment, subjects had the possibility to get used to the input controls (Wii-controller) by carrying out a tutorial. The tutorial contained an example scene made up of one ECA and three hotspots conveying dummy information. By performing the basic controls with the Wii-controller, the experimenter showed interaction possibilities. Afterward, participants were asked to maneuver within the scenery by themselves. They were told of the structure of interactive scenes and the purpose of information hotspots. Next, the stimulus was initialized by loading the required scenery. The scenery contained one ECA showing one out of four basic emotions, and three information hotspots incorporating descriptions of an emotion-eliciting situation divided into three information chunks (study 3). Participants observed the facial expressions and entered hotspot areas to read the situation-related information. As in scenarios 1 and 2, the experimenter handed out the AttrakDiff to subjects after the observation task.

Twenty participants took part in the study, 9 female and 11 male aged between 21 and 54 years (M = 31.8).

10.4 Results

We present the findings according to the three hypotheses:

(H1) The overall user experience in the interactive situation is higher than the user experience in animation scenario and the still scenario.

The evaluation of how users experience the various emotional stimuli in the varying conditions showed that the overall user experience in the interactive situation is rated at a higher level by users than in the animation scenario and still scenario (see Fig. 10.2). Comparing the overall judgment on the hedonic quality (HQ) of the users with a factor analysis shows that users rate the interactive scenarios presenting emotions as higher (M = 0.81, SD = 0.95) than for the still (M = 0.24, SD = 0.78) and the animated scenarios (M = 0.29, SD = 0.89). The post hoc analysis shows that the HQ is significantly different for the interactive scenario compared to the still scenario (LSD = 0.51, p = 0.01) and the animated scenario (LSD = 0.57, p = 0.04). We can conclude that emotions that are presented in an interactive setting lead to a higher user experience.

(H2) The animation scenario in terms of user experience is rated higher than the still scenario.

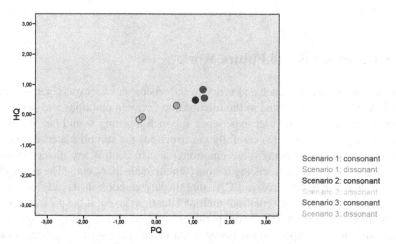

Fig. 10.2 Results of the AttrakDiff: overview of values concerning the hedonic and pragmatic quality of the three employed scenarios (consonant/dissonant)

Comparing still and animated scenario, no significant difference could be found. The animated scenario is thus not contributing to a positive user experience in the setting. The employment of animation in stimuli did not have the anticipated positive effect on UX.

> (H3) The perceived user experience will be higher for consonant settings than for settings with dissonant stimuli.

Overall, the perceived user experience is rated different for consonant and dissonant settings. The ANOVA performed showed significant differences for consonant and dissonant settings ($F = 13.6$, $p < 0.000$).

Looking into the differences in more detail, a second ANOVA showed that all scenarios were rated significantly different in terms of hedonic quality (HQ) ($F = 5.25$, $p < 0.000$), as well as for attractiveness ($F = 9.16$, $p < 0.000$) and pragmatic quality ($F = 14.23$, $p < 0.000$). Figure 10.2 shows these results in more detail: showing higher ratings for consonant scenarios (upper right) and lower ratings for dissonant scenarios (lower left). The interactive scenario is rated best in both conditions.

The type of the presentation medium is heavily influencing the overall user experience in which an emotional stimulus is shown (in this case, a facial expressions of an ECA). For research on emotional aspects in psychology, it can be concluded that the context description can have a significant influence on how an emotion is perceived, as well as the scenario the stimuli are presented in.

For the games industry, the user experience in terms of facial expression of ECAs can be enhanced by providing consonant stimuli (consonant facial expression and description) and allowing direct interaction with the ECA (not only still or animated sequences).

10.5 Conclusions and Future Work

Investigating user experience and possible influences on user experience is a difficult task. We were interested in the relationship between emotions and perception of emotions and how the user experience for such a setting would be. To investigate this aspect, we (had to) carefully construct(ed) the stimuli material (emotion descriptions, ECAs showing these emotions) and to control any unwanted influences balanced various influencing factors (female/male ECA, etc.). The experiment showed that people do perceive ECAs that display emotion differently depending on the context description (emotion-eliciting situation) given. If the presented material is consonant, the overall user experience is higher, if the presented material is dissonant, the user experience is lower (even negative). User experience can thus be influenced (and can be designed positively in a game) giving congruent information in form of (written) scenario and presented emotions of the ECA. Second, user experience is not higher for semi-animated facial expressions. In general, user experience is higher for interactive settings. The implications of this first results show that investment in small animations (for improving still images presenting emotions) is not improving the user experience, except the user is allowed to interact with the ECA. Creators in the games domain are interested in establishing an entertaining and intense gaming experience for their audience. A lot of production time is spent on creating realistic characters in detailed environments. Most situational aspects are defined without any theoretical foundation by focusing on artistic procedures. The work should show the necessity to relate to character-based communication channels (such as facial expression) with the current event the player confronts.

From the methodological perspective on how to evaluate user experience in games, we can summarize that experiments are one way to better understand the more general aspects of UX in games. As user experience is consisting of a wide variety of factors, it is difficult to find an experimental setup limiting the possible influencing experimental components. A careful experimental setup (including many prestudies) is thus a long process, and results for influencing factors on user experience are not immediately available. In general, experiments are a necessary means to understand the scientific basics of user experience, for an industrial context this kind of methodology might not be applicable. On a long-term basis, we see this kind of experiments as a necessary means to lay the foundations for understanding user experience.

References

Bailenson JN (2008) Avatars. http://www.stanford.edu/~bailenso/papers/avatars.pdf. Accessed 22 May 2008.

Bartneck C (2000) Affective expressions of machines. Master's Thesis, Stan Ackerman Institute – III, Eindhoven, Netherlands.

Bates J (1994) The role of emotion in believable agents. Communications of the ACM 37(7): 122–125.

Bernhaupt R, Boldt A, Mirlacher T et al. (2007) Using emotion in games: Emotional flowers. In: Proceedings of ACE 2007, ACM, New York, pp. 41–48.

Bernhaupt R, Ijsselsteijn W, Mueller F, Tscheligi M, Wixon D (2008) Evaluating user experiences in games. In: Proceedings of CHI 2008, ACM, New York, pp.3905–3908.

Bernhaupt R, Palanque P, Winkler M, Navarre D (2007) Model-based evaluation: A new way to support usability evaluation of multimodal interactive applications. In: Law E et al. (eds) Maturing Usability: Quality in Software, Interaction and Value. Springer, London, pp. 95–127.

Bernhaupt R, Sloo D, Migos C, Darnell M (2008) Towards new forms of iTV user experience. Workshop During EuroiTV 2008, 2nd July 2008, Adjunct Proceedings of EuroiTV 2008.

Bickmore T, Cassell J (2001) Relational agents: A model and implementation of building user trust. In: Proceedings of CHI 2001, ACM Press, New York.

Branco P (2003) Emotional interaction. In: Proceedings of CHI 2003, ACM, New York, pp. 676–677.

Cassell J (2008) Justin cassell: Research. http://www.soc.northwestern.edu/justine/jc_research.htm. Accessed 8 May 2008.

Cornelius RR (1996) The Science of Emotion: Research and Tradition in the Psychology of Emotions. Prentice Hall, Upper Saddle River, NJ.

Crane EA, Shami NS, Peter C (2007) Let's get emotional: Emotion research in human computer interaction. In: Proceedings of CHI 2007, ACM, New York, pp. 2101–2104.

Desmet P, Hekkert P (2002) Pleasure with Products, Beyond Usability, Chapter: The Basis of Product Emotions. Taylor Francis, London, pp. 60–68.

Dix A, Finlay J, Abowd G, Beale R (2004) Human–Computer Interaction. Prentice Hall, Essex, England.

Ekman P, Friesen W (1972) Emotion in the Human Face: Guidelines for Research and an Integration of Findings. Pergamon Press, New York.

Elliott C, Brzezinski J (1998) Autonomous agents as synthetic characters. AI Magazine 19(2): 13–30.

Ermi L, Mäyrä F (2005) Challenges for pervasive mobile game design: Examining players' emotional responses. In: Proceedings of ACE 2005, ACM, New York, pp. 371–372.

Fernandez-Dols JM, Carroll JM (1997) Is the meaning perceived in facial expression independent from its context. In: Russell JA, Fernandez-Dols JM (eds) The Psychology of Facial Expression (Studies in Emotion and Social Interaction). Cambridge University Press, New York, pp. 275–295.

Fischer L, Brauns D, Belschak F (2002) Zur Messung von Emotionen in der angewandten Forschung: Analysen mit den SAMs: Self-Assessment-Manikin. Pabst Science Publishers, Göttingen.

Hassenzahl M, Burmester M, Koller F (2003) AttrakDiff: Ein Fragebogen zur Messung wahrgenommener hedonischer und pragmatischer Qualität. In: Ziegler J, Szwillus G (eds) Mensch & Computer 2003. Interaktion in Bewegung. BG Teubner, Stuttgart, pp. 187–196.

Hassenzahl M, Tractinsky N (2006) User experience – A research agenda. Behaviour & Information Technology 25(2): 91–97.

ISEAR (2008) http://www.unige.ch/fapse/emotion/databanks/isear.html . Accessed 4 April 2009.

Isbister K (2006) Better Game Characters by Design: A Psychological Approach (The Morgan Kaufmann Series in Interactive 3D Technology). Morgan Kaufmann Publisher, San Francisco, CA.

Jaimes A, Sebe N (2007) Multimodal human-computer interaction: A survey. Computer Vision and Image Understanding 108(1–2): 116–134.

Law EL, Vermeeren AP, Hassenzahl M, Blythe M (2007) Towards a UX manifesto. In *Proceedings of the 21st British HCI Group Annual Conference on HCI 2008: People and Computers Xxi: Hci. But Not As We Know It - Volume 2* (University of Lancaster, United Kingdom, September 03–07, 2007). British Computer Society Conference on Human-Computer Interaction. British Computer Society, Swinton, UK, pp. 205–206.

Lee J, Marsella S (2006) Nonverbal behavior generator for embodied conversational agents. In: Lecture Notes in Computer Science: Intelligent Virtual Agents. Springer, Berlin/Heidelberg, pp. 243–255.

Lieberman H (1997) Autonomous interface agents. In: Proceedings of CHI 1997 ACM, New York, pp. 67–74.

Lime (2008) Lime surveyor. http:// www.limesurvey.org . Accessed 27 September 2008.

Mahlke S (2005) Studying affect and emotions as important parts of the user experience. http://www.emotion-inhci.net/workshopHCI2005/Mahlke_StudyingAffectAndEmotionsAs ImportantPartsOfTheUserExperience.pdf. Accessed 28 February 2008.

Mancini M, Hartmann B, Pelachaud C (2004) Non-verbal behaviors expressivity and their representation. http://pfstar.itc.it/public/doc/deliverables/pelachaud_tech_rep3.pdf . Accessed 10 February 2007.

Mandryk RL, Atkins MS, Inkpen KM (2006) A continuous and objective evaluation of emotional experience with interactive play environments. In: Proceedings of CHI 2006. ACM, New York, pp. 1027–1036.

Minge M (2005) Methoden zur Erhebung emotionaler Aspekte bei der Interaktion mit technischen Systemen. Master's Thesis, FREIE UNIVERSITÄT BERLIN Fachbereich Erziehungswissenschaften und Psychologie.

Norman D (2002) Emotion and design: Attractive things work better. Interactions 9(4): 36–42.

Picard RW (1997) Affective Computing. MIT Press, Cambridge, MA.

Picard RW, Wexelblatt A, Nass CI (2002) Future interfaces: Social and emotional. In: Proceedings of CHI 2002 ACM, New York, pp. 698–699.

Prendinger H, Ishizuka M (2004) Life-Like Characters: Tools, Affective Functions, and Applications. Springer, Heidelberg.

Pruett C (2008) The evolution of videogames. http://bcis.pacificu.edu/journal / 2003/07/pruett.php Accessed 5 April 2008.

Ravaja N, Saari T, Turpeinen M, Laarni J, Salminen M, Kivikangas M (2006) Spatial presence and emotions during video game playing: Does it matter with whom you play? Presence: Teleoperators and Virtual Environments 15(4): 381–392.

Reeves B, Nass C (2003) The Media Equation. The University of Chicago Press, Chicago, IL.

Roto V, Rautava M (2008) User experience elements and brand promise. http://research.nokia.com/ files/UXelements-v2.pdf. Accessed 5 April 2009.

Russell JA, Fernandez-Dols JM (1997) What does facial expressions mean. In: JA Russell and JM Fernandez-Dols (eds) Psychology of Facial Expression (Studies in Emotion and Social Interaction), Chapter Introduction. Cambridge University Press, New York, NY, pp. 3–31.

Scherer KR, Wranik T, Sangsue J et al. (2004) Emotions in everyday life: Probability of occurrence, risk factors, appraisal and reaction patterns. Social Science Information 43(4): 499–570.

Suk HJ (2006) Color and emotion: A study on the affective judgment of color across media and in relation to visual stimuli. PhD Thesis, Sozialwissenschaften der Universität, Mannheim.

Summerfield A, Green EJ (1986) Experiencing Emotion: A Cross-Cultural Study. Cambridge University Press, Cambridge, MA.

Wallbott HG (1990) Mimik im Kontext. Verlag für Psychologie, Dr. C. J. Hogrefe, Göttingen.

Part IV
User Experience – Evaluating Special Aspects of Games

Chapter 11
Evaluating Exertion Games

Florian 'Floyd' Mueller and Nadia Bianchi-Berthouze

Abstract Games that demand exertion of the players through bodily movements are experiencing increasing commercial success and have been attributed with many physical, mental and social benefits, thus changing the way we play computer games. However, there is a lack of understanding of how to evaluate such exertion games, mainly because the games' facilitated bodily movements are believed to be responsible for these novel experiences, but are not considered in traditional evaluation methods that primarily assume keyboard- and gamepad-style input devices. We do not believe there is a generic approach to evaluating exertion games, and therefore offer an overview of our mixed experiences in using various methods to guide the reader for future evaluations in this domain. We support the presented methods with data from case studies we undertook in order to illustrate their use and what kinds of results to expect. Methods that we have not had experience with, but which also have the potential to address the contribution of bodily involvement to the user experience, are also outlined. By identifying remaining issues in regards to evaluation methods for exertion games, we aim to provide an informed way forward for research in this area. With our work, we hope to contribute towards the advancement of such games, fostering their many benefits towards a more positive user experience.

11.1 Introduction

Gamers have recently seen the explosion of a new gaming genre that has been labelled exergaming or exertion games, which describes the emerging computer game titles that combine exerting bodily movements with computer gaming. Inspired by the success of Dance Dance Revolution, EyeToy and the Wii, computer

F. Mueller (✉)
Interaction Design Group, Department of Information Systems, The University of Melbourne, Melbourne, Australia
e-mail: floyd@floydmueller.com

R. Bernhaupt (ed.), *Evaluating User Experience in Games*, Human-Computer Interaction Series, DOI 10.1007/978-1-84882-963-3_11,
© Springer-Verlag London Limited 2010

game companies are excited about the potential of embracing physical activities in their games. Exertion games, defined as computer games that require intense physical effort from their players (Mueller et al. 2003), are believed to be able to work against the prevailing computer gaming image of facilitating the modern world's sedentary lifestyles. The use of the Wiimote and the Wii Fit by gamers to address their personal weight goals has made worldwide headlines (DeLorenzo 2007) and influenced game companies to release more interactive fitness games. Clinicians have discovered the potential of such games to address the obesity epidemic and are conducting studies to test these games' effectiveness in motivating gamers, especially children and teenagers, to incorporate more physical exercise into their daily lives by engaging them through exertion game play (Graves et al. 2007). They have also discovered the use of exertion games for rehabilitation purposes to make traditionally repetitive boring exercise tasks more fun (LeBlanc 2008, Powell 2008). These exertion games are also attracting new audiences that have previously not been catered for, offering a transition in the user experience from "high-score chasing" gaming to "party-fun", especially Nintendo Wii's bowling seems to be attractive to seniors, who organise championships in their nursing homes (Clark 2008). This new trend in gaming might ultimately challenge our understanding of the previously distinct terms of computer game, sports and exercise: The Dance Dance Revolution game, a computer game that requires exhausting jumping on dance pads, has recently been recognised as an official dance sport in Finland (Well-being Field Report), and "Sports over a Distance" applications have enabled sportive exercise between geographically distant locations (Mueller et al. 2007). Several research studies have added weight to anecdotally reported physical, mental and social health benefits (Lieberman 2006, Graves et al. 2007, Wakkary et al. 2008, Bianchi-Berthouze et al. 2007, Eriksson et al. 2007), and their proliferation appears to contribute to an understanding that these exertion games have the ability to introduce a new era in the history of computer gaming that changes the perspective for players, developers and even spectators in regards to how we see computer gaming, opening doors for new opportunities previously not imaginable.

Being able to understand what makes players engage in such exertion games could result in improved experiences (Bianchi-Berthouze et al. 2007), but also increased energy expenditure, and hence enhanced fitness (Bogost 2005), resulting in a healthier population that also benefits from mental and social benefits facilitated by these games. Studies on recreational physical activity (Wankel 1985) for non-athletes have indeed shown that flow, i.e. a form of optimal experience (Csikszentmihalyi 1990), is an important and relevant factor in maintaining the level of motivation high and reducing dropout. However, what is currently missing is an understanding of how such games should be evaluated to improve the user experience (Hoysniemi 2006). Traditional approaches to evaluating the user experience in games can fall short in providing a complete story of the user experience when it comes to exertion: Exertion games offer opportunities that mouse- and gamepad-controlled games lack, and not considering the unique aspects of exertion in such games might result in evaluation work that does not provide a complete picture of the user experience, ultimately failing in contributing towards the advancement of such games. In order to contribute to the success of exertion games, researchers and practitioners need to have an understanding not only of the opportunities but also of the challenges that arise when evaluating user experiences in exertion games. The purpose of this chapter is to contribute to this understanding.

We do not believe there is a generic approach to evaluating exertion games, and therefore offer an overview of our experiences in using various methods in order to provide the reader with a personal account that can serve as guide for future evaluations in this domain. We detail specific aspects user experience researchers and practitioners might encounter based on our results of evaluating exertion games using a range of methods. Our stories are based on over 5 years experience in designing, developing and evaluating exertion games, and we refer back when appropriate to our original work to offer the reader concrete examples, supplemented with empirical evaluation data, to offer insights into our work. The aim is to provide the interested practitioner with guidance based on completed evaluation tasks of exertion games, supplemented with some practical examples of "lessons learned". Furthermore, we hope our work can provide researchers with inspiration for further investigations into this area by contributing to an understanding of how to approach the task of evaluating such games. We conclude by suggesting a research agenda for future work on the topic of evaluating the user experience of exertion games and provide an outlook on what challenges lie ahead. With our work, we hope to contribute towards the advancement of such games, fostering their many benefits towards a more positive user experience.

11.2 Approach

Prior work has acknowledged that the evaluations of exertion games can benefit from methods that consider and accommodate for the unique characteristics of exertion games in their evaluation task design (Hoysniemi 2006). However, there is a limited understanding of what opportunities exist for the design of evaluation tasks and what shortcomings need to be considered when evaluating user experiences in such games. This lack of a comprehensive understanding of the challenges exertion brings to the evaluation process can hinder the advancement of these games, and therefore limit the benefits they can offer to their users. Our work addresses this shortcoming by exploring how the user experience in exertion games can be evaluated based on our experiences of evaluating these games and informed by our results. Our approach begins with detailing our evaluation experiences of a diverse set of existing commercial and prototypal gaming systems. Based on the game under investigation, we have chosen different evaluation approaches, which we subsequently improved and refined. We highlight personal experiences we gained from evaluating these games and provide insights into the shortcomings of some of the methods we used, a summary of which is given in Table 11.1. We also describe opportunities for further research that arose out of particular instances. Furthermore, we provide an opinioned commentary that is aimed at giving the reader a critical view of what to expect in their evaluation tasks when faced with an exertion game. Also, by describing our results, we hope to offer guidance when there is a need to choose between several methods.

Table 11.1 Summary of case studies, outcomes and challenges in evaluating post-playing and in-place user experience

Case studies	Approaches	Outcomes	Challenges
Table Tennis for Three: single condition	Semi-structured interviews, observations and coding of video data	Exertion facilitates social play in and outside game play, e.g. fosters the recollection of the experience through kinesthetic stimulation	(a) How to define coding systems? (b) How to overcome the fact that re-enacting can bring players to reinterpret their experience?
Breakout for two: exertion vs. non-exertion condition	Prisoner's dilemma and questionnaires	Exertion stimulates competition, connectedness	These measures overcome the limitations of self-reports but they are indirect
Donkey Konga: exertion vs. non-exertion conditions	Quantitative comparison of verbal and non-verbal behaviours	Exertion facilitates empathic behaviour in cooperative games: increase social interaction and emotional experience	How to define coding systems that produce high inter-rater reliability?
Guitar Hero: exertion vs. non-exertion conditions	Quantitative analysis of movement by motion capture system	Exertion facilitates emotional experience and role-taking experience. Amount of movement of the player correlates with engagement	The automatic analysis of complex movements (e.g., pointing, shrugging) is technically challenging

We acknowledge that our approach cannot and is not intended to result in a comprehensive list of all available methods, nor describes every aspect of evaluation specific to exertion games. However, with our approach, we aim to focus on providing an experience-based account of what opportunities lie ahead in this exciting new field. We believe our experiences on this topic will give the reader an extensive, although not comprehensive, view from various perspectives, contributing to an understanding that can inspire and guide future investigations.

11.3 Evaluating User Experience Post-playing

We begin by describing evaluation methods that are based on the belief that the game experience can be (self-)assessed after it has occurred, for example by interviewing the participants immediately after playing. Such approaches have the advantage that they leave the experience unaltered, as they separate the experience from the evaluation process not only temporally, but also often physically. We start with interviews, as they are also often used in non-exertion games and are a familiar tool; however, we describe what purpose they serve in contributing to our understanding of exertion games.

11.3.1 Interviews

For most of our experiments, we conducted semi-structured interviews with the participants after the gaming action. We have also videotaped these interviews, and we now describe our experiences with this method based on one particular case study. We selected this case study as it offered some unique insights into the social aspects of exertion games, as the players were geographically distant, connected only over a computer network. (We present a collocated exertion game study that also included interviews further below, but report on a different method there.)

Case study: Table Tennis for Three. We have conducted semi-structured interviews in an attempt to qualitatively analyse the social play in Table Tennis for Three. Table Tennis for Three is an exertion game that was inspired by table tennis, but can be played by three geographically distant participants. It uses a real bat and ball on a modified table tennis table that detects the ball's impact in order to modify virtual game content, projected onto the playing surface and augmented with a videoconferencing component to support a social aspect amongst the participants. A detailed description of the system can be read here (Mueller and Gibbs 2007a, Mueller and Gibbs 2007b), and the evaluation process is described here (Mueller and Gibbs 2007b). After having played the game, the participants were interviewed in one room together. The video recordings of the interviews were coded using qualitative analysis software. This approach revealed an interesting aspect specific to exertion games, which we aim to sensitise other researchers to, as it might affect the evaluation process. However, we begin by describing the study design.

Experimental setup. Forty-two participants were recruited and asked in the advertising material to organise themselves preferably in teams of three. If they were unable to do so, we matched them up randomly with other participants in order to have always three people participating at the same time. We had one last minute cancellation; in this case, we replaced the third player with a participant who had played previously, hence we report on 41 distinct participants. The participants were between 21 and 55 years old (arithmetic mean 32 years), whereas 27 were male and 14 female. After each group of three participants played for at least 30 min, they were brought together into the same room after the game, where we conducted semi-structured interviews with all three of them together. The interviews lasted from 20 to 60 min and included open-ended questions about their experience and their interactions with the other players. We took notes during the interviews as well as videotaped each session. We analysed the video data using a coding process based on grounded theory (Strauss and Corbin 1998), with the help of a database for all the video data. An iterative coding process was used to identify important themes and ideas. We also used the notes and created affinity diagrams to further refine our concepts.

Analysis and discussion. The joyful atmosphere of the exertion game carried over to the interviews, which appeared to be facilitated by the use of bodily actions as exhibited during the game by the participants. For example, players used movements not only in relation to play directly, such as throwing their hands in the air to indicate they won. A player jokingly made a fist to the other players; another participant put her tongue out. Players often applauded others on their performance, and the joyful atmosphere seemed to have carried over into the interviews. Players used their bodies to retell their experiences, and the video recordings were viable tools in capturing this retelling. For example, one team patted on each other's shoulders and slapped each other comradely several times during the interview. Another team initiated a group hug.

In addition to the theoretical concepts we identified as part of the investigation of Table Tennis for Three, we found the aspect of bodily movements facilitated by the exertion game that carried over to a retelling in the interviews particularly intriguing for an understanding of user experiences in games. Such a retelling is an element of metagaming, a social play phenomenon that refers to the relationship of a game to elements outside of the game. One way that metagaming occurs "during a game other than the game itself. . . are social factors such as competition and camaraderie" (Salen and Zimmerman 2003). The participants in Table Tennis for Three used this to turn the interview into a metagaming event by verbally and non-verbally commenting on the other players' performance and turning the post-game into a social spectacle. The retelling of what happened in a game is an important part of a "lived experience" (McCarthy and Wright 2004). Players predominantly used their exertion skills in the games, so they drew on these skills again during the reliving of the experience. This reliving of a "pleasurable kinesthetic stimulation" has been suggested to re-trigger the associated pleasurable emotions (Iso-Ahola and Hatfield 1986). Re-enacting the exertion movements can also support the players' cognitive processes, helping them to remember certain parts of the game (Lindley and Monk 2008). Players gave further meaning to these exertion actions by sharing them with others, the opportunity for metagaming provided by the interview task therefore contributed towards a meaningful social play experience. In contrast, the exertion actions supporting metagaming are missing in keyboard- and gamepad-controlled computer games, and the players have to rely on their cognitive skills to remember their experiences and associated affective responses. Furthermore, Moen (2006) believes that movement literacy can be improved not only by physically exploring movement, as our players did during game play, but also by verbally reflecting on it, which they did through the interviews. This suggests that the interview task might have contributed to the participants' movement literacy.

Our observations during post-game interviews suggest implications for evaluation methods used in exertion games. Researchers need to be aware that retelling, in particular as part of metagaming, is an important aspect of the user experience, and players will use opportunities to enable such an experience. We believe user experience researchers should be aware of such effects in order to be able to consider them in their experimental designs and be sensitive towards them during the interview process. If the game to be investigated features exertion actions, researchers should anticipate that bodily movements will play a role in the interview process as well. Any capturing should accommodate for this: We valued the use of video, as a traditional audio-only recording and analysis would have neglected the bodily actions we observed, which revealed valuable insights into the game experience.

11.3.2 Prisoner's Dilemma Task

We now report on our findings on a distributed soccer-like game called Breakout for Two (Mueller et al. 2003) that allows two participants to engage in a ball sports activity although being apart. In the accompanied study, we were interested in understanding if the required exertion to play the game has an effect on the sense of connectedness between the participants, and hence compared the exertion game with a similar game that is played with a keyboard. We present an element of a larger evaluation study: a Prisoner's Dilemma task.

Measuring social effects between participants based on short periods of gaming activity can be difficult, as many outside factors such as personality types and situational context can affect social behaviour. Social interaction is one aspect of it, but even measuring this is not trivial: Humans use many cues to express social needs, and a comprehensive account of all social elements within human communication is an almost insurmountable task. The Breakout for Two study consequently focused on investigating whether the system could facilitate a sense of trust between the participants. This sense of trust was probed with a variation of a Prisoner's Dilemma task (Palameta and Brown 1999). A between-subjects experimental design tested the effects of the exertion game on performance in the Prisoner's Dilemma task in comparison with a non-exertion version of the game. There are many interpretations and alteration of the traditional Prisoner's Dilemma task; however, they mostly follow the same principle. The variation used in the study requires to make a decision based on another person's decision; however, their decision is not accessible when the decision needs to be made, because the participants cannot communicate during the process. Such a task is a commonly used measure of trust and cooperation, and multi-round Prisoner's Dilemma tasks have been successfully used to assess levels of trust established between participants in remote locations (Zheng et al. 2002, Zheng et al. 2001, Rocco 1998).

Case study: Breakout for Two. Facilitating exertion as part of a gaming experience is believed to positively influence social factors between the participants. The case study of Breakout for Two was designed to investigate if the positive effects on sociality transfer to mediated communication scenarios; in other words, does the addition of an exertion interface still facilitate social benefits even if the players can only interact with one another over a videoconference? The research answered this by conducting a study that allowed distributed players to exert themselves with a physical ball that was the interface to a shared virtual game: The players had to kick the ball at certain targets before the other player did, and these targets were interconnected over the network. The players could comment on each other's play and see their progress through an integrated large-scale videoconference. The winner was the player who hit the ball the hardest and most accurately, thereby scoring the most points.

Experimental setup. Fifty-six volunteers were recruited through flyers and email postings at local universities, sports clubs and youth hostels. The average age of the participants was 26, the youngest being 17 and the oldest 44. Thirty-four volunteers were asked to play the physical game and 22 played the non-exertion, keyboard-controlled game. Seventy-seven percent of the participants were male in the exertion group, 64% in the non-exertion group. This equal distribution was not deliberate, but opportune. After the participants played Breakout for Two, they were escorted to a different area where they could not see nor hear each other. They were faced with written instructions, which explained that their task was to choose if they wanted to put a big X on the back of a sheet of paper or not. If both of the players chose not to put anything down, they would both receive an additional 5 Euros to their payment, in order to ponder their choice seriously. If only one of them would mark an X, this person would receive an additional 10 Euros, but if both of them would draw an X, they would receive nothing.

Analysis and discussion. In the exertion group, 15 players put an X on the back of their sheet (44%). This comprises 11 pairs where only one person put an X down (resulting in this person receiving an extra 10 Euros), 2 teams where both participants wrote an X (resulting in no extra payment) and 4 teams where both players left the page blank (resulting in an extra 5 Euros for each of them). In the non-exertion group, only five players put down an X (23%). In each case, their partner left the page blank, resulting in an extra 10 Euros payment for the first player. Six pairs put nothing down, receiving an additional 5 Euros each and no team had an X on both sheets.

We expected that the participants in the exertion condition would be more likely to cooperate in the Prisoner's Dilemma task than their non-exertion counterparts, based on the higher levels of connectedness that were recorded in the questionnaire survey and interviews within the same setup (Mueller 2002). It seems plausible to anticipate that participants who play a team sport are more likely to cooperate in a Prisoner's Dilemma task. After all, a correlation between sport and trust has been previously studied (Clark and Gronbegh 1987). However, the results showed that players were *less* likely to cooperate if they participated in the exertion game.

Further investigations with larger user numbers are necessary to shed light on this surprising result; however, we have a hunch about what have caused the players' reactions. We believe it could be speculated that the exertion component increased the competitive aspect of the game. The game in both conditions was identical in terms of its competitive element; however, investing bodily actions might have triggered the participants to "take it more seriously" and value the competitive aspect higher. In order to strengthen this claim, we would like to draw attention to the element of competition in traditional exertion sports games: Most sports are of a competitive nature, and almost all organised sports have provisions such as overtime or penalty shootouts to determine a winner, if not at the end of a game, at least at the end of the season. It seems competition and exertion go hand in hand; however, this does not imply that physical games cannot foster non-competition: Collaborative physical games experienced a high in the 1970s as the New Games movement and augmented derivatives exist (Lantz 2006). However, these games have slowly faded and lack the widespread success of competitive sports.

Reflecting upon the pervasive role of competition in traditional exertion sports, it could be hypothesised that the introduction of exertion activity in a game context amplifies any competitive element. This is underlined by anecdotal incidents observed during game play, in which some participants appear to become "more into it" and were more eager to win once they have achieved a certain level of exertion. This would extend the findings that exertion can amplify competiveness by a virtual game play component. However, further empirical research is needed to investigate whether augmented exertion can amplify any competitive aspect in games.

We are aware that a Prisoner's Dilemma task does not measure user experience in games per se. However, our investigation demonstrates that using such a task to test for social effects as an outcome of exertion gaming has its caveats. In particular, it leads to the speculation that exertion can amplify competitive notions developed during game play. If further research confirms this assumption, this can have implications on how to evaluate competitive games in which the bodies are involved, whether the evaluation includes a Prisoner's Dilemma or any other task, as the investigated concept, here trust, might be skewed by the altered competitiveness that the exertion aspect facilitated.

11.3.3 Questionnaire

Finally, we conclude this section by discussing the use of questionnaire to gather data for evaluation purposes since this approach is a common practice and has been increasingly used for an understanding of games as well. As part of our research, we have also used questionnaires and have acquired experience from using established questions. We have also developed our own set of questions to gather data depending on the context, research question and study design we faced. Although questionnaires may seem to be a generic tool for evaluating user experience, and its use for exertion games might not appear to require any specific attention, we have observed that using questionnaires within the context of exertion games can pose some interesting caveats that we believe researchers should be aware of in order to account for them in their analysis.

One aspect that makes the use of questionnaires particular in the context of exertion games is related but not identical to the critique of using questionnaires for games in general. The use of questionnaires for evaluating user experience has been criticised for its inadequacy of capturing a user state during the game, as players answer questions regarding their experience after they have played the game, "outside" their immediate engagement with it, a critique in common with post-interviews. The participants need to divert their focus of attention to the evaluation task, diverting from the experience; the same experience they are now asked to self-assess. This criticism is common amongst questionnaire approaches, whether the game facilitates exertion or not. However, if the players exerted themselves as part of the game play, several factors influence their answers in ways different to a keyboard or gamepad experience: First, as exertion games are believed to facilitate more emotional play (Bianchi-Berthouze et al. 2007), these affected states of emotions could influence the assessment players give, in particular if the questions are asked immediately after the game. We acknowledge that these altered emotional states could be a desired effect of the game, worth capturing in the evaluation process; however, we want to point out that researchers should be aware that the emotional change could occur not only from the game content, but also from the physical exertion the game facilitates, which might have different implications for the analysis. Second, a possibly lower recovery curve from a heightened state of arousal based on exertion might affect an effective comparison with non-exertion game data. To explain: The emotions facilitated by the involvement of the body interact with the physiological functions of the body in a bidirectional relationship, and it has been suggested that this relationship can affect the emotional engagement with the game for longer than in a traditional non-exertion game, in which the engagement is mainly regulated by cognitive functions (Lehrer 2006). This prolonged engagement with the game is not limited to emotional aspects, for example in our investigations of Breakout for Two (Mueller et al. 2003), we have observed that players needed a break to physically recover from the activity before they were able to fill out a questionnaire. This suggests that the exertion aspect can affect the time between the game experience and answering questions, possibly altering the recall capability of the experience. Furthermore, research has shown that cognitive functions are improved after exercise (Ratey 2008), which might also impact upon how the subjects answer, independent from the experience under investigation. These potential effects do not eradicate the use of questionnaires as evaluation method for exertion games, but researchers might benefit from being aware of these potential influences that are quite different than what is expected in traditional questionnaire experiences in order to address them in their evaluation design.

11.4 Evaluating User Experience In-Place

In the previous sections, we have focused on methods that rely on data gathered after the gaming action. We are now describing our experiences with directly observing exertion actions while they are taking place. We focus on how the analysis of participants' non-verbal behaviour can give insights into their experience, in particular, we describe how it helped us to quantify and reason about the effect of a game's design on social and emotional experiences.

11.4.1 Coding Body Movement

Case study: Donkey Konga. We carried out a study to investigate how the use of whole body game controllers would change the way players engage in a game (Lindley et al. 2008). An experiment was thus designed to observe and compare the behaviour of players playing the same game but using different types of controllers: controllers that require only finger movement to control the game and controllers that require larger body movement.

Experimental setup. Levels of engagement and the degree of emotional and social interactions between players were explored in a game of Donkey Konga (Lindley et al. 2008). The input devices were bongos and a standard dual-pad controller. When bongos were used, players were encouraged to tap the bongos and clap their hands in time with the music; when the dual-pad controller was used, these actions were performed through button pressed using fingers and thumbs. We are aware that playing augmented bongos does not necessarily result in intense physical exhaustion; however, the involved body movements and their reliance on rhythmic coordinated kinesthetic actions have many characteristics similar to sportive behaviour and have been previously compared to exertion games (Bogost 2005), and hence the results should be able to contribute to an understanding of movement-based activities in general.

Ten pairs of participants were asked to play in both conditions, and the order of the two conditions was counterbalanced across the pairs. Being all beginners, the players played in two-player cooperative mode ("Duet") at the easiest skill setting. The playing sessions were videotaped and an existing engagement questionnaire (Chen et al. 2005) was used. The scores for the participants in each pair were summed. To measure the emotional and social engagements of the participants, their verbal and non-verbal behaviours were coded using the Autism Diagnostic Observation Schedule (Lord et al. 2000). We found this scheme particularly useful; however, other researchers seem to prefer Laban's notations, especially when concerned with dance-like movements (Loke et al. 2007). The length of time that each participant spent producing speech and other utterances was measured. Non-verbal behaviours were also classified according to two categories: Instrumental gestures were defined as those in which the action conveyed a clear meaning or directed attention (e.g., pointing, shrugging, and nods of the head); empathic gestures were defined as those in which the action was emotive (e.g., placing the hands to the mouth in shock). These gestures were selected as they indicate the players' social and emotional involvements.

Analysis and discussion: To understand the magnitude of the effect the body movements has on the players, a statistical analysis of the non-verbal and verbal behaviours was performed. Prior to this, scores on the game were compared across the two conditions to ensure that possible effects were not due to variations in performance. Wilcoxon's two-tailed matched-pairs signed-ranks test showed that the type of controller had no significant effect on performance ($Z = -0.889$, $p = 0.414$). All further differences were evaluated for statistical significance using Wilcoxon's one-tailed matched-pairs signed-ranks tests, with the pair as the sampling unit.

The participants produced more speech ($Z = -1.478$, $p = 0.08$) and significantly more other utterances ($Z = -2.599$, $p < 0.01$) when using the bongos. Participants also made significantly more instrumental ($Z = -1.895$, $p < 0.05$) and empathic ($Z = -2.5273$, $p < 0.01$) gestures when using the bongos rather than the wireless controller, lending further weight to the idea that there was more social interaction in this condition. The participants rated themselves as experiencing a significantly higher level of engagement ($Z = 2.803$, $p < 0.01$) when using the bongos (mean = 248.80, max score = 336, std. dev. = 23.03) rather than the wireless controller (mean = 198.50, max score = 336, std. dev. = 25.33).

This study has contributed to an understanding of the quality of engagement in the game. Whereas the engagement questionnaire informed us of a statistically significant higher level of engagement in the bongo condition, the players' behaviour informed us that the dynamics of the experience differed between the two conditions, an important implication for our understanding of how to evaluate such games. As shown by the number of instrumental gesture and utterances, players in the bongo condition were socially more interactive. It is important to note that the increased number of gestures cannot simply be accounted for by the fact that players have their hands free. They still need to use them to control the game (i.e., clapping and tapping). The fact that the number of emotional expressions (e.g., dancing) and emphatic gestures was statistically higher in the bongo condition compared with the traditional controller condition suggests that playing the bongos facilitated more emotional and social experiences. We believe our results can inform the choice of future evaluations, because they shed light on characteristics unique to exertion. For example, other measuring techniques, such as biosensors, might have captured emotional engagement and increased physical activity; however, we believe it is unlikely that they would have detected how the social and emotional interactions between players unfolded, a very important information for usability purposes. Whilst Mueller et al. (2003) have proposed that arousal associated with physical movement might support social interaction, Mandryk and Inkpen (2004) have shown that the presence of a friend results in higher engagement. Lindley and Monk (2008) have argued further that social behaviour and experience are intertwined to the extent that measures of conversation can be used to tap into unfolding experience. By affording realistic movements, the bongos may have facilitated a willing suspension of disbelief during game play, and their flexibility may have promoted enjoyment by encouraging clapping and dancing.

11.4.2 Automatically Coding Body Movement

In the previous section, we have shown how the statistical analysis of non-verbal and verbal behaviours enabled us to investigate the effect that changes in the design of a game's interface may have on the emotional and social experiences of the player. In this section, we discuss how this approach can be improved: We describe how such an analysis could be facilitated by using a motion capture system to obtain a more objective analysis of the behaviour and to reduce the amount of time necessary to analyse the captured video footage. To our knowledge, this is the first time such a device has been used to evaluate exertion gaming experiences.

Case study: Guitar Hero. Here, we present a study in which movement actions captured by using an exoskeleton were quantitatively analysed to understand the relation between movement and the level and quality of player engagement.

Experimental setup. Participants were asked to play Guitar Hero, a guitar simulation game for Sony's PlayStation (Hero). This game sees the player perform a song by pressing in sequence a number of colour-coded buttons on a guitar-shaped controller. Twenty players were randomly assigned to two different playing conditions. In one condition (called D hereafter), the guitar-shaped controller was used as a dual-pad controller, i.e. the participants were taught all of those features that are controlled solely with the hands (i.e., fret buttons, strut bar and whammy bar). In the second condition (called G hereafter), instead, the participants were informed that to gain "star power" they could make use of a tilt sensor in the neck of the guitar, i.e. by raising the guitar upward. The participants were fitted with a lightweight exoskeleton so as to provide angular measurements for each of the upper-body joints. In addition, a video camera was placed in front of them to record their body movements during play. After playing two rock songs (for about 10 min) at the beginner level, the player's engagement level was assessed using the previously mentioned engagement questionnaire.

The engagement scores were analysed using a t-test revealing that the G condition returned significantly higher engagement scores ($t = 5.123$, $p < 0.001$), thus suggesting that body movement imposed in the G condition affected the player's engagement level. To further clarify this finding, we correlated the engagement scores with the amount of motion measured with the motion capture system. We identified a negative correlation in the D condition and a positive correlation in the G condition.

Analysis and discussion. The results seem to indicate that the amount of movement could be a measure of engagement, at least for certain types of movement-based games. However, the amount of movement alone is not sufficient, as specific types of movements, e.g. fidgeting, could be an indication of boredom as reported in Bianchi-Berthouze et al. (2006). By analysing the video footage of this experiment, we observed that in condition G players displayed more, even if briefly, guitar-like player movements (e.g., dancing), showing a tendency to take over the role play offered by the game (e.g., being a rock-star). They also showed expressions of higher levels of arousal and positive experience, such as expressions of excitement. In condition D, players seemed more driven by a desire to win the game (hard fun), leading to an increased focus on the display and to emotional expressions of frustration when a mistake was made. They displayed more still behaviour and some rhythm-keeping foot behaviour that may have facilitated control of the game. The amount of movement that possibly contributed to a different type of engagement could be identified in more positive emotional expressions and movements that reflect the role the player assumes in the game. Even though in this study we were yet unable to automatically perform such an analysis, new tools for gesture and affective movements detection are becoming available, and a motion capture system could facilitate the capturing of these different types of behaviour automatically. Berthouze and colleagues (2003) proposed a low-level description of body posture and movement that enables the mapping of bodily expressions into emotion categories or emotion dimensions. By using low-level descriptions of posture, motion capture, and connectionist or statistical modelling techniques to these descriptions, they have suggested that mapping models can easily be adapted to detect different types of expressions irrespective of the context in which these expressions are displayed. Using this approach, they explored whether the style of play of the players could be a factor affecting the players' experience.

Although this study has only shown the use of simple measures of movement, the use of a motion capture system paves the way for more complex analyses of bodily movement. Furthermore, it might enhance our understanding of how the type of movements that the game either imposes or affords can affect the strategies adopted by players and hence the emotional and social experiences. The use of an exoskeleton could in fact facilitate the analysis of movement strategies (e.g., smooth and long movement vs. jerky and fast movement) (Pasch et al. 2008) and help produce movement measures that can be indicators of user experience. This approach is thus promising, as it offers a more objective way to measure movement. The use of motion capture devices to measure non-verbal behaviour is increasingly becoming available, but given the challenge gesture recognition technology still faces when dealing with unpredictable scenarios whereby the set of movements and gestures cannot be predefined, we believe this approach still needs to be used in connection with other measures such as video analysis when the meaning of movement needs to be interpreted.

11.5 Other Approaches of Evaluating Exertion Games

Other researchers have also been concerned with investigating user experience when evaluating interactive technology that involves exertion. However, most of the work evolved from a physiological perspective, primarily concerned with the physical health outcomes that result from participating in such experiences. When applied to gaming applications, these investigations mainly focus on any physical health effects that the game can facilitate, for example whether an exertion game can lead to weight loss (Graves et al. 2007, Tan et al. 2002). In order to shed light on the contribution the game makes to a physiological benefit, the exertion level of the player has been measured. We now describe a few approaches that are derived from these studies, but have potential to be useful and practical for evaluating user experience. Although mostly new to the context of games, we believe they hold promise for exertion games due to their special characteristics. The following outline is by no means comprehensive, but should give the reader a starting point for thought. We believe future investigations will shed light on our understanding of such approaches in the context of games, in particular when combined with more traditional methods.

11.5.1 Physiological Measurements

So far, we have highlighted how our work suggests that movement and engagement can be intertwined in exertion games. However, capturing objective movement might only tell one story: different people exert themselves differently when performing the same physical movement, depending on their fitness level and bodily capabilities. Physiological measurements could create a more objective measure as to how much exertion players invested into the game, possibly contributing to a more complete understanding of engagement and user experience. One cost-effective way of measuring a participant's exertion intensity is to use a heart rate monitor. Heart rate monitors are widely available, and a few models allow interfacing with a PC for subsequent analysis. Athletes and hobby sports people often use heart rate monitors in their training, hence study subjects can often already be familiar with such devices, and knowledge about their advantages and shortcomings is widely available. Human–computer interaction research has previously used heart rate monitors not only for measuring, but also for controlling games (Nenonen et al. 2007, Mandryk et al. 2006), furthering acceptance in the community through its pervasive use. Heart rate monitors are also small, lightweight and battery powered, making them suitable for mobile use (Mueller et al. 2007). They can provide physiological user data for little cost and are easy to administer; however, the type of exertion activity that is involved during the game play can determine its utility, as heart rate monitors are best utilised in aerobic activities. It should also be noted that a player's heart rate can be affected by other factors outside the game environment, too. Hart gives a few examples: Outside temperature, too much clothing or caffeine drinking can affect heart rate data (Hart 2003). If such data are not useable, researchers have suggested to use performance measurements to evaluate exertion activities, for example, through measurement devices in the participants' shoes or by using GPS data to track a player's movements (Mueller et al. 2007). We believe these approaches can, if supplemented with body data from the user, give insights into the energy expenditure during game play, contributing to a wider picture of game experience.

11.5.2 Borg's Perceived Exertion Scale

Another way of measuring a participant's exertion level is by using Borg's scale (1998), which aims to acquire the rate of perceived physical exertion by the participant. It is a simple scale, requiring no technical equipment, which was designed for athletes and sports coaches to be used to assess the intensity of training and competition. The Borg scale, or often referred to as "Rating of Perceived Exertion", is presented to the participant in form of a chart. The participant then has to select how hard she/he feels, she/he is working by giving a rating such as "Light" or "Maximal". The original scale has 21 points of exertion, but variations with less points exist (Hart 2003). The Borg scale has the advantage that it is easy to administer and understand by participants. It has also been demonstrated that the scale correlates well with more reliable indicators of exercise intensity such as blood lactate, VO2, ventilation and respiration rates, and it is also not affected by the environmental factors associated with skewed heart rate monitor data (see above). The results are subjective, however, and the players need to give their rating during or right after the exertion activity. For example, asking a subject during a treadmill-based game to rate her/his exertion level seems doable; however, chasing a player on a football pitch to acquire an intensity rating might seem impractical.

It should be noted, however, that such a focus on the outcome of the game experience, whether through heart rate monitors or Borg's scale, might aid in offering recommendations as to which exertion games support the most intense workout; however, they fall short in contributing to an understanding of whether and how the game facilitates an intrinsic motivation for the participants to play in the first place. Hence, we believe such approaches should not be used exclusively, but rather complement the methods we described in more detail above. By doing so, they might be able to contribute to a more complete story of the user experience in exertion games.

11.5.3 Evaluating Exertion Games Based on User Groups

We also would like to point the reader to the work by Höysniemi (2006), who describes the design and evaluation of physically interactive games she has been involved in designing herself. The author argues that different user groups can benefit from different evaluation methods and that the unique characteristics of exertion games demand a critical reflection on which method to choose. Next to interviews and questionnaires, she has used observational as well as Wizard-of-Oz and peer tutoring methods to evaluate exertion games. Similar to Loke et al. (2007), she has also attempted to describe the bodily movements exhibited in a game using dance-derived movement analysis. She selected specific methods depending on the user group, children, dancers or martial art athletes and argues that each has potential for unique insights.

11.5.4 Evaluating Using Blogs

As users have appropriated exertion games for their personal weight loss goals, it might be possible to use their self-reported progress reports to evaluate such games. For example, upon its release, the Nintendo Wii inspired many avid gamers who described themselves as reluctant exercisers to use the accompanied exertion games to increase their energy expenditure through gaming. Many of these gamers reported their progress in blogs (see for example, DeLorenzo 2007) and used the social support they gained from comments and page-view statistics as motivational tools. Although these data need to be trusted, the sheer amount of user data and worldwide availability could make such an approach an intriguing tool to evaluate games in terms of their effectiveness not only to reduce players' waistlines, but also to investigate any long-term effects to engage players, based on their dedication to report about it.

11.6 Future Challenges

Parts of our work involve affective notions of user experience and their relationships with exertion activity. Most often, emotional engagement with games is associated with increased bodily activity. An additional way forward to understanding this inter-relationship could be a view from the opposite direction: By examining the exertion component, researchers might be able to infer affective aspects from the gaming experience. This appears to be a valid approach, as bodily expressions are an important index of emotional experience. For example, past research has shown that body movement and posture can be an important modality in the human judgment of behavioural displays including affective states and moods (Argyle 1988, Bernhardt and Robinson 2008). Although most work in this area has focused on facial expressions (Ambady and Rosenthal 1992, Ekman and Rosenberg 2005), recent studies embraced a more body-centric approach and found that the perception of emotion is often biased towards the emotion expressed by the body (Meeren et al. 2005), meaning the inference of affective states through body posture in exertion games could yield improved results compared to facial-expression approaches. It should be noted, however, that unlike the recognition of facial expressions, which has been generally based on quantitative models that map pattern of muscle activation into emotions (e.g., Ekman and Rosenberg 2005), recognition of bodily expressions of emotions has long been mostly qualitative. Recent advances make the process of identifying emotions from basic movement and posture units more objective and measurable. For example, Berthouze et al. (Bianchi-Berthouze and Kleinsmith 2003, De Silva and Bianchi-Berthouze 2004) proposed a general description of posture based on angles and distances between body joints to support the mapping of body postures into emotions. Although such approaches might suffer from the general limitations of any automatic recognition systems, their ability to mature through a demand of supporting the creation of technology that can adapt to the affective states of the user can make them a powerful new avenue for evaluation.

11.7 Final Thoughts

We have described our work on the topic of evaluating user experiences of exertion games. We do not believe there is a generic approach to evaluating exertion games, and therefore we offered a diverse set of results with the intention to contribute towards an understanding of this new emerging area from varied viewpoints. By supporting our experience reports with concrete data from case studies, we hoped to be able to provide the reader with practical guidance on what kind of effects one can expect, which are unique to evaluating exertion games. Our aim was to provide a lively account in order to inspire researchers for further investigations into this area and present them with opportunities for future work encouraged by our results.

We have presented methods known from traditional evaluation tasks and described their different use in an exertion game setup. We found that whether asking a participant interview or questionnaire-style questions, any post-experience evaluation should take into account that the player will be exhausted after the game. The exertion activity demanded the investment of physical effort, and players can be expected to be out of breath, tired and in an altered emotional state. This altered state can show in many ways, and although mostly beneficial when it comes to the well-being of the player, it can also affect the evaluation task, an issue we believe researchers should be aware of in future studies. Evaluators should also be aware that motivation to play these exertion games can be facilitated not only through the game play, but also by an intrinsic drive to improve one's health: Many players have subscribed to a weight-loss goal and use their game as a more "fun" way to achieve this goal, instead of exercising in a traditional gym. The user experience might be affected if such an internal motivation is dampened by the weight scale not responding in the expected direction: It could be that the game facilitated increased energy expenditure; however, environmental factors outside the magic circle of the game (Salen and Zimmerman 2003) might have caused a weight gain. Gyms that use such exertion games to combine the advantages of engaging game play with the social aspects of working out in a dedicated space are emerging (XRtainment), and evaluating exertion games in such contexts is a new and exciting area that provides novel opportunities to understand these games with a holistic view on health and social aspects. Measuring physiological or bodily performance data might not only enhance our understanding of physical health implications, but also supplement results from other methods to help paint a more complete picture of the user experience. Making such data available to the user, for example through displaying the heart rate, could also contribute to the experience itself, as the users' intrinsic motivation might benefit from an immediate feedback showing the game "works" for their goals.

Using the body's actions to not only facilitate, but also understand affective experience is an exciting new area. Technological advances will contribute towards rapid evolvement of this field. Using the inter-relationship between affect and body movements for evaluation purposes not only might provide new opportunities for understanding how exertion games engage players, but also be used in other areas of human–computer interaction to create more affective-aware technology. Combining some of the other methods with their individual advantages will also contribute to being able to tell a story that gives justice to the many benefits exertion can offer to its players. By learning from past experiences and appreciating perspectives from various research views, an understanding of exertion games will unfold that, in turn, can offer an exciting new outlook on how we play and interact with technology. We hope with our work that we have contributed towards such advancement and we were able to excite other researchers to explore this emerging new field further.

Acknowledgements   Some of the case studies presented in this chapter have been supported by the Marie Curie International Re-Integration Grant "AffectME" (MIRG-CT-2006-046434). The authors also wish to acknowledge the role of Media Lab Europe and the MIT Media Lab in supporting initial work on Breakout for Two, together with Stefan Agamanolis, Rosalind Picard and Ted Selker. Thanks also to the University of Melbourne and CSIRO Collaborative Research Support Scheme in supporting initial development work on Table Tennis for Three. Special thanks to Martin R. Gibbs and Frank Vetere in the Interaction Design Group at the University of Melbourne.

References

Ambady N, Rosenthal R (1992) Thin slices of expressive behavior as predictors of interpersonal consequences: A meta-analysis. Psychological Bulletin 111: 256–274.

Argyle M (1988) Bodily Communication. Methuen, London.

Bernhardt D, Robinson P (2008) Interactive control of music using emotional body expressions. In: CHI '08 Extended Abstracts on Human Factors in Computing Systems, ACM, New York.

Bianchi-Berthouze N, Cairns P, Cox A, Jennett C, Kim WW (2006) On posture as a modality for expressing and recognizing emotions. Workshop on the Role of Emotion in HCI, HCI 2006.

Bianchi-Berthouze N, Kim W, Patel D (2007) Does body movement engage you more in digital game play? and why? Affective Computing and Intelligent Interaction.

Bianchi-Berthouze N, Kleinsmith A (2003) A categorical approach to affective gesture recognition. Connection Science 15: 259–269.

Bogost I (2005) The rhetoric of exergaming. Digital Arts and Cultures (DAC) Conference, Denmark.

Borg G (1998) Borg's Perceived Exertion and Pain Scales. Human Kinetics, Champaign, IL.

Chen M, Kolko B, Cuddihy E, Medina E (2005) Modelling and measuring engagement in computer games. Presentation at the Annual Conference for the Digital Games Research Association (DiGRA), Vancouver, Canada.

Clark R (2008) Seniors trump barriers in Wii bowling tourney. http://www.nj.com/sunbeam/index.ssf?/base/news-4/1222587621327110.xml&coll=9. Accessed 20 April 2009.

Clark M, Gronbegh E (1987) The effect of age, sex and participation in age group athletics on the development of trust in children. International Journal of Sport Psychology 18: 181–187.

Csikszentmihalyi M (1990) Flow: The Psychology of Optimal Performance. Harper and Row, New York.

De Silva PR, Bianchi-Berthouze N (2004) Modeling human affective postures: An information theoretic characterization of posture features. Computer Animation and Virtual Worlds 15: 269–276.

DeLorenzo M (2007) Wii sports experiment. http://wiinintendo.net/2007/01/15/wii-sports-experiment-results/. Accessed 20 April 2009.

Ekman P, Rosenberg EL (2005) What the Face Reveals: Basic and Applied Studies of Spontaneous Expression Using the Facial Action Coding System (FACS). Oxford University Press, New York.

Eriksson E, Hansen T, Lykke-Olesen A (2007) Movement-based interaction in camera spaces: A conceptual framework. Personal and Ubiquitous Computing 11: 621–632.

Graves L, Stratton G, Ridgers ND, Cable NT (2007) Comparison of energy expenditure in adolescents when playing new generation and sedentary computer games: Cross sectional study. British Medical Journal 335: 1282–1284.

Hart M (2003) Borg scale gets 'thumbs up'. http://www.torq.ltd.uk/pfm_disp.asp?newsid=18. Accessed 20 April 2009.

Hero G (2009) Guitar Hero. http://guitarhero.com. Accessed 20 April 2009.

Hoysniemi J (2006) Design and evaluation of physically interactive games. Tampere University.

Iso-Ahola SE, Hatfield BD (1986) Psychology of Sports: A Social Psychological Approach. Wm. C. Brown Publishers, Dubuque, IA.

Lantz F (2006) Big games and the porous border between the real and the mediated. http://www.vodafone.com/flash/receiver/16/articles/indexinner07.html. Accessed 20 April 2009.

LeBlanc C (2008) Nintendo Wii fits in neurorehabilitation. http://72.14.235.132/search?q= cache:-AMXr3ZD4DAJ:healthcarereview.com/index.php%3Fsrc%3Dnews%26refno%3D2366 %26category%3DCover%2520Story%26PHPSESSID%3D...+%22Nintendo+Wii+Fits+in+ Neurorehabilitation%22&hl=en&ct=clnk&cd=2&gl=au. Accessed 20 April 2009.

Lehrer J (2006) How the Nintendo Wii will get you emotionally invested in video games. Seedmagazine.com. Brain & Behavior. http://www.seedmagazine.com/news/2006/11/a_ console_to_make_you_wiip.php. Accessed 20 April 2009.

Lieberman DA (2006) Dance games and other exergames: What the research says. http://www.comm.ucsb.edu/faculty/lieberman/exergames.htm. Accessed 20 April 2009.

Lindley SE, Le Couteur J, Berthouze NL (2008) Stirring up experience through movement in game play: Effects on engagement and social behaviour. In: Proceeding of the twenty-sixth annual SIGCHI conference on Human factors in computing systems, ACM, Florence, Italy.

Lindley SE, Monk AF (2008) Social enjoyment with electronic photograph displays: Awareness and control. International Journal of Human-Computer Studies 66: 587–604.

Loke L, Larssen A, Robertson T, Edwards J (2007) Understanding movement for interaction design: Frameworks and approaches. Personal and Ubiquitous Computing 11: 691–701.

Lord C, Risi S, Lambrecht L, Cook EH, Leventhal BL, DiLavore PC, Pickles A, Rutter M (2000) The autism diagnostic observation schedule-generic: A standard measure of social and commu- nication deficits associated with the spectrum of autism. Journal of Autism and Developmental Disorders 30: 205–223.

Mandryk R, Atkins S, Inkpen K (2006) A continuous and objective evaluation of emotional expe- rience with interactive play environments. In: CHI '06: Proceedings of the SIGCHI Conference on Human Factors in Computing Systems, ACM Press, New York.

Mandryk RL, Inkpen KM (2004) Physiological indicators for the evaluation of co-located collabo- rative play, In: Proceedings of the 2004 ACM Conference on Computer Supported Cooperative Work, ACM, New York.

McCarthy J, Wright P (2004) Technology as Experience. MIT Press, Boston, MA.

Meeren HKM, van Heijnsbergen C, de Gelder B (2005) Rapid perceptual integration of facial expression and emotional body language. Proceedings of the National Academy of Sciences 102: 16518–16523.

Moen J (2006) KinAesthetic movement interaction: Designing for the pleasure of motion. KTH, Numerical Analysis and Computer Science, Stockholm.

Mueller F (2002) Exertion interfaces: Sports over a distance for social bonding and fun. Massachusetts Institute of Technology.

Mueller F, Agamanolis S, Picard R (2003) Exertion interfaces: Sports over a distance for social bonding and fun. In: Proceedings of the SIGCHI Conference on Human Factors in Computing Systems, ACM, Ft. Lauderdale, FL.

Mueller F, Gibbs M (2007a) A physical three-way interactive game based on table tennis. In: Proceedings of the 4th Australasian Conference on Interactive Entertainment, RMIT University, Melbourne, Australia.

Mueller F, Gibbs M (2007b) Evaluating a distributed physical leisure game for three players. Conference of the Computer-Human Interaction Special Interest Group (CHISIG) of Australia on Computer-Human Interaction: OzCHI'07, ACM, Adelaide, Australia.

Mueller F, Stevens G, Thorogood A, O'Brien S, Wulf V (2007) Sports over a distance. Personal and Ubiquitous Computing 11: 633–645.

Nenonen V, Lindblad A, Häkkinen V, Laitinen T, Jouhtio M, Hämäläinen P (2007) Using heart rate to control an interactive game. In: Proceedings of the SIGCHI Conference on Human Factors in Computing Systems, ACM Press, New York.

Palameta B, Brown WM (1999) Human cooperation is more than by-product mutualism. Animal Behaviour 57: 1–3.

Pasch M, Berthouze N, van Dijk EMAG, Nijholt A (2008) Motivations, strategies, and movement patterns of video gamers playing Nintendo Wii boxing. Facial and Bodily Expressions for Control and Adaptation of Games (ECAG 2008), Amsterdam, the Netherlands.

Powell W (2008) Virtually walking? Developing exertion interfaces for locomotor rehabilitation. CHI 2008. Workshop submission to "Exertion Interfaces".

Ratey J (2008) Spark: The Revolutionary New Science of Exercise and the Brain. Little, Brown and Company, Boston, MA.

Rocco E (1998) Trust breaks down in electronic contexts but can be repaired by some initial face-to-face contact. In: Proceedings of the SIGCHI Conference on Human Factors in Computing Systems. ACM Press/Addison-Wesley Publishing Co., New York.

Salen K, Zimmerman E (2003) Rules of Play: Game Design Fundamentals. MIT Press, Cambridge, MA.

Strauss A, Corbin J (1998) Basics of Qualitative Research: Techniques and Procedures for Developing Grounded Theory. SAGE Publications, Thousand Oaks, CA.

Tan B, Aziz AR, Chua K, Teh KC (2002) Aerobic demands of the dance simulation game. International Journal of Sports Medicine 23: 125–129.

Wakkary R, Hatala M, Jiang Y, Droumeva M, Hosseini M (2008) Making sense of group interaction in an ambient intelligent environment for physical play. In: Proceedings of the 2nd International Conference on Tangible and Embedded Interaction, ACM, Bonn, Germany.

Wankel LM (1985) Personal and situational factors affecting exercise involvement: The importance of enjoyment. Research Quarterly for Exercise and Sport 56: 275–282.

Well-being Field Report (2009) http://nsg.jyu.fi/index.php/Well-being_Field_Report. Accessed 20 April 2009.

XRtainment (2009) XRtainment – Where working out is all play! http://www.xrtainmentzone.com/. Accessed 20 April 2009.

Zheng J, Bos N, Olson JS, Olson GM (2001) Trust without touch: Jump-start trust with social chat. Short Paper at the Conference on Human Factors in Computing Systems CHI-01, ACM, New York.

Zheng J, Veinott E, Bos N, Olson JS, Olson GM (2002) Trust without touch: Jumpstarting long-distance trust with initial social activities. In: Proceedings of the Conference on Human Factors in Computing Systems, CHI-2002, ACM, New York, pp. 141–146.

Chapter 12
Beyond the Gamepad: HCI and Game Controller Design and Evaluation

Michael Brown, Aidan Kehoe, Jurek Kirakowski, and Ian Pitt

Abstract In recent years, there has been an increasing amount of computer game-focused HCI research, but the impact of controller-related issues on user experience remains relatively unexplored. In this chapter, we highlight the limitations of current practices with respect to designing support for both standard and innovative controllers in games. We proceed to explore the use of McNamara and Kirakowski's (2006) theoretical framework of interaction in order to better design and evaluate controller usage in games. Finally, we will present the findings of a case study applying this model to the evaluation and comparison of three different game control techniques: gamepad, keyboard, and force feedback steering wheel. This study highlights not only the need for greater understanding of user experience with game controllers, but also the need for parallel research of both functionality and usability in order to understand the interaction as a whole.

12.1 Introduction

Over its brief history, human–computer interaction (HCI) has developed a multitude of techniques for measuring and evaluating user experience with technology (Kirakowski and Corbet 1993, Nielsen 1993, Rubin 1994, ISO 1998a, Brown 2008). Many of the design considerations and usability issues that arise in game software are significantly different from those encountered in other software genres. For example, a game that allows a player to complete quests quickly and easily might score highly with respect to ISO 9241-11 (1998b) software efficiency and effectiveness measures, but it would probably rate very low with respect to user satisfaction because of the lack of challenge. As a result, in recent years we have seen the emergence of HCI research focused on computer games, addressing the unique

M. Brown (✉)
People and Technology Research Group, Department of Applied Psychology, University College Cork, Cork, Ireland
e-mail: mab@campus.ie

R. Bernhaupt (ed.), *Evaluating User Experience in Games*, Human-Computer Interaction Series, DOI 10.1007/978-1-84882-963-3_12,

challenges that this area presents (Desurvivre et al. 2004, Federoff 2002, Jørgensen 2004, Kavakli and Thone 2002).

The visual and audio presentation capabilities of gaming platforms have increased dramatically over the last 20 years, and much of the associated research has focused on these aspects of games. However, the game controller, and how that controller is supported in the game, can have a significant impact on the player's gaming experience. Mastery of the control system is an important part of most games (Johnson and Wiles 2003). In order to have an enjoyable game play experience, it is important that players feel a sense of control over the game interface and the associated game controls.

In this chapter, we describe how McNamara and Kirakowski's (2006) theoretical framework for understanding interactions with technology can be applied to the evaluation of controllers in games. Using this model as a guide, a user study was performed to explore the use of a range of game controllers in terms of functionality, usability, and user experience. The framework is described in Section 12.3, below. The results of this study are presented and discussed in Section 12.4.

12.2 The Evolution of Game Controllers

As far back as the 1950s, general purpose computing platforms have been used for the development and playing of computer games. The pre-existing input and output capabilities of the computing platforms were leveraged for game play purposes. For example, in 1961, the initial implementations of the "Spacewar!" game, running on the DEC PDP-1, used the test-word toggle switches for player input (Graetz 1981).

However, even in those early game environments the opportunities for specialized game controllers were recognized. The location of the toggle switches on the DEC PDP-1 (c. 1960), relative to the visual display, gave one of the players the advantage of being able to see the display more easily. To overcome this problem, a dedicated control box incorporating these switches was constructed. In addition to implementing the required switch functionality, the control box configuration also utilized more natural and intuitive mappings for the controls, e.g., the rotation switch was configured so that moving the switch to the right resulted in the craft being rotated to the right; a lever-style control could be moved to accelerate the craft. Graetz, one of the "Spacewar!" developers, stated that the new control mechanism "improved ones playing skills considerably, making the game even more fun" (Graetz 1981).

Over the past decades, the improvements in processor speeds and storage have been matched by developments in the field of input and output devices. During this time, the evolution of game software and game controllers has been inextricably linked. Games have influenced the design of game controllers, and game controllers have influenced the design of games (Cummings 2007). Many games, especially those played on general purpose computing platforms, have been designed to use the pre-existing control methods for the platform. However, the development of new generations of dedicated gaming platforms, and sometimes specific games, has often incorporated innovation in the area of game controllers.

12.2.1 Standard Game Controllers

The majority of games have been designed to operate with standardized (or de facto standardized) platform-specific controllers, e.g., each game console has an associated standardized first-party controller. Today, most games running on consoles support the standard console controller; most games running on personal computers support input via the keyboard and mouse; mobile phone games are played using the standard phone controls; and the recent proliferation of devices incorporating a touch screen have also supported that interaction method in games. Thus, the majority of games are designed to incorporate support for existing control methods.

Much of the innovation in the area of game controllers has been associated with dedicated gaming platforms. There are a number of popular-press books that document the development of the console games industry and technology (Sheff 1993, Kent 2001, Forster 2005). Throughout this almost 40-year development of game consoles, newer generations of consoles were typically accompanied by some degree of development and innovation in the associated game controller. In many cases, the level of controller innovation for a new console was relatively minor, and in some cases there was significant change and innovation, e.g., Nintendo Wii Remote, Nintendo Entertainment, and System gamepad.

Controllers for dedicated gaming platforms have traditionally been very tightly integrated with the console system electronics, supporting firmware/software and games. Through the 1970s and early 1980s, players used a variety of controls (switches, dials, and sliders) that were an integral part of the console itself, e.g., Magnavox Odyssey 100–500 series, and Coleco Telstar series. From the early 1980s onward, it became increasingly common for the controllers to be distinct separate physical entities (usually gamepads or joysticks) that were connected to the game console through a cable, or in more recent systems, a wireless link.

Each of today's game consoles has a "standard" controller that was designed with the capabilities of its console in mind and is tightly coupled to that system. A "standard" controller, with support implemented in games in a uniform manner, can help ensure a consistent interface for the user while playing games on that platform. Most games take a conservative approach and adhere to the recommended controller guidelines for their target platforms. The widespread use of standard controllers, together with the use of common control mechanisms within many game genres, results in controls being one of the most difficult areas in which to innovate within a game (Rabin 2005).

12.2.2 Focus on Innovative Game Controllers

While uniformity of game controller support can be beneficial, it can also be very limiting for both the game designer and the player (Rabin 2005). Even in the early years of game console systems, when the console and game controls were part of the same mechanical enclosure, there were attempts to make controllers that were targeted toward a particular game or genre of game, e.g., Atari Stunt Cycle (Atari Inc. 1977) and steering wheel controller. These types of developments mirror what was also happening in the arcade machine arena, i.e., the use of dedicated controllers for flying games, racing games, etc.

In recent years, an increasing number of games have added support for new and innovative controllers in their games. Incorporating support for innovative controllers in games offers opportunities for a game to distinguish itself in the market place (Kane 2005, Marshall et al. 2006). Custom controllers, designed to operate with specific games, offer possibilities to enhance the user experience in games by enabling interaction styles that are not possible using standard controllers, as described above.

While designing and implementing a custom controller offers opportunities to greatly enhance a game, it also introduces significant additional work, more project schedule risk, and probably an increased retail price for the game-plus-controller bundle. However, apart from platform-specific checklists, the advice available to guide designers and developers considering new or innovative controllers is very limited. Support for innovative controllers must be carefully planned and designed, and their performance evaluated. Problems associated with developing and implementing support for custom controllers have been listed in the postmortem reports which are published on a monthly basis in Game Developer magazine (Game Developer Magazine 2008). For example, Guitar Hero in February 2006 edition, Metal Gear Solid in May 2006 edition, and Tony Hawk in January 2007 edition.

12.3 Evaluating Game Controllers: Experience, Usability, and Functionality

As with all technology, the interaction between humans and game controllers is multifaceted and complex. This section describes McNamara and Kirakowski's (2006) theoretical framework for understanding interactions with technology and discusses the implications of applying this model to game controllers.

12.3.1 Introduction to the Components of Human–Computer Interaction

Recent developments in HCI have highlighted the importance of focusing on user experience in the design of technology. This need for high-quality user experience is especially important for computer games, as their primary function is to entertain. This revelation has led to some theoretical difficulties, as the concept of user experience does not easily fit into the traditional HCI fields of usability and ergonomics. In order to fully understand interactions with technology, we must understand the various components of the interactions and how these components impact on each other.

McNamara and Kirakowski (2006) propose a three-factor model for understanding the interactions between humans and technology, represented in Fig. 12.1.

Fig. 12.1 Components of technology usage from McNamara and Kirakowski (2006)

This theoretical framework presents three separate but codependent components of human–computer interaction. "Functionality" describes the technology side of the interaction, focusing on the technological possibilities of the interaction. Conversely, "experience" describes the purely human side of the interaction. This factor looks at how the interaction impacts on the person involved by asking questions such as "Do they enjoy the interaction?" and "Does it make them happy?". Finally, "usability" looks at the dynamics of the interaction itself, is it efficient, effective, and satisfying? They propose that in order to fully understand an interaction we must study each of these three components.

12.3.2 Functionality and Game Controllers

This aspect describes the purely technology-based part of the interaction. Key questions in this area are "Does it work?" and "What does it do?" This is the one aspect of the interaction that is relatively independent of both environment and user.

Looking at game controllers, it becomes clear that the primary function is to facilitate user interaction with computer game software. Traditionally, controllers only supported a one-way interaction from the user to the game, with audio visual devices providing feedback from the game to the user. However, the recent development of in-controller feedback means that the interaction with game controllers is now bidirectional. For example, haptic gamepads, steering wheels, and speakers integrated in the WiiMote. These developments mean that when considering game controller functionality, we must consider the range of input and feedback that a given control method can provide.

In some cases, controllers may not have the required number of controls to allow the player to invoke all the game commands. For example, flight simulator games typically support a larger number of game commands (often more than 30) than there are physical controls on a low-end joystick. In this case, the player must select a subset of the game commands to be assigned to their joystick controls, and the remaining commands can be invoked via the keyboard (or perhaps not used at all by the player).

Another important issue of game controller functionality is the level of support for the controller in a given game. A controller with a wide range of possible inputs and outputs is of little benefit if game software does not support it. Assessing controller functionality in isolation from software is fairly straightforward, as the range and sensitivity of various inputs and outputs can be easily tested. However, relating this to in-game functionality is a more complex issue, as the range and sensitivity of a controller may not be supported or necessary for a given game.

12.3.3 Usability and Game Controllers

A classic description of usability is "The extent to which a product can be used by specified users to achieve specified goals with effectiveness, efficiency and satisfaction in a specified context of use" (ISO 1998a). This definition highlights four core concepts central to interaction: effectiveness, efficiency, satisfaction, and context of use. Each of these concepts is important when discussing game controller design.

Effectiveness describes the ability of the user to complete specific tasks with the technology. This goes further than basic functionality, as not only must the technology have the potential to perform tasks, the user must also be able to operate the technology sufficiently to actually complete these tasks. The importance of effectiveness in game controller design is obvious: If users cannot use a controller to perform game tasks, they will be unable to interact with the game in any meaningful way.

The importance of efficiency in game controller design is a more complex issue. Efficiency considers the resources that must be expended by the user to complete tasks. These resources can be mental effort, physical effort, or time. In terms of computer games, this is closely linked to concept of difficulty: i.e., if a game requires a large amount of resources (time, skill, mental effort, etc.), then it is described as difficult and, conversely, if it requires few resources, it is described as easy. This might seem to be of limited importance when discussing game controllers, as the main focus of games is to enjoy playing them, not to effectively complete tasks. However, as Csikszentmihalyi (1975) reports, completing tasks that are easy can become boring and tasks that are difficult can become frustrating. This need for balance of effectiveness presents a dilemma in game controller design.

The concept of satisfaction deals with how the interaction impacts the user; are they free from discomfort and do they have a positive attitude toward the interactions? Once again the importance of this concept to game controller design is fairly obvious, as playing computer games is an entertainment-driven activity, and the interaction should be satisfying. Unlike efficiency, effectiveness, and context of use, satisfaction is purely subjective. While the other core concepts of usability can to some degree be directly observed, satisfaction must be assessed solely on the basis of user feedback. This can cause problems in game controller design, as variables such as context of use can influence user report and distort findings.

Context of use is unlike the other concepts discussed as it is not a vital part of usability, but is a factor that must be considered when studying efficiency, effectiveness, and satisfaction. Basically, context of use describes the situation in which an interaction is happening (Bevan and McLeod 1993). It is important to consider that this refers not only to the physical environment, but also to the individual differences and the social environment in which the interaction is taking place. While this concept is vital when studying all forms of technology, it is especially important when working with control devices because, as interaction facilitation devices, they introduce additional complexity that must be considered. The device a controller is being used to control has a huge influence on the usability of the interaction. In terms of game controllers, this means both the hardware (PC or console) and software (the specific game) must be considered in design.

12.3.4 Experience and Game Controllers

This final aspect of interaction design is perhaps the most recent to be explored. Experience refers to the psychological and social impact technology has on users. While this is related to the usability concept of satisfaction, it has a much wider scope, looking at interaction in a much broader sense than merely task completion. When studying experience, concepts external to the interaction must be considered, for example aesthetics, marketing, social impact, attachment, and mood can all affect users' experience of interacting with technology.

Once again, the nature of game controllers as intermediary devices can make studying this aspect of user interaction difficult. In addition to the social, psychological, and environment factors that must be considered when looking at experience of any technology, the hardware and software that is being controlled may also impact on user experience with game controllers. Little research or theory exists relating to user experience with game controllers, making it impossible to predict what factors are key to users' experiences in this area. However, the tools needed to explore this area do already exist; qualitative psychological methods such as critical incidents technique, semi-structured interview, grounded theory, content analysis, and ethnography have been used to evaluate experience in a wide range of fields (McCarthy and Wright 2004), and their flexible nature means they can be easily applied to the study of game controllers.

12.3.5 Evaluation and Design of Game Controllers

This section discusses the impact of the McNamara and Kirakowski's framework on research and design in this field. First, current literature is explored and then the implications for design are discussed.

Looking at recent research into controllers in general reveals that a significant number of research papers have explored the performance of pointing devices (including mice, touch pads, and trackballs), keyboards in traditional desktop/laptop computing scenarios, and keypads usage on handheld devices (Card et al. 1978, MacKenzie 1992, Silfverberg et al. 2000). In recent years, HCI researchers have also explored a variety of increasingly popular interaction methods including gesture, touch, haptics, and styluses (Dennerlein et al. 2000, Forlines et al. 2007,

Albinsson and Zhai 2003). Most of this work has been concerned with the effectiveness and efficiency of the input methods, but user satisfaction has also been considered (Brewster et al. 2007, ISO 1998b).

Despite the fact that game control has been highlighted by many studies as an important aspect of game design (Federoff 2002, Johnson and Wiles 2003, Desurvivre et al. 2004, Adams 2005, Hoysniemi 2006, Pinelle et al. 2008, Falstein and Barwood 2008), little research has been conducted that focuses on game controllers. Some work has studied the development of input devices and how they affect user performance (Kavakli and Thone 2002, Pagulayan et al. 2003, Klochek and MacKenzie 2006); however, the effects of game controllers on user experience have yet to be explored in detail. According to McNamara and Kirakowski's (2006) model, we will not be able to fully understand the interaction involved with game controllers until it has been studied in terms of functionality, usability, and user experience.

Current game controller design practice continues this pattern, with an emphasis on the functionality aspects but little attention paid to usability, still less to user experience. For example, the game play and console compliance checking activities incorporate evaluation of controller support. The associated checklists typically contain very specific advice with respect to assignment of functionality to buttons. Apart from this very platform-specific advice, the guidelines and heuristics related to support of standard controllers are very limited.

The next question that must be answered is how adopting this model impacts game controller design? Currently, little research exists to help focus game controller evaluation on the aspects of game controllers that have the greatest effect on user interaction. This lack of focus leaves controller designers with two choices when it comes to evaluation: either perform a broad range of evaluations to ensure that all aspects of the controller are examined, or perform a few tests and hope that most of the important issues are found. Neither of these are ideal solutions, as the first is costly to perform and it may be even more costly to correct all the issues found, and the second is likely to miss key issues and produce a poor product. The McNamara and Kirakowski (2006) model highlights the distinct components of the interaction, allowing designers to perform fewer evaluations but still investigate each of the components of the interaction. Ensuring that controller functionality, usability, and user experience are all evaluated means that all the vital aspects of the controller can be assessed without performing a huge range of evaluations.

12.4 Case Study

In order to further explore this area, a case study was designed to evaluate both standard and innovative computer game controllers usages in a game. This study focused on control of racing games and evaluated keyboard and mouse, standard gamepad, and force feedback steering wheel control methods with respect to each aspect of user interaction, as described by McNamara and Kirakowski (2006). This study is designed in order to highlight the benefits of evaluating user experience, within the context of a multi-component game controller evaluation.

12.4.1 Justification

In order to fully explore the interaction between user and game controller, each controller was assessed in terms of functionality, usability, and user experience. Measuring each of these component measures brings with it unique challenges.

12.4.1.1 Functionality

Functionality describes the purely technology-based part of the interaction. Since this component is relatively independent of both environment and user, it can be measured by an inspection of the technical limitations of each game controller This inspection was done by comparison of the quantity and range of outputs produced by each controller relative to possible inputs recognized by the game. In addition to this, the use of inputs was measured with custom logging software.

12.4.1.2 Usability

This quality is dependent not only on the user, but also on the environment in which the interaction takes place. Each aspect of usability as described by the ISO (1998b) was measured independently. Efficiency was measured in terms of mental effort required to use the controllers: the lower the mental effort required, the more efficient the interaction with the controller. Mental effort was measured using the self-report Subjective Mental Effort Questionnaire (Arnold 1999). Effectiveness was measured via lap time. The faster users can complete a lap using a controller, the more effective the interaction, as fast lap completion is the primary task in racing games. Satisfaction was measured via the Consumer Product Questionnaire (CPQ) (McNamara 2006), a standardized measure for evaluating user satisfaction with electronic consumer products.

12.4.1.3 Experience

As this aspect is purely subjective in nature, it can be difficult to measure and is dependent on a huge range of psychological and social factors external to the interaction itself, including aesthetics, advertising, and social desirability (McCarthy and Wright 2004). Critical Incidents Technique (CIT) (Flanagan 1954) was used to collect qualitative data describing user experience. This method involves asking each user to report his/her three most positive and three most negative experiences with the controller in an open-ended questionnaire. This method was chosen for two key reasons. First, as a postgame play measure, it will not interfere with the game play experience itself. Many during-play methods such as talk out loud can alter the experience of game play and reduce the validity of any findings. Second, CIT is open-ended and does not require a knowledge base in the area being explored. This is important, as a lack of previous research in this area means that other researcher-lead methods are not appropriate. In addition to the CIT evaluation, each subject was asked to report his/her preference between the controllers on a set of three two-way controller preference scales (ranging from "much preferred controller A" to "much preferred controller B").

12.4.2 Methodology

A total of 12 subjects took part in this study. Gender balance was reasonably equal with five female and seven male subjects. The mean age of the participants was 24.6, with ages ranging from 19 to 30. Participants were also asked if they drive regularly as this may give them an advantage with the steering wheel controller; five responded that they did. They were also asked if he/she had any experience of racing games, all except subject 1 responded that he/she had little or none.

The test system was an HP Compaq dc7800p running Windows XP. The following three controllers were evaluated in the study:

Keyboard. Dell USB keyboard.

Gamepad. The Logitech Dual Action is a USB gamepad, with two mini-joysticks (similar to those commonly used on game consoles) and 12 digital buttons.

Steering wheel. The Logitech MOMO Racing is a USB force feedback device, with an analog steering wheel, analog accelerator and brake pedals, and 10 digital buttons.

A single game was used in the study, Colin McRae Rally DiRT (Codemasters 2007). In order to minimize the impact of game-specific artifacts on the evaluation, a number of the game settings were fixed. The same difficulty level (amateur), control assignment, view (behind the car), car (Subaru Impreza), and track (Avelsbachring) were used for all subjects.

This study used a repeated measures type design, with each subject taking part in every condition. The independent variable was the type of control method used and was operationalized in three conditions: Gamepad, Keyboard, and Force Feedback Steering wheel.

In order to reduce confounding variables between conditions, a number of controls were used. The order of conditions was counterbalanced in order to counteract any effects due to learning. Each condition used the same software and hardware, except for the control method, so reducing the effect these may have on the evaluation.

12.4.2.1 Procedure

After completing a short demographic questionnaire, the subjects were introduced to the game and the first control method they would use. They were then asked to play the game until they felt comfortable with the control method. How long this step took was left to the participants' discretion and varied from 5 to 20min. Then the participant performed two timed laps of the test track. Once they had done this the participant was asked to complete the CPQ, SMEQ, and CIT questionnaires. This procedure was repeated for each control method.

12.4.3 Results

12.4.3.1 Functionality

When comparing the controllers in terms of functionality, there are two issues to be considered. First, "Are all the game commands supported by the controller?" and second, the issue of exactly how the control is supported. The DiRT game has only a small set of commands. In addition to steer, accelerate, and brake, a small number of extra commands are also supported (change camera, handbrake, look left/right/back, and gear up/down). Even though the use of all the game commands was not examined in the study, the various controllers had sufficient controls for all of these game commands to be assigned, i.e., 100% of the game commands can be assigned to the controllers.

Both the gamepad and steering wheel support analog steering. However, as Table 12.1 highlights, their response characteristics are very different, with the wheel being several times more precise in terms of angular resolution. This data show that in terms of functionality in the context of this game, the steering wheel is the superior control method, with the widest range of motion and sensitivity. Conversely, the keyboard has the poorest functionality, only accommodating binary input for both steering and acceleration.

12.4.3.2 Usability

The usability of each game controller was measured in terms of effectiveness, efficiency, and user satisfaction.

Table 12.2 shows the results for each component of the usability analysis of the three controllers. It indicates poorer performance for the steering wheel compared to the other two control methods in terms of both completion time and SMEQ (low values of SMEQ indicate mental effort required). Gamepad and Keyboard results for these two measures appear to be much closer. In terms of CPQ results, the Keyboard reports an extremely low result for satisfaction, with the Gamepad and Steering Wheel performing slightly better (50% on the CPQ is an average device score, according to the CPQ database). A series of one-way repeated measure ANOVAs were used to determine the statistical significance of these results. ANOVA was used as it is a robust method of difference testing, and performing multiple t-tests would increase the likelihood of a type II error. For this exploratory study, an alpha level of 0.05 was used.

Table 12.1 Functional differences between gamepad and wheel controllers

Control parameter	Gamepad	Wheel
Physical range (approximately)	25	240
Analog counts	255	1024
Deadzone	Yes (center)	No
Angular resolution (approximately)	<10.2	4.3

Table 12.2 Means scores on usability measures

Controller type	Completion time	SMEQ score	CPQ score (%)
Steering wheel	04:39	72.92	20.83
Gamepad	02:59	34.42	15.08
Keyboard	03:13	42.58	6.25

Table 12.3 ANOVA results for usability measures

	Completion time	SMEQ score	CPQ score
F value	5.876	7.258	3.268
Degrees of freedom	10	10	10
P	0.021	0.011	0.081

Table 12.4 P-values for STEP analysis of completion time ANOVA

Completion time	Steering wheel	Gamepad	Keyboard
Steering wheel	–	0.014	0.027
Gamepad	–	–	0.4
Keyboard	–	–	–

Table 12.3 shows that the ANOVA results indicate significant results at an alpha level of 0.05 for completion time and SMEQ scores. Results for CPQ scores show the data approach significance, but fail to reject the null hypothesis at a 0.05 alpha level. In order to further investigate the differences, a post hoc STEP analysis was performed on each of the significant ANOVA results.

Table 12.4 shows the probability values for the STEP analysis of the completion time data and reveals significant differences between Gamepad and Wheel, and Keyboard and Wheel. This shows that the steering wheel performed significantly worse than the other two methods in terms of effectiveness.

Table 12.5 reveals similar results for the STEP analysis of the SMEQ data. Significances were found between Steering wheel and Gamepad and between steering wheel and keyboard. This shows that the steering wheel also performed significantly worse than the other control methods in terms of efficiency.

In summary, the usability data collected show an interesting trend in terms of the steering wheel. This controller scored significantly worse than both of the other control methods in terms of efficiency and effectiveness (as measured by Completion

Table 12.5 P-values for STEP analysis of SMEQ ANOVA

SMEQ results	Steering wheel	Gamepad	Keyboard
Steering wheel	–	0.014	0.027
Gamepad	–	–	0.4
Keyboard	–	–	–

Time and SMEQ), but scored the highest in the measure of user satisfaction. This set of results suggests that while the steering wheel was not an effective or efficient controller, the participants enjoyed using it. Keyboard data show the opposite trend, with good efficiency and effectiveness scores, but the poorest satisfaction results. Finally, the Gamepad performed the best of three controllers in terms of usability, producing the best lap times, the lowest SMEQ scores, and a reasonable score in the CPQ, compared to the other controllers. It is also worth noting that all three control systems performed poorly in terms of user satisfaction, with means scores ranging from 6.25 to 20.83%. The lack of statistical significance may be due to a "floor" effect, i.e., the CPQ scores could hardly get much worse.

12.4.3.3 User Experience

The data collected to measure user experience took two forms: First, user preference was gauged and second CIT was used to report user attitudes toward the devices.

Table 12.6 presents the mean user preference scores and shows a preference toward the gamepad compared to the other two controllers and a preference for the keyboard over the steering wheel. In order to test the significance of these results, one-way repeated measures ANOVA was performed at alpha level 0.05, producing an F value of 3.015 with 10 degrees of freedom. This falls outside the critical region and so does not show statistical significance.

As the CIT produces quantitative data, a more detailed analysis is required. The responses for each game controller were formed into categories using content analysis. This method involved grouping the comments collected into categories, based on the content of those categories, in order to identify the key areas of the users' experience with the game controllers.

Table 12.7 shows the results of the content analysis of the steering wheel comments. This table highlights *Sensitivity*, *Feedback*, *Easy to pick up*, and *Realism* as the most reported aspects of users experience with this device.

The *Sensitivity* comments highlight the high sensitivity of left/right steering using the wheel. For example:

"... impressive accuracy while playing." (Subject 1, positive)
"Controller is very sensitive to movement, it takes a while to judge accurately how much force is required." (Subject 7, negative)
"Hard to control. The steering was highly sensitive." (Subject 11, negative)

While the majority of these comments are negative, showing frustration at the highly sensitive controls, three of the subjects listed this as a positive feature that actually enhanced their game play experience.

Table 12.6 User preferences scores on a 1–5 scale

User preference	Keyboard – gamepad	Keyboard – steering wheel	Steering wheel – gamepad
Mean	4	2.5	3.92
Standard deviation	1.28	1.57	1.44

Table 12.7 Content analysis of steering wheel comments

Steering wheel categories	Positive comments	Negative comments	Total
Sensitivity	3	9	12
Feedback	7	4	11
Easy to pick up	7	4	11
Realism	9	2	11
Physical characteristics	4	3	7
Learning potential	1	3	4
Miscellaneous	0	1	1
Total	31	26	57

Comments in the *Feedback* category discuss the force feedback produced when using the steering wheel. For example:

"The motion of the wheel when on rough terrain (vibration) added to the experience of crashing." (Subject 6, positive)
"The vibrations of the wheel were a nice effect in making it seem like you were really on the terrain, like the grass." (Subject 12, positive)
"The motion/vibration of the wheel often made turning the wheel very difficult – it moved a lot less smoothly" (Subject 6, negative).

Again, the comments in this category are both positive and negative. The positive comments show an appreciation of the fun and realism that force feedbacks add to the interaction, while the negative comments mention situations where it got in the way of playing the game. This shows the care with which innovative controller features should be applied so that they add to the game experience without getting in the way of the basic features of the game, in this example steering.

The *Easy to pick up* comments mention instances where this control system was or wasn't easy to pick up and use. Some subjects found the familiar steering wheel and pedals provided an intuitive control system, but for others the reproduction of driving conditions was not accurate enough to make it easy to pick up. For example:

"Using a steering wheel is quite intuitive; it's obvious how it works." (Subject 6, positive)
"The accelerator and brake pedals were awkward to use at first and I never really got comfortable with them." (Subject 3, negative)

The *Realism* category produced the most positive comments for the steering wheel, with only two negative comments from 11. These comments mainly praise the realism of this control method, and two of the comments call for even more realism. For example:

"The wheel combined with the pedals made it seem like a very realistic driving system." (Subject 6, positive)
"Steering wheel only had half turn each way rather than the 1.5 as I am used to when driving." (Subject 8, negative)

Table 12.8 Content analysis of keyboard comments

Keyboard/categories	Positive comments	Negative comments	Total
Ease of use	10	3	13
Sensitivity	3	8	11
Physical characteristics	5	6	11
Realism	0	3	3
Comfort	0	2	2
Feedback	0	2	2
Familiarity	2	0	2
Total	20	24	44

Table 12.8 shows the results of the content analysis of the keyboard comments. It is worth noting that this is the only control method that received more negative comments than positive ones. The categories that contain the most comments and are the focus of the evaluation are *Ease of use*, *Sensitivity*, and *Physical characteristics*.

The *Ease of use* category contains comments discussing how easy the keyboard was to use. Most of these are positive comments focusing on the simplicity of the interface, but some mention the limited control that is afforded by keyboard control. For example:

"Actions didn't translate well to game. Even though controls are simple, car was difficult to control and judge." (Subject 7, negative).

The category containing the most negative remarks was *Sensitivity*, which contained comments relating to the binary nature of the keyboard input. A few comments praised this as easy to use, while most of them criticized the lack of sensitivity. For example:

"Easier to make incremental adjustments during steering." (Subject 2, positive)
"Breaking was instantaneous, I had no control over slowing down, it was stop or nothing." (Subject 3, negative)

Comments in the *Physical characteristics* category discuss the implication of the physical layout of the keyboard, either praising the localized controls or criticizing it for being cramped. For example:

"Small choice space-i.e. arrow keys within easy range of fingers" (Subject 2, positive)
"Spacing of input keys is a small bit cramped." (Subject 9, Negative)

Table 12.9 shows the results of the content analysis of the gamepad comments and reveals that the comments in this category are more evenly spread across the categories produced; this suggests that there were not any aspects of the interaction that were experienced by all the users. The categories that contain the most comments are *Comfort*, *Learnable*, *Sensitivity*, *Personal preference*, and *Ease of use*.

Table 12.9 Content analysis of gamepad comments

Gamepad – categories	Positive comments	Negative comments	Total
Comfort	8	2	10
Learnable	4	3	7
Sensitivity	3	4	7
Personal preference	2	5	7
Ease of use	6	1	7
Feedback	0	3	3
Realism	1	1	2
Misc	2	0	2
Total	26	19	45

Comfort is the largest category produced and contains the most positive comments. These comments simply talk about how comfortable the gamepad is. For example:

"Very comfortable. I could hold it all day long." (Subject 3, positive)
"Makes my thumb sore after playing for a while." (Subject 1, negative)

Comments in the *Learnable* category talk about how easy or difficult it is to get used to using the gamepad controller. For example:

"Very familiar. I knew exactly how it worked within very little time" (Subject 3, positive).
"Maybe if someone used this for the very first time it would be difficult to figure out" (Subject 7, negative).

It is interesting to note that while several users mention this method is easy to learn, none talk about how intuitive it is, as they did with both the steering wheel and the keyboard. This may suggest that it may be familiarity with this device rather than an intuitive interface that makes learning easier.

The *Sensitivity* comments highlight the positive and negative effects of steering, acceleration, and break sensitivity. For example:

"Natural feeling, right sensitivity" (Subject 1, Positive)
"The acceleration and brakes didn't seem to work well together. It was hard to brake slightly; you had to come to a complete stop." (Subject 11, negative)

Comments in the *Personal preference* category discuss issues relating to control assignment setting in the game. Most of these comments are negative, perhaps representing the fact that the participants were not allowed to alter these settings during the study. For example:

"Would have preferred to accelerate on the 'trigger' buttons" (Subject 2, negative)
"The button for the break should be to the right side, not above the accelerator." (Subject 8, negative)

The *Ease of use* category contains comments relating the simplicity (or lack of) using this control method. Most of these comments are positive, with only a single comment stating that this device is difficult to use. For example:

"Very easy to use. Actions were displayed accurately in the game. It was easy to judge how much movement/force was required." (Subject 7, positive)
    "The joystick seems sometimes a little bit difficult to use." (Subject 5, negative)

In addition to highlighting some of the key issues in game controller user experience, these data have revealed an interesting trend, the mixture of positive and negative comments throughout the categories relating to all three control methods. The vast majority of categories discovered contain both positive and negative comments; this trend highlights the importance of individual differences when analyzing game controllers. What some users may see as a positive feature or aspect of a game controller, others may view in an extremely negative light. For example, when discussing the binary nature of the keyboard, one subject found it much easier to steer with, while another found the lack of sensitivity frustrating.

"Easier to make incremental adjustments during steering." (Subject 2, keyboard, positive)
    "Very difficult to control the strength of the control/action by simply pressing one key." (Subject 4, keyboard, negative)

12.4.4 Combining the Results

While each of the evaluations produced interesting results, a more complete picture can be gained by looking at a combination of all three measures. While a complete analysis of all the data collected falls outside the scope of this chapter, this section highlights a single issue that was reported by several of the analysis methods and explores it in more detail.

The issue of controller sensitivity is one that seems to have an impact on all three components of the interaction. The user experience analysis highlighted controller sensitivity as an important aspect of experience for each of the control methods. Categories within each analysis revealed each control method's advantages and disadvantages in terms of sensitivity. The results suggest that this aspect of the interaction was the most influential when using the steering wheel, as nine comments mentioned sensitivity as a problem. However, in terms of functionality the steering wheel is clearly superior, being sensitive to small gradations in terms of steering, acceleration, and braking.

To examine this in more detail, an analysis of the data collected by the logging software for subject 1 (the subject with the best laps times using the wheel) and subject 5 (a subject with close to average lap times with the wheel) was conducted.

Figure 12.2 shows the reports captured by the logging software for subjects 1 and 5, while using the gamepad and steering wheel to control the steering axis while driving the two timed laps of the track. The chart is a frequency distribution of the range of controller reports. Both controllers report a different range of values in response to movement. In order to display them all on the same X-axis scale, the data from both controllers have been normalized; −1000 is the controller axis at the extreme left; +1000 is the controller axis at the extreme right; and 0 is the center position for the controller. The Y-axis represents the total number of reports of a given value.

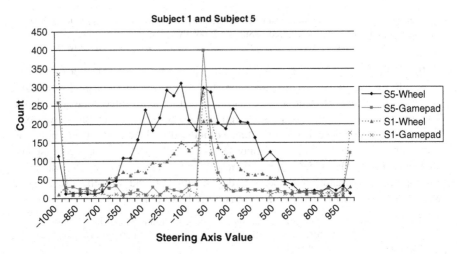

Fig. 12.2 Device steering reports for subjects 1 and 5

The bias of data toward the left-hand side of the chart is a result of the track being driven in an anticlockwise direction. As can be seen in Fig. 12.2, the profile of reports generated by both subject 1 and subject 5 while using the gamepad is very similar. The distribution of the data shows that little of the analog capability of the mini-joystick on the gamepad is being used. Most of the reports are either close to the axis center (mini-joystick is moved to the center "deadzone") or at the limit of the device range, i.e., the gamepad mini-joystick is essentially being used as a digital control in a manner similar to the keyboard.

The profiles of reports generated by both subjects while using the steering wheel are obviously different. The increased number of wheel reports for Player 5 vs. Player 1 is a reflection of the fact that Player 5 took more time to complete the two laps while using the wheel, and thus generated more reports. In contrast to the gamepad data, the analog capability of the wheel is being utilized. The graph for Player 1, who had the fastest drive time for the wheel, shows a concentration of reports about the center position of the wheel. In contrast, the graph for Player 5 shows a wider distribution of data, as he/she struggled to control the vehicle using the wheel, i.e., significant over steering.

This suggests that, although a more sensitive control method is a useful tool for a more skilled user, it is of little benefit to those of less skill. As few of the participants had much experience with steering wheels in games; this could explain the negative comments regarding the steering wheel, as they found it frustrating to use without the time to master. The distraction caused by this unfamiliar sensitivity could also go some way toward explaining the poor usability scores reported for the steering wheel. The analog nature of the brakes and pedals on the steering wheel controller allows the player to perform a variety of real-world rally driving techniques in a game, such as the "heel-and-toe" and "left foot braking". However, none of the subjects in the study used these techniques.

This example highlights the main advantage of using this multi-component analysis: the ability to fully explore an issue that has been highlighted by one of the methods and find its root cause. While a traditional usability or user experience evaluation would probably discover that sensitivity is a key issue for these control devices, they would not be able to explore this issue in its entirety, as this multi-component evaluation has.

12.4.5 Critique

When considering the results of this study, there are several possible short weaknesses that must be considered. The most obvious of these is the range of methods used. While this allows a great deal of data to be collected for each component of the interaction, it also means that compromises have to be made when assessing each component. For example, when exploring user experience, McCarthy and Wright (2004) suggest evaluations in the field, but the present study used a laboratory environment so that usability evaluations could be performed simultaneously. The lab was set up to closely resemble a home environment, but it is impossible to recreate the exact conditions of a field study.

Another factor that must be considered is the inexperienced participants. Only 1 of the 12 subjects reported having regularly played racing games, and none of them had more than a few hours of experience with steering wheel controllers. The results must be interpreted with this in mind, and may not be generalizable to more experienced gamers.

12.4.6 Conclusions

The steering wheel is an attractive device which supports all the functions needed by the game commands, and therefore may be a selling point for the game. In the hands of an inexperienced user, however, it will lead to poor game performance. Nonetheless, at least initially, users will feel satisfied with it.

Although the gamepad comes out above the steering wheel and the keyboard on usability performance measures, the keyboard has the advantage that it is regarded as very easy to learn. "Experience" and "usability" in this case seem to be telling different stories. Which should the game designer go for if there is a choice to be made? If there is a trade-off between the keyboard and the gamepad, the designer may well choose not to support the gamepad if user experience is the key issue.

The issue of controller sensitivity shows the complexity involved in understanding a small aspect of user experience with game controllers. It highlights not only the need for greater understanding of user experience with game controllers, but also the need for parallel research of both functionality and usability in order to understand the interaction as a whole.

Overall, all three of the devices studied were able to support the game command functions, and the steering wheel was also able to transmit extra output using haptic feedback. Thus, we may infer that for the game and devices studied, the game controller was working at 100%. However, the devices differed in the way the user interacted with them in the game. This study shows that the method of user interaction is actually an important aspect of game play, and how one may be able to assess its impact in a simple and direct laboratory evaluation. With experienced facilitators, a study such as this need not take more than two elapsed days.

In terms of game controller user experience, several issues were highlighted that appear to be important for all of the controllers evaluated. These include: Sensitivity, Ease of use, Realism, and Comfort. This information represents an initial baseline of game controller user experience, which can be further explored with future research.

12.5 Discussion

Much of on-going game play testing that is performed as a regular part of the development process is accomplished using informal techniques. Such informal evaluation could also be complemented by more a structured evaluation of controller support, as outlined in the user study. It is relatively quick and easy to perform and could be especially useful during the early stages of development to benchmark controller support.

12.5.1 Implications and Recommendations

Between discussion and the case study presented here, the advantages and disadvantages of a multi-method evaluation have been highlighted. The main advantage shown is the ability to identify the root cause of the issues discovered in any of the evaluations. The main disadvantage is that when performing a range of evaluations simultaneously, compromises such as the use of a laboratory setting must be made.

In terms of practical implications, these findings suggest that a multi-component model such as this could be useful within a game development process, where it is important not only to highlight issues, but also to discover their root causes and fix them. However, the compromises that must made in the evaluation process means that focused user experience evaluations may be more appropriate in academic setting, where understanding of the intricacies of an issue is more important.

12.5.2 Future Research

In terms of user experience, the case study presented has laid the ground work for exploring how game controller affects user experience. Having discovered some of the key issues in this area, the next step is to explore these issues in more detail with more in-depth data collection and analysis, such as interview and grounded theory.

This user study was deliberately constrained in that it only explored the initial stages of game play for each of the controllers in a single game. However, with extended game play, the players will become more familiar with both the game and the controllers. As a result, longitudinal studies would be required to explore the issues that arise in the context of longer game play durations over an extended period of time. The same techniques applied in this user study could also be applied in the context of longitudinal studies, and the data then analyzed to explore change over time.

The data collected in the study consist of both data collected during game play (with logging software) and data collected afterward as subjects complete questionnaires. The data collected during game play in the study were limited to the reports generated by the game controllers. It would be useful to complement this in-game data with biometric and video capture data (with emphasis on facial expressions and body movement). This could perhaps allow better interpretation of the in-game reports and complement the information collected postgame play in the questionnaires.

Future studies should seek to elaborate on the effects of functionality on usability and experience. For instance, where possible, to observe the effects on game players in setups where the game controls, controllers, and support devices offer different levels of functionality as defined in this chapter.

References

Adams E (2005) Bad game designer, no twinkie! VI. Gamasutra designer's notebook. http://www.gamasutra.com/features/20050603/adams_01.shtml Accessed 23rd August 2008.

Albinsson P, Zhai S (2003) High precision touch screen interaction. In: Proceedings of SIGCHI on Human Factors in Computing Systems, ACM, New York, pp. 105–112.

Arnold A (1999) Mental effort and evaluation of user interfaces: A questionnaire approach. In: Proceedings of 8th International Conference on Human-Computer Interact, ACM, New York, pp. 1003–1007.

Atari Stunt Cycle {computer software} (1977). Atari Inc.

Bevan N, Mcleod M (1993) Usability measurement in context. Behaviour & Information Technology 13: 132–145.

Brewster S, Faraz C, Brown L (2007) Tactile feedback for mobile interactions. SIGCHI Conference on Human Factors in Computing Systems CHI 2007, ACM, New York, pp. 159–162.

Brown M (2008) Evaluating computer game usability: Developing heuristics based on user experience. In: Proceedings of IHCI conference 2008, University College Cork, Ireland, pp. 16–21.

Card S, English W, Burr BJ (1978) Evaluation of mouse, rate-controlled isometric joystick, step keys, and text keys for text selection on a CRT. Ergonomics 21: 601–613.

Colin McRae: Dirt {computer software} (2007) Codemasters.

Csikszentmihalyi M (1975) Beyond Boredom and Anxiety. Jossey-Bass Publishers, London.

Cummings A (2007) The evolution of game controllers and control schemes and their effect on their games. In: Proceedings of 17th Annual University of Southampton Multimedia Systems Conference.

Dennerlein J, Martin D, Hasser C (2000) Force-feedback improves performance for steering and combined steering-targeting tasks. In: CHI Letters, ACM, New York, 2 (1), pp. 423–429.

Desurvivre H, Caplan M, Toth JA (2004) Using heuristics to evaluate the playability of games. Extended Abstracts, Conference on Human Factors in Computing Systems. ACM Press, New York, pp. 1509–1512.

Falstein N, Barwood H (2008) The 400 project.   http://theinspiracy.com/400_project.htm Accessed 6th November 2008.

Federoff M (2002) Heuristics and usability guidelines for the creation and evaluation of fun in video games. Thesis, Indian University.

Flanagan JC (1954) The critical incident technique. Psychology Bulletin 51(4): 327–358.

Forlines C, Wigdor D, Shen C, Balakrishnan R (2007) Direct-touch vs. mouse input for tabletop displays. In: Proceedings of SIGCHI Conference on Human Factors in Computing Systems 2007, ACM, New York, pp. 647–656.

Forster W (2005) The Encyclopedia of Game Machines – Consoles, Handheld and Home Computers 1972–2005. Hagen Schmid, Berlin.

Game Developer Magazine (2008) http://www.gdmag.com/homepage.htm Accessed 8th November 2008.

Graetz JM (1981) The origin of spacewar. Creative computing, August 1981. http://www. atarimagazines.com/ Accessed 12 November 2008.

Hoysniemi J (2006) International survey on the Dance Dance Revolution game. Computer Entertainment. April 2006.

ISO (1998a) 9241 Ergonomic requirements for office work with visual display terminals (VDTs) – Part 9 – Requirements for non-keyboard input devices (ISO 9241–9).

ISO (1998b) 9241 Ergonomic requirements for office work with visual display terminals (VDTs) – Part 11 – Guidance on usability (ISO 9241–11).

Johnson D, Wiles J (2003) Effective affective user interface design in games. Ergonomics 46(13/14): 1332–1345.

Jorgensen AH (2004) Marrying HCI/Usability and computer games: A preliminary look. In: Proceedings of 3rd Nordic Conference in HCI, pp. 393–396.

Kane C (2005) Beyond the gamepad. http://www.gamasutra.com/features/20050819/kane_pfv.htm accessed 20th October 2008.

Kavakli M, Thone J (2002) A usability study of input devices on measuring user performance in computer games. In: Proceedings of First International Conference on Information Technology and Applications 2002, pp. 291–295.

Kent LS (2001) The Ultimate History of Video Games: From Pong to Pokémon. The Story Behind the Craze That Touched Our Lives and Changed the World. Three Rivers Press, Roseville, CA.

Kirakowski J, Corbet M (1993) SUMI: The software usability measurement inventory. British Journal of Educational Technology (Blackwell Synergy) 24(3): 210–212.

Klochek C, MacKenzie IS (2006) Performance measures of game controllers in a three-dimensional environment. Proceedings – Graphics Interface 137: 73–79.

MacKenzie S (1992) Fitts' law as a research and design tool in human–computer interaction. Human-Computer Interaction 7: 91–139.

Marshall D, Ward T, McLoone S (2006) From chasing dots to reading minds: The past, present, and future of video game interaction. ACM Crossroads 13(2): 10, December 2006.

McCarthy J, Wright P (2004) Technology as Experience. MIT Press, London.

McNamara N (2006). Measuring user satisfaction with consumer electronic products. Doctoral Thesis, University College Cork, Ireland.

McNamara N, Kirakowski J (2006) Functionality, usability, and user experience: Three areas of concern. Interactions 13(6): 26–28, November 2006.

Nielsen J (1993) Usability Engineering. Academic Press Inc., Oxford.

Pagulayan RJ, Keeker K, Wixon D, Romero RL, Fuller T (2003) User-centered design in games. In: JA Jacko and A Sears (eds) The Human-Computer Interaction Handbook: Fundamentals, Evolving Technologies and Emerging Applications. Human Factors and Ergonomics. L. Erlbaum Associates, Hillsdale, NJ, pp. 883–906.

Pinelle D, Wong N, Stach T (2008) Heuristic evaluation for games: Usability principles for video game design. ACM SIG CHI '08, pp. 1453–1462.

Rabin I (2005) Introduction to Game Development. Charles River Media, Hingham, MA, p. 125.

Rubin J (1994) Handbook of Usability Testing. John Wiley & Sons, Inc., New York.

Sheff D (1993) Game Over – How Nintendo Zapped an American Industry, Captured Your Dollars, and Enslaved Your Children. Random House, New York.

Silfverberg M, MacKenzie IS, Korhonen P (2000) Predicting text entry speed on mobile phones. In: Proceedings of SIGCHI Conference on Human Factors in Computing Systems, CHI '00, ACM, New York, pp. 9–16.

Chapter 13
Using Heuristics to Evaluate the Overall User Experience of Video Games and Advanced Interaction Games

Christina Koeffel, Wolfgang Hochleitner, Jakob Leitner, Michael Haller, Arjan Geven, and Manfred Tscheligi

Abstract This chapter describes an approach to evaluating user experience in video games and advanced interaction games (tabletop games) by using heuristics. We provide a short overview of computer games with a focus on advanced interaction games and explain the concept of user-centred design for games. Furthermore, we describe the history of heuristics for video games and the role of user experience of games in general. We propose a framework consisting of three sets of heuristics (game play/game story, virtual interface and tabletop specific) to detect the most critical issues in video games as well as advanced interaction games. To assess its applicability, we compare the results of expert evaluations of five current games with the user experience-based ratings of various game review sites. In the conclusion, we provide an outlook on possible extensions of our approach.

13.1 Introduction

The computer games industry has remarkably increased in importance over the last years (ESA 2008). The number of units sold climbs up steadily, and video games have changed from being a product for a small minority to a widely used and accepted medium. The expanding game market also opens the door for a series of research-related activities. Especially the term user experience (UX) has become increasingly important. Researchers and human-computer interaction (HCI) experts want to find out how computer gamers experience the game situation (Clarke and Duimering 2006), and the industry is interested in finding ways to measure the user experience and to interpret the collected data (e.g. to acquire new target groups). The evaluation of the user's experience and the closely connected user-centred development of video games have been addressed in numerous publications (cf. Marsh et al.

C. Koeffel (✉)
Center for Usability Research and Engineering, Vienna, Austria
e-mail: christina@c-na.net

R. Bernhaupt (ed.), *Evaluating User Experience in Games*, Human-Computer
Interaction Series, DOI 10.1007/978-1-84882-963-3_13,
© Springer-Verlag London Limited 2010

2005). Several researchers have designed methods for game evaluation by adopting techniques from the field of usability such as usability tests and heuristic evaluations. In recent years, several documents on heuristic evaluations of video games have been proposed, all treating overlapping subject areas but diverse in detail and quality of description (cf. Federoff 2002, Desurvire et al. 2004, Röcker and Haar 2006, Koivisto and Korhonen 2006, Pinelle and Gutwin 2007, Schaffer 2007, Pinelle et al. 2008, Jegers 2008, Bernhaupt et al. 2007, 2008).

Social and physical interactions are a new frontier in entertainment. Today, countless applications are built that provide entertainment to the masses, but very few support truly new user experiences. Nintendo's Wii[1] controller is an excellent example for a novel interface that allows a very intuitive and natural interaction leading to a completely new user experience. This even motivates non-traditional target audiences like elderly players to try playing video games. However, people also still love traditional board games, such as Risk or Monopoly, mostly due to the rich social interaction. Instead of sitting solely in front of a screen, playing with friends over the internet or even having a shoulder-by-shoulder experience, people still enjoy having a face-to-face experience (Amaya and Davis 2008). Most traditional board games are multiplayer games and game sessions are organised as social events. Experiencing close social interactions like laughter, cheering, discussions or even shouting makes classical board games interesting enough to prevail against video games, despite limits in interactivity and complexity.

On the one hand, today's video game consoles and video games lack all sorts of nonverbal communication which are crucial to face-to-face communication. On the other hand, traditional board games are limited because of static game media hindering the implementation of complex game scenarios and truly interactive game environments. Therefore, the logical consequence is to combine the advantages of both, video games and traditional board games for a new gaming experience. In various areas, digital tabletops have already been used successfully. For example, interactive tabletop interfaces have already emerged as an effective tool for colocated collaboration over digital artefacts (Scott and Carpendale 2006). Related research shows that in the case of collaborative work, a tabletop device can have a significantly higher job performance than a traditional desk (Scott and Carpendale 2006) and encourages a higher level of creativity and interaction among users (Buisine et al. 2007). Microsoft's Surface[2] table and Smart's SmartTable[3] are trying to bring digital tabletop applications to the next level by releasing commercially available platforms to the market.

In the past few years, tabletop installations and games have become more and more popular (Kojima et al. 2006, Lee et al. 2005, Loenen et al. 2007, Magerkurth et al. 2004, Tse et al. 2007). Most recent work on interactive surfaces deals with

---

[1] http://wii.nintendo.com/

[2] http://www.microsoft.com/surface/

[3] http://www2.smarttech.com/st/en-US/Products/SMART+Table/

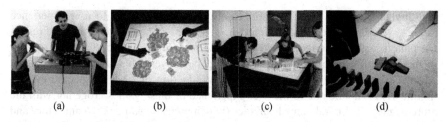

Fig. 13.1   Different tabletop games. (**a**) NeonRacer[4] is an interactive car-racing game, (**b**) PenWars is a sketch-based tank-war game,[5] (**c**) Comino[6] is a domino game that combines the physical and digital world, and (**d**) IncreTable[7] is a follow-up game from Comino and allows one modifying the digital terrain using physical (tangible) objects

merging the real with the virtual (digital), enabling people to share the same experience (Dietz and Leigh 2001, Morris et al. 2006). Example applications are the STARS platform (Magerkurth et al. 2004), Augmented Coliseum (Sugimoto et al. 2005), PlayAnywhere (Wilson 2005), PlayTogether (Wilson and Robbins 2006) or MonkeyBridge (Barakonyi et al. 2005)

Over the past four years, we developed different tabletop games (see Fig. 13.1), focusing mainly on interaction techniques. During the development we found that it is even more important for game designers to get a framework for identifying usability problems both in early designs and in more mature prototypes.

There is little research about the user performance of tabletop devices, and only few formal user studies are performed to demonstrate the real benefits of tabletop games. Most studies so far focus more on tabletop setups in general, and researchers evaluate interactive tables more on a technical level (e.g. comparing different interaction metaphors). Besides our focus on measuring user experience with heuristics of a broad variety of games, we provide methods for a more narrow and specific field of games: tabletop games.

13.1.1 Overview

Few approaches are currently linking the results of heuristic evaluation methods to user experience. Especially in the field of computer games, where the experience is the leading factor, different aspects can be evaluated using heuristics. Therefore, we first put the main focus of this chapter on demonstrating the connection between heuristics for games and a game's user experience. Next, we provide an overview of previously available heuristics and introduce summarised heuristics

---

[4] http://www.neonracer.net/

[5] http://mi-lab.org/projects/penwars/

[6] http://mi-lab.org/projects/comino

[7] http://mi-lab.org/projects/incretable

of a higher quality. To test the applicability of our heuristics to user experience ratings, we conduct heuristic evaluations on several games and compare the resulting data to user experience-based game reviews. Finally, we critically assess our method and offer improvements and future perspectives. This discussion of current advanced interaction games leads to the introduction of a set of specific evaluation heuristics applicable to the user experience of these games. Together with the aforementioned general game heuristics (which focus on game play/game story and the virtual interface), we deliver a complete framework usable for evaluating the user experience of games either generally or specifically for advanced interaction games.

13.2 Video Game Definition and Genres

Before discussing heuristics for video games, we want to get a clear understanding of the terminology "video game". Esposito provides an interesting definition for a video game:

> A video game is a game which we play thanks to an audiovisual apparatus and which can be based on a story (Esposito 2005).

Esposito's definition contains four important elements that classify a video game: *game*, *play*, *audiovisual apparatus* and *story*. These elements are derived from literature such as Huizinga (1950), Callois (1961) and Zimmerman (2004).

We second this definition in most of its statements but want to add that the mentioned audiovisual apparatus is not necessarily limited to two senses. Touch-based input and haptic feedback mechanisms allow a broader range of video game devices. We also want to point out the need to clearly distinguish games from productivity applications as done in Pagulayan et al. (2003). Finally, to avoid misunderstandings about the term itself, we consider video games as an umbrella term for all electronic games, independent of their platform (computer, console, arcade, etc.). Still there is need to put games into certain categories to be able to unite titles of similar type.

There are many different distinctions available, some more common than others. Wolf defined a set of 41 genres in Wolf (2001), being sometimes too specific (e.g. when defining Diagnostic Cartridges as a genre). Ye proposes to adapt the genre term and certain genre conventions from movies to games, but does not give a clear genre definition himself (Ye 2004). A common and well-established genre definition has been created by the NPD group and is mentioned amongst others in Pagulayan et al. (2003) and used by ESA (2008) for their market statistics. This classification contains eleven well-known and established (super-) genres such as role-playing game (RPG), action or shooters, and abstains from introducing fine-grained subcategories. We propose the use of theses genres in order to be able to classify games in accordance with the market/industry for our test in Section 13.6.2.

13.3 User-Centred Design in Games

User-centred design is a design philosophy which describes a prototype-driven software development process, where the user is integrated during the design and development process. The approach consists of several stages which are iteratively executed: requirements analysis, user analysis, prototyping and evaluation. User-centred design is specified in EN ISO 13407–Human Centred Design Processes for Interactive Systems (ISO 13407:1999). This approach is also used for game design as described in Fullerton et al. (2004) and a central topic at Microsoft Game Studios[8]. It contains three distinct development phases: conceptualisation, prototyping and playtesting. The first phase typically involves the complete planning such as identification of goals, challenges, rules, controls, mechanics, skill levels, rewards and story (Pagulayan et al. 2003). These specifications are done by game designers and are put on record in game design documents.

The second phase–prototyping–is used to quickly generate playable content, which can be efficiently used to do playtesting and measure attributes such as user experience, the overall quality (commonly denoted as fun), the ease of use or the balancing of challenge and pace (Pagulayan et al. 2003).

To gather results for these variables, a range of usability methods such as structured usability tests (Dumas and Redish 1999) and rapid iterative testing and evaluation (RITE, Medlock et al. 2002) can be applied. Pagulayan et al. propose additional evaluation methods such as prototyping, empirical guideline documents or heuristics (Pagulayan et al. 2003). We believe that especially heuristics can be a fast and cost efficient but still effective and accurate evaluation method for user experience in games. Therefore, we will present our own set of heuristics in Sections 13.5 and 13.7 and verify them by conducting an expert evaluation. Before that we will give a short introduction to heuristic evaluation as an expert-based usability approach.

Heuristic evaluation is one of the so-called expert-based usability inspection methods (Nielsen and Mack 1994). It is an efficient analytical and low-cost usability method to be applied repeatedly during a development process, starting at the very beginning of a project design circle (Nielsen and Mack 1994). In general, heuristics can be considered as rules of thumb that describe the affordances of the users to a particular system. The formulation of heuristics is more universal than the one of usability guidelines (Koeffel 2007). The heuristics should provide enough information to enable the evaluator to judge all possible problems of a system (Sarodnick and Brau 2006). During a traditional user-interface evaluation, three to five experts (in the field of the application, usability or both) inspect a system according to recognised and established usability principles (i.e. the heuristics). Heuristics allow for an evaluation of systems in a very early stage of the design process (e.g. paper mockups). Although numerous heuristics are available for the evaluation of video games

---

[8] http://mgsuserresearch.com/

(see following section), no particular work on how to evaluate user experience through the application of heuristics has been introduced.

13.4 History of Heuristics for Video Games

In the following, a brief overview of the history of heuristics for video games will be presented, starting with Malone who was the first one to introduce the idea of using heuristics to evaluate games (Malone 1980, 1982). His heuristics mainly focused on educational games, not possessing the graphical, acoustic and computational possibilities that current video games offer. Malone categorised his heuristics into challenge, fantasy and curiosity.

Although Malone has introduced his heuristics as early as 1980, this method was adopted by a wider audience with Jakob Nielsen's 10 heuristics introduced in 1994 (Nielsen 1994). Since then, these 10 heuristics are the mostly referenced set of heuristics and frequently used for different kinds of applications. Originally, they have been developed for traditional interfaces, nevertheless they are also (to a certain extent) applicable to several other areas such as pervasive games or video games. Federoff assessed the applicability of these heuristics to the area of video games (Federoff 2002). She discovered that they were usable and developed a set of 40 heuristics which were partially based on Nielsen's heuristics. For a better overview and easier assignment of single problems to heuristics, she categorised them into game interface, game mechanics and game play. We think that the heuristics published by Federoff appear slightly superficial and sometimes do not cover the entire extent of facets offered by video games, especially when considering the capabilities of state-of-the-art video games. Furthermore, they appear to concentrate on role-playing games and are therefore not applicable to all possible game genres.

In 2004 Desurvire et al. released a new set of verified heuristics, the HEP (heuristic evaluation of playability), which were based on the heuristics introduced by Federoff (Desurvire et al. 2004). In contrast to Federoff's approach, these heuristics were categorised into four sections: game story, game play, game mechanics and game usability. Through further evaluations, these heuristics have proven to be effective. We think that the heuristics by Desurvire et al. do not consider the important impact of challenge on the user's experience. Nevertheless, the categorisation of heuristics for video games into game play, game story, game mechanics and game usability has been taken into account when formulating our framework. Two years after Desurvire et al. designed their heuristics, Röcker and Haar tested the adaptability of these heuristics to the area of pervasive games (Röcker and Haar 2006). It was their basic assumption that no aspects related to the game platform were to be found in the heuristics for game play and game story. Furthermore, they expected this information to be contained in the categories game mechanics and game usability, which were deemed to be platform dependent. For this reason, these heuristics had to be reconsidered. The results of a study connected to their investigations revealed that the heuristics concerning the game mechanics are the same for all types of games. Besides the evaluation of pervasive games, the evaluation of mobile games has also been of interest to researchers. In 2006, Nokia released a framework for the evaluation of the playability of mobile games (Koivisto and Korhonen 2006). Their framework is split into modules containing heuristics for game play, game usability and mobility. The modules do not have to be evaluated at the same time, and at least the modules concerning game play and game usability should be able to be applied to other kinds of games, not only mobile games.

Another approach towards the evaluation of groupware has been published in Pinelle and Gutwin (2007). They developed the Table-Collaboration Usability Analysis (T-CUA) which is based on the Collaboration Usability Analysis (CUA). It is especially designed to evaluate collaborative groupware and concentrates on issues in connection with teamwork. In April 2007, Schaffer released a white paper introducing a new version of heuristics for video games (Schaffer 2007). According to him, the heuristics introduced so far were too vague, difficult to realise, more suitable to postmortem reviews and not applicable during the design process. He provides a set of detailed heuristics with graphical examples for each heuristic which eases the evaluation significantly, especially when it is not conducted by an expert in the field of computer games. Pinelle et al. introduced a set of heuristics based on game reviews in 2008 (Pinelle et al. 2008). For their work, five researchers reviewed 108 game reviews of the GameSpot[9] website and categorised the issues found into 10 final heuristics. According to Pinelle et al., this approach offers the possibility to evaluate a game's usability without reviewing unnecessary technical issues and issues related to entertainment.

Based on the idea of heuristics for pervasive games by Röcker and Haar (2006), Jegers has introduced a study investigating the special characteristics and issues of pervasive games (Jegers 2008). He criticises the approach of Röcker and Haar as being too focused on Smart Home technology and the evaluation as being too theoretical. Therefore, Jegers has developed a pervasive game and conducted an iterative evaluation using different methods. When comparing his findings to Desurvire's HEP (Desurvire et al. 2004) and to traditional usability issues, he found out that there are several problems that are not covered by the aforementioned principles. Therefore, he suggests further methodological research in this area.

13.5 User Experience of Games

Within recent years, the term "user experience" has become a buzzword within the community focusing on HCI. According to Hassenzahl and Tractinsky (2006), this is the counter-reaction to the more dominant task and work-related usability paradigm. Still, this is not a completely new concept. The American philosopher and psychologist John Dewey described experiences to be "not mere feelings; they

---

[9] http://www.GameSpot.com

are characteristics of situations themselves, which include natural events, human affairs, feelings, etc." as early as 1934 (Dewey 1934).

Nevertheless, a clear definition and grounded understanding of this term is still missing (Law et al. 2008). According to Law et al., the main problem is that user experience treats non-utilitarian aspects of interactions between humans and machines. This means that user experience mainly focuses on affect and sensation–two very subjective impressions. It encompasses areas from traditional usability to beauty, hedonic, affective or experimental aspects of technology use (Forlizzi and Battarbee 2004). Hassenzahl and Law, leading researchers in the field of user experience, define it as "a momentary, primarily evaluative feeling (good–bad) while interacting with a product or service" (Hassenzahl 2008). Therefore, user experience is designing for joy and fun instead of designing for the absence of pain (Hassenzahl and Tractinsky 2006). Thus, the community has recently undertaken measures to better understand the meaning of user experience and to find a unified definition through different conferences, workshops (Law et al. 2008, Roto and Kaasinen 2008), forums and the like. Especially, the MAUSE COST Action 294[10] has aimed for finding a definition and measurement of user experience.

According to literature, user experience in games can be measured using the following qualitative and quantitative methods (Federoff 2002, Desurvire et al. 2004, Sweetser and Wyeth 2005, Hazlett 2006, Koivisto and Korhonen 2006, Mandryk and Atkins 2007): physiological measurements; expert evaluation (heuristics, etc.); subjective, self-reported measures; and usability tests.

Integral factors of user experience are the state of flow and immersion defining the level of enjoyment and fun (IJsselsteijn et al. 2007).

The measurement of the state of flow through different methods is one of the major topics of user experience in games and by many seen as the optimal experience when playing games (cf. Sweetser and Wyeth 2005). According to Hassenzahl, the concept of flow is very close to the idea of user experience and he describes flow as "a positive experience caused by an optimal balance of challenges and skills in a goal-oriented environment" (Hassenzahl 2008). The concept of flow was first introduced in Csikszentmihalyi (1975) and further refined to fit to video games and player enjoyment in Cowley et al. (2008), Sweetser and Wyeth (2005). Whereas Cowley et al. introduce a framework to map flow of the game play, Sweetser and Wyeth try to integrate heuristics into a model to help design and evaluate enjoyment in games. They found out that there is a certain overlap of the heuristics investigated and the concept of flow. Based on this, Jegers introduced the pervasive game flow model that enhances the game flow idea from Sweetser and Wyeth, with aspects that are particular to pervasive games (Jegers 2007).

Another concept that is tightly linked to user experience is immersion. One definition of immersion and its stages has been proposed in Brown and Cairns (2004). Through a semi-structured interview with seven gamers, they were able to

---

[10]http://www.cost294.org/

distinguish immersion into three phases: engagement, engrossment and total immersion. Engagement is the first stage of immersion. According to Brown and Cairns, the players have to be interested in the game to reach this state. When the user continues to play a game after the stage of engagement, she will reach engrossment. When engrossed in a game, the player's emotions are directly affected by the game. Total immersion is the most immersed a user can get. She will be completely involved in the game and will experience absolute presence, where only the game and the emotions produced by the game matter. In a follow-up work, Cheng and Cairns have further investigated the different stages of immersion (Cheng and Cairns 2005). They tested a game with changing graphics and behaviour on 14 different users. Through this experiment, Cheng and Cairns found out that when a user is immersed in a game, she would oversee usability issues and even not notice changes in the game's behaviour.

Our work is influenced by the first approach described in Sweetser and Wyeth (2005) to integrate heuristics into the game design process and especially to use it for the evaluation of user experience. Sweetser and Wyeth accomplished this by integrating common known heuristics into the eight steps of flow as proposed by Csikszentmihalyi. Nevertheless, we will not try to measure the user experience through the factor flow, especially since the GameFlow approach has been criticised by Cowley et al. (2008) stating that through the employed mapping important, if not elementary issues got lost and also question the necessity of social interaction as a central point. Instead, we will provide a set of heuristics that are independent of the flow approach and will target usability and user experience of the evaluated games. A comprehensive overview of this process will be given in Section 13.6.

13.6 Overview and Review of Existing Video Game Heuristics and Their Impact on User Experience

As introduced in Section 13.3 and further discussed in Section 13.4, heuristics can be a valuable method in video game design. In this section, we want to present a modular framework which is based on previous literature and was introduced in Koeffel (2007). The framework consists of the sections game play/game story, virtual interface, and device- and application-specific heuristics. The review of existing literature as introduced in Section 13.4 has indicated that separating the heuristics into different categories appears to be most effective. Especially, since a categorisation allows for a better readability by experts and therefore for more clarity during the review.

The section game play/game story contains heuristics regarding these very topics. In the section about the virtual interface, heuristics concerning the displayed virtual and not physical interface that the player interacts with are presented. The device- and application-specific heuristics are supposed to symbolise an exchangeable part that can be substituted with heuristics that are specific for a special area, such as tabletop games (see Section 13.7) or mobile games. Hence, the heuristics treating game play/game story and the virtual interface are generally applicable to video games as they are formulated in Table 13.1. For use with other devices (i.e., input devices, setups, etc.), the third (device- and application-specific) part was formulated. Therefore, all possible eventualities offered by those games can be covered.

In the following, the heuristics of the sections game play/game story and virtual interface of the framework will be listed. As an example for the modularity of the framework, the heuristics concerning special properties of tabletop games will be introduced in Section 13.7.

Table 13.1 Heuristics concerning game play/game story and virtual interface

	No.	Heuristic	Source
Game play/game story	1	The player should be presented with "clear goals" early enough or be able to create her own goals and "should be able to understand and identify them". There can be "multiple goals on each level" so that there are more strategies to win. Furthermore, the player should know how to reach the goal without getting stuck	(Federoff 2002, Desurvire et al. 2004, Koivisto and Korhonen 2006, Schaffer 2007)
	2	The player should receive meaningful rewards. "The acquisition of skills" could also be a reward	(Federoff 2002, Koivisto and Korhonen 2006)
	3	The player should "feel that she is in control". That includes the "control over the character" as well as the "impact on the game world". "The controls should allow management that is appropriate to the challenge." "Changes the player makes to the game world should be persistent and noticeable." Furthermore, the player should be able to "respond to threats and opportunities"	(Desurvire et al. 2004, Koivisto and Korhonen 2006, Schaffer 2007, Pinelle et al. 2008)
	4	"Challenge, strategy and pace should be in balance." "Challenges should be positive game experiences"	(Desurvire et al. 2004, Koivisto and Korhonen 2006)
	5	"The first-time experience is encouraging"	(Koivisto and Korhonen 2006)
	6	The "meaningful game story should support the game play" and be "discovered as part of the game play"	(Desurvire et al. 2004, Koivisto and Korhonen 2006)
	7	"The game does not stagnate" and the player feels the progress	(Koivisto and Korhonen 2006, Schaffer 2007)

Table 13.1 (continued)

No.	Heuristic	Source
8	The game should be consistent and "respond to the user's action in a predictable manner". This includes "consistency between the game elements and the overarching settings as well as the story". The story should "suspend disbelief" and be perceived as a single vision, i.e. the story should be planned through to the end	(Desurvire et al. 2004, Koivisto and Korhonen 2006, Pinelle et al. 2008)
9	"It should be clear what's happening in the game, the player should understand failure conditions and be given space for making mistakes"	(Schaffer 2007)
10	"There should be variable difficulty levels" for a "greater challenge". The game should be "easy to learn, but hard to master"	(Federoff 2002, Desurvire et al. 2004, Pinelle et al. 2008)
11	The game and the outcome should be perceived as being fair	(Federoff 2002, Desurvire et al. 2004)
12	The game itself should be replayable and the player should enjoy playing it. Nevertheless, "challenging tasks should not be required to be completed more than once". The challenge should create the desire to play more. This includes also the possibility to skip non-playable and repeating content if not required by the game play	(Desurvire et al. 2004, Schaffer 2007, Pinelle et al. 2008)
13	"The artificial intelligence should be reasonable", "visible to the player, consistent with the player's expectations" and "yet unpredictable"	(Federoff 2002, Desurvire et al. 2004, Röcker and Haar 2006, Pinelle et al. 2008)
14	The game should be "paced to apply pressure but not frustrate the player"	(Federoff 2002, Desurvire et al. 2004)
15	The "learning curve should be shortened". The "user's expectations should be met", and the player should have "enough information to get immediately started". Tutorials and adjustable levels should be able to involve the player quickly and provided upon request throughout the entire game	(Federoff 2002, Desurvire et al. 2004, Röcker and Haar 2006, Schaffer 2007, Pinelle et al. 2008)
16	"The game emotionally transports the player into a level of personal involvement (e.g., scare, threat, thrill, reward and punishment)"	(Desurvire et al. 2004)

Table 13.1 (continued)

	No.	Heuristic	Source
	17	"The game play should not require the player to fulfil boring tasks"	(Koivisto and Korhonen 2006)
	18	"The game mechanics should feel natural and have correct weight and momentum." Furthermore, they should be appropriate for the situation the user is facing	(Federoff 2002, Pinelle et al. 2008)
Virtual Interface	19	"The player should be able to identify game elements such as avatars, enemies, obstacles, power-ups, threats or opportunities." The objects "should stand out, even for players with bad eyesight or colour blindness and should not easily be misinterpreted". Furthermore, the objects "should look like what they are for"	(Koivisto and Korhonen 2006, Schaffer 2007, Pinelle et al. 2008)
	20	The "acoustic and visual effects should arouse interest" and provide meaningful feedback at the right time. Hence, the effects should give feedback to create a challenging and exciting interaction and involve the player by creating emotions. The feedback should be given immediately to the user's action	(Federoff 2002, Desurvire et al. 2004, Röcker and Haar 2006)
	21	The interface should be "consistent in control, colour, typography and dialogue design" (e.g., large blocks of text should be avoided, no abbreviations) and "as non-intrusive as possible"	(Federoff 2002, Desurvire et al. 2004, Schaffer 2007)
	22	The player should not have to "count resources like bullets, life", score, points and ammunition. This "relevant information should be displayed and the critical information should stand out". Irrelevant information should be left out. The user should be provided enough information to recognise her status and to make proper decisions. Excessive micromanagement by the user should be avoided	(Federoff 2002, Desurvire et al. 2004, Schaffer 2007, Pinelle et al. 2008)
	23	The menu should be "intuitive and the meanings obvious" and "perceived as a part of the game"	(Desurvire et al. 2004, Schaffer 2007)

Table 13.1 (continued)

No.	Heuristic	Source
24	"The player should know where she is on the mini-map if there is one and should not have to memorise the level design"	(Schaffer 2007)
25	The player "should be able to save the games in different states" (applies to non-arcade-like games) and be able to "easily turn the game off and on"	(Federoff 2002, Desurvire et al. 2004, Röcker and Haar 2006)
26	"The first player action is obvious and should result in immediate positive feedback"	(Desurvire et al. 2004)
27	Input methods should be easy to manage and have an appropriate level of sensitivity and responsiveness. The input methods should allow customisation concern the mappings	(Schaffer 2007, Pinelle et al. 2008)
28	The visual representation (i.e., the views) should allow the user to have a clear, unobstructed view of the area and of all visual information that is tied to the location	(Pinelle et al. 2008)
29	The game should allow for an appropriate level of customisation concerning different aspects	(Pinelle et al. 2008)

13.6.1 Video Game Heuristics

In Section 13.4, existing heuristics for video games have been summarised and criticised. As mentioned before, our heuristics for video games are literature based and derive from work and research by Nielsen and Molich (1990), Federoff (2002), Desurvire et al.(2004), Sweetser and Wyeth (2005), Koivisto and Korhonen (2006), Röcker and Haar (2006), Schaffer (2007) and Pinelle et al. (2008). These heuristics do therefore originate in the field of usability.

The major part of the heuristics introduced in Section 13.4 is also part of the approach introduced in Sweetser and Wyeth (2005). Nevertheless, it is their main goal to establish a method to measure the state of flow that a game offers to the player. Moreover, they set usability equal to user experience, which has proven to be a different concept (see Section 13.4). Furthermore, they only have applied their heuristics to the area of real-time strategy games, whereas we seek to generate a set of heuristics that are applicable to multiple game genres.

The previously presented heuristics do focus not only on usability but also on playability, fun and enjoyment–factors closely connected to user experience. In their work, Pinelle et al. focus solely on usability issues (Pinelle et al. 2008). Through their selection process based on game design reviews, they have eliminated all aspects related to fun, enjoyment and technical issues. Since it is our goal to evaluate user experience as well as the usability of a game, we decided not only to base our heuristics on the aforementioned literature, but also to include the usability issues distinguished by Pinelle et al. We therefore want to create a more holistic set of heuristics that do not solely concentrate on either user experience or usability. Moreover, we want to focus on all aspects offered by video games, especially as occurring problems have an impact on the user experience, and the quality of a game can hardly be determined by usability only. In their conclusion, Pinelle et al. even recommend the inclusion of user experience-based heuristics. Furthermore, they base their heuristics only on reviews of the website GameSpot.com. We believe that although GameSpot is one of the largest and most comprehensive video game review sites, it is not recommendable to rely solely on its reviews. The site has been under heavy criticism in November 2007 for allegedly firing a reviewer due to negative reviews of a game published by a financial sponsor of GameSpot.[11] Relying on multiple sources can help to attenuate possibly biased reviews. Table 13.1 contains the final heuristics concerning game play/game story and the virtual interface. These heuristics have been chosen based on a qualitative review of the sources mentioned in Section 13.4.

As mentioned before, the 29 heuristics introduced in Table 13.1 are the result of an extensive literature review of several different existing sets of heuristics in the field of video games. Furthermore, the authors' experience in the area of video games has influenced the selection of the heuristics. For reasons of redundancy and simplicity, the literature-based heuristics have been narrowed down to the 29 statements as shown in Table 13.1. Moreover, the most important aspects of video games are reflected in these heuristics. Especially, through the literature review it has become clear that certain aspects such as learning phase, mental load or a reasonable artificial intelligence have been addressed by several sources. Thus, they have been summarised into one heuristic and have been given the according level of importance. Additionally, we tried to keep the number of heuristics short, to allow for a more efficient review of the games. From the first draft to their current status, the heuristics have been continuously expanded to cover all necessary areas, resulting in our final set of 29 heuristics.

We assume that it is necessary to investigate the usability as well as the user experience of a video game to detect its overall quality. As mentioned before, heuristics have already been employed in Sweetser and Wyeth (2005) to detect the flow potential of games. But on the contrary to our approach presented here, they base their results on the concept of flow. They have taken the eight elements of Csikszentmihalyi's concept of flow (Csikszentmihalyi 1975) and mapped them onto computer games (Sweetser and Wyeth 2005), creating the GameFlow approach to flow. As described in Section 13.5, this method has been criticised amongst others

---

[11] http://www.shacknews.com/onearticle.x/50134

by Cowley et al. (2008). Using the approach described in this chapter, we are able to overcome the described weaknesses such as the possibility to lose elementary issues.

First, we do not use any kind of mapping to the flow concept. The 29 heuristics as introduced in Table 13.1 represent a summary of existing heuristics, without any direct connection or modification towards the flow theory. Second, the above-mentioned ambiguities of social interaction are not treated in the heuristics. Moreover, they are part of the device- and application-specific part of the framework introduced above. Especially, since games on different devices offer different kinds of social experiences, this particular area has been relocated to this separate part of our framework as shown in Section 13.7.

The work introduced in this section leads us to the conclusion that it is possible to detect a computer game's user experience through heuristic evaluation. Our assumption is that a game that is enjoyable to play has to a large extent be free of usability issues that keep the user from enjoying a game. Especially, the heuristics targeting game play/game story deem appropriate not only for classical usability issues (missing feedback, etc.), but also to issues connected to enjoyment and fun of a game (challenge, fairness, etc.).

In order to be able to estimate the user experience through heuristics, we have set up a methodology to prove this concept (see following section). Our approach states that the overall user experience of video games can be determined by conducting an expert-based evaluation of the game in question, using the heuristics shown above. The more heuristics are met, the higher the overall user experience is, the more heuristics point to flaws in the game, the worse the user experience is.

13.6.2 Heuristic Approach to User Experience

To prove our assumption that an expert-based heuristic usability evaluation of a game can be used to determine its user experience, we have chosen to conduct an evaluation. Larsen states in his work that common game reviews are to a major part based on the subjective evaluation of a game's user experience from the game reviewer's point of view (Larsen 2008). Game reviewers have been unwittingly evaluating user experience of games for nearly two decades.

Following this idea, we chose to evaluate a number of computer games using our 29 heuristics and compare the results to common game reviews. Therefore, we were able to compare the heuristics–primarily designed to detect usability issues– with the user experience-oriented game reviews. In order to be able to make a quantitative statement, we tried to establish a connection between the number of problems found through the heuristic evaluation and the numerical rating obtained from several different game reviews. The process of our evaluation was designed as a heuristic evaluation for video games. To obtain meaningful results, two evaluators conducted the study. Both of them were experienced in the area of computer games and usability, with one being a usability expert with gaming experience and the other vice versa. To avoid gender-specific ambiguities, a female and a male researcher were selected. Since gaming habits and preferences could influence the outcome, we have selected evaluators with different gaming habits and backgrounds. One evaluator can be considered as a so-called core-gamer who frequently plays games of different genres. The second evaluator was rather a representative of the casual gaming scene with experience in different genres (among them also core-games). For the evaluation, we decided to choose games from several different genres in order to avoid biasing towards one genre, as experienced in some of our analysed work (cf. Federoff 2002, Sweetser and Wyeth 2005). Furthermore, the chosen games had to be rather recent ones to exhaust all current technical possibilities. To allow for a reliable comparison of our testing results with a large number of reviews, we chose five popular games. Therefore, the following games have been selected:

- Shooter: Team Fortress 2^{12} (Valve Software)
- Role playing game: Sacred 2^{13} (Ascaron)
- Adventure: Sam and Max, Season one, Ep. 5: Reality 2.0^{14} (Telltale Games)
- Racing: Racedriver GRID[15] (Codemasters)
- Realtime Strategy: Die Siedler: Aufbruch der Kulturen[16] (Funatics)

The five genres above mentioned were chosen due to their popularity in terms of video game units sold (ESA 2008). "Family Games", although being among the top five genres, has been deliberately omitted, since games in this genre usually rely on a greater number of people playing at the same time (e.g., Wii party games), and our heuristics were primarily developed for traditional single-player video games. Nevertheless, we decided to include one multiplayer game (Team Fortress 2) to prove the applicability of our heuristics to this type of game too. Due to the lack of literature on the correct conduction of heuristic evaluations of video games, we defined our evaluation protocol according to available literature in heuristic evaluation (Nielsen and Mack 1994), with adaptations towards the affordances of video games. Each evaluator obtained a list with the according heuristics and an evaluation report for the found usability issues. Previous to the evaluation, the reviewers met and previewed the heuristics in order to get familiar with them and to avoid misapprehensions. Both reviewers evaluated each single game by playing single-player campaigns or Internet matches with Team Fortress 2. Issues found while playing were noted in the evaluation report. After playing the game, the experts again reviewed the game and their perceived experience according to the heuristics. For the assessment of the games, two different ratings were applied: a Nielsen severity scale and a point-scale ranking (to enable a better comparison to the game-review site).

---

[12] http://www.teamfortress.com/

[13] http://www.sacred2.com/

[14] http://www.telltalegames.com/samandmax

[15] http://www.racedrivergrid.com

[16] http://siedler.de.ubi.com/

Table 13.2 The results of the evaluation ranked according to issues found, points obtained and compared to the results of Metacritic.com

Rank	Ranking according to found issues	Ranking according to points	Metacritic.com ranking
1	Team Fortress 2 (18)	Team Fortress 2 (82.9%)	Team Fortress 2 (92%)
2	Sam and Max, GRID (22)	Die Siedler (79.65%)	GRID (87%)
3		GRID (77.93%)	Sam and Max (82%)
4	Die Siedler (26)	Sam and Max (77.7%)	Die Siedler (80.6%)
5	Sacred 2 (29)	Sacred 2 (75.17%)	Sacred 2 (78%)

First, the researchers reviewed each game after playing it, using the heuristics to rank the found issues according to Nielsen and Mack's severity scale (Nielsen and Mack 1994), which led to the number of total usability issues found per game as displayed in Table 13.2:

0. Not a usability problem at all.
1. Cosmetic problem only: It does not have a profound impact on the game.
2. Minor problem: It has a slight impact on the game and influences the experience a bit.
3. Major problem: This problem has a severe impact on the game and negatively influences the user experience.
4. Usability catastrophe: This problem has to be fixed in order to allow for a decent user experience.

Second, the evaluators assigned a score from 1 to 5 (1 being worst, 5 being best) to every single heuristic to determine how well the game fulfilled each of them. For this rating, the severity ranking of the found issues was used as an indicator for the degree of fulfilment. In general, the problems and their severity, which were found during the rating according to the above-mentioned scale, helped to determine which heuristics were the least satisfied ones. After the ranking of the heuristics, the evaluators met again and discussed possible inconsistencies in their evaluation. These problems were resolved through discussions, and when necessary evaluation and/or ranking was adapted. The achieved overall score was obtained by the summation of the ratings by the single evaluators and the calculation of an average ranking. This score was then converted into a percentage scale indicating to which degree the game complied with the heuristics (100% would mean the achievement of maximum points). The resulting ranking is shown in Table 13.2.

To compare the results of the expert-based heuristic evaluation, we chose to select at least 10 game reviews (on average 20) for each game to avoid biasing of the single reviewers and therefore guarantee a more objective rating. Metacritic.com[17] exactly fulfils these requirements by accumulating scores from different reviewing sites and

---

[17] http://www.metacritic.com/

calculating a weighted average. Their score reaches from 0 to 100 and can therefore be seen as a percentage rating which is very common among reviewing sites. Unfortunately, Metacritic.com did not have a rating for "Die Siedler: Aufbruch der Kulturen". Therefore, we gathered 13 different review scores from several review pages through our own research and calculated the average rating.

The resulting ranking of our study can be seen in Table 13.2. It shows that the sequence of the games evaluated according to process described above is similar to the sequence obtained from Metacritic.com. This tendency shows the connection between heuristic evaluations and user experience (which is the main focus of the review from Metacritic). Especially, the ranking according to usability issues found during the evaluation appears to comply with the user experience-based results from Metacritic.com. In relation to the results from Metacritic.com, we can state that the more the usability issues are found during a heuristic evaluation, the worse the user experience is. The fact that the ranking according to points is not as high as the ranking according to Metacritic.com can be caused by the fact that our heuristics focus on usability issues which might not be detected during a game review or which might not be weighted that dramatically. On the other hand, we also acknowledge that the testing time of about 2 hours per game was most likely not long enough to achieve total immersion. Therefore, certain effects as described in Cheng and Cairns (2005) such as overlooking usability issues when being totally immersed did not occur. Nevertheless, to further prove this concept more extensive evaluations (with more games from different genres and for longer periods of time) are proposed. This could also lead to a definite number of heuristics that have to be fulfilled in order to grant an optimised user experience. In order to combine research conducted both in the area of video games and tabletop applications and to complete the framework as introduced in this section, Koeffel and Haller introduce 10 heuristics for the development of tabletop games, which are described in more detail in the next section (Koeffel and Haller 2008).

13.7 A Framework of Heuristics for the Evaluation of a Tabletop Game's User Experience

While the heuristics introduced in Section 13.6 are very well suited for most video games such as standard platform PC or console games, they lack tabletop-specific aspects. According to Jegers (2008), pervasive games differ in many ways from traditional computer games. This principle also applies to tabletop games, especially since they include new social and physical experiences as described in Section 13.1. Therefore, within this section a set of device-specific heuristics will be introduced, which include the social issues as pointed out in Jegers (2008), Sweetser and Wyeth (2005) as well as particular issues that arise when interacting with a tabletop game. This section completes the aforementioned framework (see Section 13.6) with tabletop-specific aspects, some of which might seem similar to other heuristics in the framework at first. Nevertheless, the here selected 10 heuristics are tailored to tabletop games and can profoundly influence experience as well as the usability of such a game. To emphasise this aspect, these heuristics are deliberately placed in the device-specific part of the framework.

To achieve a set of rules as complete as possible, an iterative approach based on existing tabletop-related work has been chosen. Our approach, first described in Koeffel (2007), began with the creation of a first set of 12 heuristics, based on existing literature work and research trials in the field of usability. After additional research, these heuristics have been checked for weaknesses, refined and paraphrased. The second iteration focused on comprehensibility and tried to better fulfil the original concept of heuristics as "rules of thumb". Additional feedback from experts initiated the creation of a third iteration of heuristics.

These now 11 rules were used to conduct a heuristic evaluation. Six different games were evaluated. Twelve participants (3 usability experts, 3 double experts, 3 game experts and 3 medium experienced users) were presented with the 11 heuristics from the third set and then instructed to play each of the games. They were asked to identify problems and assign them to the matching heuristics afterwards. The results and findings of this evaluation led to the final version of our proposed heuristics for tabletop games.

This final set of tabletop-specific heuristics emanated from the third set after the heuristic evaluation was conducted. It saw an inclusion of subcategories to further aid evaluators by clarifying potential obscurities. Table 13.3 shows the final heuristics we achieved:

A full description of all 10 heuristics (illustrated with pictures to display occurring issues) can be found in Koeffel (2007).

Table 13.3 Device-specific heuristics for tabletop games

No.	Heuristic
1	*Cognitive workload:* The cognitive workload which is not connected to the game play (i.e., in connection with the acquisition of skills, the view, the screen orientation and the input methods) should be minimised.
2	*Challenge:* The system should be designed in a way that the challenge satisfies the preconditions of a tabletop setup and the target group.
3	*Reach:* The reach of the players should be adapted to the requirements of the game play.
4	*Examinability:* The players should not be hindered to examine the area required by the game play.
5	*Adaptability:* The system should be adaptable to the player in terms of the setup.
6	*Interaction:* The interaction method should satisfy the expectations of the player and follow the game logic.
7	*Level of automation:* The player should be able to execute all actions relevant to the game by herself.
8	*Collaboration and communication:* The interpersonal communication and collaboration should be supported by the entirety of the game (such as game play and setup).
9	*Feedback:* Feedback and feedthrough should be adapted to the possibilities of tabletop games, used adequately and provided to the players when appropriate.
10	*Comfort of the physical setup:* The construction of the setup (including the display) should be comfortable to use and not require the player to take an awkward position.

Our approach of using usability-based heuristics to determine the user experience of video games can also be adapted to tabletop games. As introduced above, the heuristics concerning the tabletop-specific aspects of games focus on particular attributes and circumstances that can be offered by tabletop games. Especially, social aspects and issues connected to the physical setup such as comfort are factors that are deeply influencing the user experience when playing tabletop games. We therefore deem the 10 heuristics as introduced above together with the rest of the framework (see Section 13.6) to be appropriate to evaluate the overall user experience of modern tabletop games. In order to establish an optimum combination between the three areas of the framework, further studies have to be designed. The coverage of all possible issues by the heuristics has to be assured. Since there are no possible mechanisms for comparing the results to established reviews, such as game reviews, the reference values have to be obtained by already investigated means to distinguish a game's user experience, such as physiological measurements.

13.8 Summary and Future Challenges

This chapter introduces a possibility to evaluate the overall user experience of traditional video games and advanced interaction games using heuristic evaluation. The term user experience has significantly gained in importance in the HCI community and although a standardised definition is missing, research strives to employ it in the evaluation of modern interfaces. The experience a user perceives when playing a computer game has been one of the central issues of many recent publications. Although being a subjective impression, researchers seek to objectively evaluate and properly describe it (Phillips 2006). The current possibilities include mostly subjective measures but also objective means such as physiological measurements are applied. An area increasing in importance, not only in the field of video games, but also in the field of advanced interfaces, is the evaluation based on heuristics.

Therefore, we analysed and reviewed the most common heuristics for video games and advanced interaction games and built a framework upon our findings. This framework consists of the following three parts: game play/game story, virtual interface and device- and application-specific properties of a system. We demonstrated the application of the device- and application-specific heuristics with a set of heuristics developed for the application of tabletop games.

We used the video game-related part of our framework to conduct an expert-based heuristic evaluation of five different video games to determine weaknesses and problems. We then tried to prove that heuristics can be used to measure the level of user experience by comparing the results of our study with accumulated reviews from several different gaming sites. Since these reviews focus on explaining how the user experience of a game was perceived by the respective author, we see it as a legitimate description of a game's user experience.

We do however acknowledge that we use a quantitative score from the reviews and not the qualitative data represented by the actual content of the review. Such a score cannot represent the written review in its entirety and is therefore less accurate. Still, using the review score allows us to draw the conclusion that the user experience of a game is worse the less it adheres to the heuristics. To further prove this statement, we suggest more extensive empirical evaluations involving more games that belong to several different genres other than the five tested so far. Also, games with a greater variety of review ratings (e.g. extremely low-rated games) should be included. Additionally, testing games still under development could further prove the concept of applying heuristics during all stages of the development process. The ideal outcome of such tests could then be a definitive number of heuristics which have to be fulfilled in order to grant an optimised user experience. Further studies are also suggested to investigate the best possible combination of the three areas covered by our framework and to advance the heuristics for tabletop games which offer a new possibility to evaluate advanced interaction games. Additionally, an evaluation of the tabletop-specific heuristics according to a similar collection of reviews such as Metacritic.com would allow for a more reliable rating of our heuristics. For a broader applicability of the entire framework, application- and device-specific heuristics for advanced interaction games other than tabletop games could be developed. Therefore, the overall usefulness of the framework for different kinds of games can be evaluated.

For the heuristics in particular, experience has shown that an additional category concerning the graphics quality and connected issues could be needed for an extensive evaluation of a game. Furthermore, differentiation regarding the various aspects of the virtual interface (e.g. main menu or in-game menu) is needed. To allow for a better comprehension of the single heuristics, the inclusion of exemplary graphics is recommended.

References

Amaya G, Davis JP (2008) Games user research (GUR): Our experience with and evolution of four methods. In: Isbister K, Schaffer N (eds) Game Usability. Morgan Kaufmann, San Francisco, CA.

Barakonyi I, Weilguny M, Psik T, Schmalstieg D (2005) MonkeyBridge: Autonomous agents in augmented reality games. In: Proceedings of the 2005 ACM SIGCHI International Conference on Advances in Computer Entertainment Technology (Valencia, Spain, 15–17 June 2005). ACE '05, Vol. 265, ACM, New York, pp. 172–175.

Bernhaupt R, Eckschlager M, Tscheligi M (2007) Methods for evaluating games – How to measure usability and user experience in games? In: Proceedings of the International Conference on Advances in Computer Entertainment Technology (Salzburg, Austria, 13–15 June 2007). ACE '07, Vol. 203, ACM, New York, pp. 309–310.

Bernhaupt R, Ijsselsteijn W, Mueller F, Tscheligi M, Wixon D (2008) Evaluating user experiences in games. In: CHI '08 Extended Abstracts on Human Factors in Computing Systems (Florence, Italy, 5–10 April 2008). CHI '08, ACM, New York, pp. 3905–3908.

Brown E, Cairns P (2004) A grounded investigation of game immersion. In: CHI '04 Extended Abstracts on Human Factors in Computing Systems (Vienna, Austria, 24–29 April 2004). CHI '04, ACM, New York, pp. 1297–1300.

Buisine S, Besacier G, Najm N, Aoussat A, Vernier F (2007) Computer-supported creativity: Evaluation of a tabletop mind-map application. Harris D (ed) Engineering Psychology and

Cognitive Ergonomics, HCII 2007, LNAI 4562, Lecture Notes in Computer Science. In.
Springer-Verlag, Berlin Heidelberg.

Callois R (1961) Man, play and games, Free Press of Glencoe, Illinois.

Cheng K, Cairns PA (2005) Behaviour, realism and immersion in games. In: CHI '05 Extended
Abstracts on Human Factors in Computing Systems (Portland, OR, 2–7 April 2005). CHI '05,
ACM, New York, pp. 1272–1275.

Clarke D, Duimering PR (2006) How computer gamers experience the game situation: A
behavioral study. ACM Computers in Entertainment (CIE) 4(3), July 2006.

Cowley B, Charles D, Black M, Hickey R (2008) Toward an understanding of flow in videogames.
ACM Computers in Entertainment (CIE) 6(2): 1–27, July 2008.

Csikszentmihalyi M (1975) Beyond Boredom and Anxiety. Jossey-Bass, San Francisco, CA.

Desurvire H, Caplan M, Toth JA (2004) Using heuristics to evaluate the playability of games. In:
CHI '04 Extended Abstracts on Human Factors in Computing Systems (Vienna, Austria, 24–29
April 2004). CHI '04, ACM, New York, pp. 1509–1512.

Dewey J (1934) Art as Experience. Minton, Balch, New York.

Dietz P, Leigh D (2001) DiamondTouch: A multi-user touch technology. In: Proceedings of the
14th Annual ACM Symposium on User Interface Software and Technology (Orlando, Florida,
11–14 November 2001). UIST '01, ACM, New York, pp. 219–226.

Dumas J, Redish J (1999) A Practical Guide To Usability Testing. Intellect Books, Exeter.

ESA (2008) Essential facts about the computer and videogame industry, 2008 sales, demographic and usage data. Entertainment Software Association, http://www.theesa.com/facts/
pdfs/ESA_EF_2008.pdf. Accessed 07 December 2008.

Esposito N (2005) A short and simple definition of what a videogame is. In: Proceedings of DiGRA
2005 Conference: Changing: Views – Worlds in Play (Vancouver, British Columbia, Canada,
16–20 June 2005) DiGRA'05, University of Vancouver, BC.

Federoff MA (2002) Heuristics and usability guidelines for the creation and evaluation of fun in
videogames. Master's Thesis, Department of Telecommunications, Indiana University.

Forlizzi J, Battarbee K (2004) Understanding experience in interactive systems. In: Proceedings
of the 5th Conference on Designing interactive Systems: Processes, Practices, Methods, and
Techniques (Cambridge, MA, 1–4 August 2004). DIS '04, ACM, New York, pp. 261–268.

Fullerton T, Swain C, Hoffman S (2004) Game Design Workshop: Designing, Prototyping, and
Playtesting Games. CMP Books, San Francisco, CA.

Hassenzahl M (2008) User experience (UX): Towards an experiential perspective on product quality. Keynote IHM, http://www.uni-landau.de/hassenzahl/pdfs/hassenzahl-ihm08.pdf. Accessed
7 December 2008.

Hassenzahl M, Tractinsky N (2006) User experience – A research agenda. Behavior & Information
Technology 25(2): 91–97, March–April 2006.

Hazlett RL (2006) Measuring emotional valence during interactive experiences: Boys at videogame
play. In: Proceedings of the SIGCHI Conference on Human Factors in Computing Systems
(Montréal, Québec, Canada, 22–27 April 2006). CHI '06, ACM, New York, pp. 1023–1026.

Huizinga J (1950) Homo Ludens: A Study of the Play-Element in Culture. Beacon Press,
Boston, MA.

IJsselsteijn WA, Kort YAW de, Poels K, Jurgelionis A, Belotti F (2007) Characterising and measur-
ing user experiences. In: Proceedings of the international Conference on Advances in Computer
Entertainment Technology (Salzburg, Austria, 13–15 June 2007). ACE '07, Vol. 203, ACM,
New York.

ISO 13407:1999 (1999) Human-centred design processes for interactive systems. International
Organization for Standardization, Geneva, Switzerland. http://www.iso.org/iso/iso_catalogue/
catalogue_tc/catalogue_detail.htm?csnumber=21197. Accessed on 7 December 2008.

Jegers K (2007) Pervasive game flow: Understanding player enjoyment in pervasive gaming. ACM
Computers in Entertainment (CIE) 5(1): 9, January 2007.

Jegers K (2008) Investigating the applicability of usability and playability heuristics for evaluation
of pervasive games. In: Proceedings of the 2008 Third International Conference on Internet

and Web Applications and Services (Athens, Greece, 8–13 June 2008). ICIW, IEEE Computer Society, Washington, DC, pp. 656–661.

Koeffel CA (2007) Heuristics for tabletop games. Master's Thesis, Department of Digital Media, Upper Austria University of Applied Sciences Hagenberg.

Koeffel C, Haller M (2008) Heuristics for the evaluation of tabletop games. In: Evaluating User Experiences in Games, Workshop at the 2008 Conference on Human Factors in Computing Systems (Florence, Italy, 5–10 April 2008). CHI '08.

Koivisto EMI, Korhonen H (2006) Mobile game playability heuristics. Forum Nokia. http://www.forum.nokia.com/. Accessed 07 December 2008.

Kojima M, Sugimoto M, Nakamura A, Tomita M, Inami M, Nii H (2006) Augmented coliseum: An augmented game environment with small vehicles. In: Proceedings of the First IEEE International Workshop on Horizontal Interactive Human-Computer Systems (Adelaide, Australia, 5–7 January 2006). TABLETOP, IEEE Computer Society, Washington, DC, pp. 3–8.

Larsen JM (2008) Evaluating user experience – How game reviewers do it. In: Evaluating User Experiences in Games, Workshop at the 2008 Conference on Human Factors in Computing Systems (Florence, Italy, 5–10 April 2008). CHI '08.

Law E, Roto V, Vermeeren AP, Kort J, Hassenzahl M (2008) Towards a shared definition of user experience. In: CHI '08 Extended Abstracts on Human Factors in Computing Systems (Florence, Italy, 5–10 April 2008). CHI '08, ACM, New York, pp. 2395–2398.

Lee W, Woo W, Lee J (2005) TARBoard: Tangible augmented reality system for table-top game environment. In: PerGames2005 (Munich, Germany, 11 May 2005). PerGames '05, ACM, New York.

Loenen E van, Bergman T, Buil V, Gelder K van, Groten M, Hollemans G, Hoonhout J, Lashina T, Wijdeven S van de (2007) Entertaible: A solution for social gaming experiences. In: Tangible Play: Research and Design for Tangible and Tabletop Games, Workshop at the 2007 Intelligent User Interfaces Conference (Honolulu, HI, 28–31 January 2007) ACM, New York, pp. 16–19.

Magerkurth C, Memisoglu M, Engelke T, Streitz N (2004) Towards the next generation of tabletop gaming experiences. In: Proceedings of Graphics interface 2004 (London, Ontario, Canada, 17–19 May 2004). ACM International Conference Proceeding Series, Vol. 62, Canadian Human-Computer Communications Society, School of Computer Science, University of Waterloo, Waterloo, ON, pp. 73–80.

Malone TW (1980) What makes things fun to learn? Heuristics for designing instructional computer games. In: SIGSMALL '80: Proceedings of the 3rd ACM SIGSMALL Symposium and the First SIGPC Symposium on Small systems (Palo Alto, CA, 18–19 September 1980) ACM, New York, pp. 162–169.

Malone TW (1982) Heuristics for designing enjoyable user interfaces: Lessons from computer games. In: Proceedings of the 1982 Conference on Human Factors in Computing Systems (Gaithersburg, MD, 15–17 March 1982). ACM, New York, pp. 63–68.

Mandryk RL, Atkins MS (2007) A fuzzy physiological approach for continuously modeling emotion during interaction with play technologies. International Journal of Human-Computer Studies 65(4): 329–347, April 2007.

Marsh T, Yang K, Shahabi C, Wong WL, Nocera L, Carriazo E, Varma A, Yoon H, Kyriakakis C (2005) Automating the detection of breaks in continuous user experience with computer games. In: CHI '05 Extended Abstracts on Human Factors in Computing Systems (Portland, OR, 2–7 April 2005). CHI '05, ACM, New York, pp. 1629–1632.

Medlock MC, Wixon D, Terrano M, Romero R, Fulton B (2002) Using the RITE Method to improve products: A definition and a case study. Usability Professionals Association, Orlando, FL.

Morris MR, Piper AM, Cassanego A, Huang A, Paepcke A, Winograd T (2006) Mediating group dynamics through tabletop interface design. IEEE Computer Graphics & Applications 26 (5): 65–73.

Nielsen J (1994) Usability Engineering. Morgan Kaufmann, San Francisco, CA.

Nielsen J, Mack RL (1994) Usability Inspection Methods. John Wiley & Sons, New York.

Nielsen J, Molich R (1990) Heuristic evaluation of user interfaces. In: Proceedings of the SIGCHI Conference on Human Factors in Computing Systems: Empowering People (Seattle, Washington, United States, 1–5 April 1990). CHI '90, ACM, New York, pp. 249–256.

Pagulayan RJ, Keeker K, Wixon D, Romero R, Fuller T (2003) User-centered design in games. In: Jacko J, Sears A (eds) Handbook for Human-Computer Interaction in Interactive Systems. Lawrence Erlbaum Associates, Inc., Mahwah, NJ.

Phillips B (2006) Talking about games experiences: A view from the trenches. Interactions 13(5): 22–23, September 2006.

Pinelle D, Gutwin C (2007) Evaluating teamwork support in tabletop groupware applications using collaboration usability analysis. Personal and Ubiquitous Computing 12(3): 237–254, January 2008.

Pinelle D, Wong N, Stach T (2008) Heuristic evaluation for games: Usability principles for videogame design. In: Proceeding of the Twenty-Sixth Annual SIGCHI Conference on Human Factors in Computing Systems (Florence, Italy, 5–10 April 2008). CHI '08, ACM, New York, pp. 1453–1462.

Röcker C, Haar M (2006) Exploring the usability of videogame heuristics for pervasive game development in smart home environments. In: Proceedings of the Third International Workshop on Pervasive Gaming Applications – PerGames 2006 (Dublin, Ireland, 7–10 May 2006), Springer-Verlag, Heidelberg, pp. 199–206.

Roto V, Kaasinen E (2008) The second international workshop on mobile internet user experience. In: Proceedings of the 10th international Conference on Human Computer interaction with Mobile Devices and Services (Amsterdam, The Netherlands, 2–5 September 2008). MobileHCI '08, ACM, New York, pp. 571–573.

Sarodnick F, Brau H (2006) Methoden der Usability Evaluation, Wissenschaftliche Grundlagen und praktische Anwendung. Hans Huber Verlag, Bern, Switzerland.

Schaffer N (2007) Heuristics for usability in games. Technical report, Rensselaer Polytechnic Institute. http://friendlymedia.sbrl.rpi.edu/heuristics.pdf. Accessed 7 December 2008.

Scott SD, Carpendale S (2006) Guest editors' introduction: Interacting with digital tabletops. IEEE Computer Graphics & Applications: Special Issue on Interacting with Digital Tabletops 26 (5): 24–27.

Sugimoto M, Kagotani G, Kojima M, Nii H, Nakamura A, Inami M (2005) Augmented coliseum: Display-based computing for augmented reality inspiration computing robot. In: ACM SIGGRAPH 2005 Emerging Technologies (Los Angeles, California, 31 July–4 August 2005). SIGGRAPH '05, ACM, New York, p. 1.

Sweetser P, Wyeth P (2005) GameFlow: A model for evaluating player enjoyment in games. ACM Computers in Entertainment (CIE) 3(3): 1–24, July 2005.

Tse E, Greenberg S, Shen C, Forlines C (2007) Multimodal multiplayer tabletop gaming. ACM Computers in Entertainment (CIE) 5(2): 12, April 2007.

Wilson AD (2005) PlayAnywhere: A compact interactive tabletop projection-vision system. In: Proceedings of the 18th Annual ACM Symposium on User Interface Software and Technology (Seattle, WA, 23–26 October 2005). UIST '05, ACM, New York, pp. 83–92.

Wilson A, Robbins DC (2006) PlayTogether: Playing games across multiple interactive tabletops. In: IUI Workshop on Tangible Play: Research and Design for Tangible and Tabletop Games (Honolulu, HI, 28–31 January 2007). IUI '07, ACM, New York.

Wolf MJP (2001) The Medium of the Videogame. University of Texas Press, Austin, TX.

Ye Z (2004) Genres as a tool for understanding and analyzing user experience in games. In: CHI '04 Extended Abstracts on Human Factors in Computing Systems (Vienna, Austria, 24–29 April 2004). CHI '04, ACM, New York, pp. 773–774.

Zimmerman E (2004) Narrative, interactivity, play, and games. In: Wardrip-Fruin N, Harrigan P (eds) First Person. MIT Press, Cambridge, UK.

Index

R. Bernhaupt (ed.), *Evaluating User Experience in Games,* Human-Computer
Interaction Series, DOI 10.1007/978-1-84882-963-3,
© Springer-Verlag London Limited 2010